# Scott, Foresman Mathematics

L. Carey Bolster
Supervisor of Mathematics
Baltimore County Public Schools
Towson, Maryland

E. Glenadine Gibb
Professor of Mathematics Education
The University of Texas at Austin
Austin, Texas

Viggo P. Hansen
Professor, Mathematics Education
California State University
Northridge, California

Joan E. Kirkpatrick
Professor, Elementary Education
University of Alberta
Edmonton, Alberta, Canada

Charles R. McNerney
Professor of Mathematics
University of Northern Colorado
Greeley, Colorado

David F. Robitaille
Professor
of Mathematics Education
University of British Columbia
Vancouver, British Columbia, Canada

Harold C. Trimble
Professor of Education, Emeritus
The Ohio State University
Columbus, Ohio

Irvin E. Vance
Associate Professor of Mathematics
New Mexico State University
Las Cruces, New Mexico

Ray Walch
Teacher of Mathematics
Florida Institute of Technology
Jensen Beach, Florida

Robert J. Wisner
Professor of Mathematics
New Mexico State University
Las Cruces, New Mexico

Scott, Foresman and Company
Editorial Offices: Glenview, Illinois

Regional Offices: Palo Alto, California •
Tucker, Georgia • Glenview, Illinois •
Oakland, New Jersey • Dallas, Texas

## Consultants, Grades 1–8

**Linda Cox**
Coordinator, Special Education
Seattle Public Schools
Seattle, Washington

**Jane Gawronski**
Director
Department of Education
San Diego County
San Diego, California

**Alejandro Gonzalez**
Chairman, Mathematics Department
Gay Junior High School
Harlingen, Texas

**Harriet Haynes**
Mathematics Staff Developer
School District 19
Brooklyn, New York

**William Nibbelink**
Professor of Early Childhood
and Elementary Education
University of Iowa
Iowa City, Iowa

**Thomas Pagan**
Executive Director
William E. Wilson Education Center
Jeffersonville, Indiana

**Glenn Prigge**
Professor of Mathematics
University of North Dakota
Grand Forks, North Dakota

**Sidney Sharron**
Supervisor in the Educational
Media and Resources Branch
Los Angeles Unified School District
Los Angeles, California

## Advisors, Grade 3

**Pat Sutherland**
Teacher
Neoga, Illinois

**Mary Penn**
Parent
Raleigh, North Carolina

## Acknowledgments

For permission to reproduce indicated information on the following pages, acknowledgment is made to:

Riddle on 95 from MORE RIDDLES, RIDDLES, RIDDLES by Helen Hoke, copyright 1976 by Helen Hoke. Used by permission of the Publisher. Riddle on 115 from RIDDDLE RAT by Donald Hall. Text Copyright © 1977 by Donald Hall. Reprinted by permission of Frederick Warne & Company, Inc. and Curtis Brown, Ltd. Tongue twister on 162 from A TWISTER OF TWISTS, A TANGLER OF TONGUES. Text Copyright © 1972 by Alvin Schwartz. Reprinted by permission of J. B. Lippincott Company and Curtis Brown, Ltd. Riddle on 176 from A POCKETFUL OF RIDDLES by William Wiesner. Copyright © 1966 by William Wiesner. By permission of the publisher, E. P. Dutton. Mountain elevations on 226 courtesy Rand McNally & Co. Data on 228 from *U.S. Mileage Chart.* Copyright © Rand McNally & Company, R. L. 78-Y-125. Reprinted by permission. Riddle on 248 reprinted by permission of Charles Scribner's Sons from WHAT? A RIDDLE BOOK by Jane Sarnoff and Reynold Ruffins. Copyright © 1974 Jane Sarnoff and Reynold Ruffins.

For permission to reproduce the photograph on the cover, acknowledgment is made to Randy Bennett/Experimental Aircraft Association.

ISBN: 0-673-20213-5

# Unit 1

# Unit 2

# Unit 3

# Unit 4

# Unit 5

# Unit 6

# Unit 1

# Chapter 1  Numbers

## Using Numbers

I see numbers throughout each day
And their uses vary in every way:

Numbers on the street signs keep
    me from being lost,
Numbers on the price tags tell
    me how much the cost.

Numbers on school doorways tell
    where my classes are,
And numbers on the road map
    show me yet how far.

We tell the time of day from the
    numbers on the clock,
And numbers are on the houses of
    the neighbors in my block.

Numbers on scales and rulers
    give me my height and weight,
And numbers on the calendar
    help me find day and date.

Numbers for each telephone help
    me call my friends,
And numbers on paper money can
    tell us fives from tens.

In fact, I hope you've noticed
    (why don't you take a look?)
The number at the bottom is a
    page name in this book.

by Robert J. Wisner

For each picture tell if the number is used
to locate, to count, or to identify.

**Here's how**

1. 2.

*identify*

3. 4. 5.

6. 7. 8.

9. List five ways you use numbers during the day.

# Ordinal Numbers

**A.** Some numbers are used to tell order.

1st   first

2nd   second

3rd   third

4th   fourth

5th   fifth

6th   sixth
7th   seventh
8th   eighth
9th   ninth
10th   tenth

11th   eleventh
12th   twelfth
13th   thirteenth
14th   fourteenth
15th   fifteenth
16th   sixteenth
17th   seventeenth

30th   thirtieth
31st   thirty-first

B. The red car was third. How many finished ahead of the red car?

2 cars

C. 15 people are ahead of Tim in a line. Name his place in line.

Number: 16th
Word: sixteenth

D. Give the position of the letter Z in the alphabet.

Number: 26th
Word: twenty-sixth

Each number gives a position.
Give the number and the word.

**Here's how**   21   *21st twenty-first*

1. 7   2. 9   3. 12   4. 18   5. 19   6. 20   7. 23

8. 32   9. 47   10. 54   11. 66   12. 75   13. 88   14. 91

Give the position of the given letter in each word.

**Here's how**   M in MUMPS   *1st and 3rd*

15. P in PUMPS   16. N in NOON   17. O in BOOK

18. L in CALLS   19. A in BANANAS   20. E in ELEVENTH

Give the answer.

21. Luis is tenth in line. How many are ahead of him?

22. Nan is the 13th person. How many are before her?

23. Give the 10th letter of the alphabet.

24. Give the twentieth letter of the alphabet.

Use these numbers.
0, 1, 2, 3, 4, 5, 6, 7, 8, 9

*25. Give the sum of the 3rd and 7th numbers.

*26. Give the sum of the 2nd, 4th, and 9th numbers.

# Comparing Numbers

**A.** The Twins have fewer runs than the A's.

3 is less than 4.

## 3 < 4

The A's have more runs than the Twins.

4 is greater than 3.

## 4 > 3

**B.** The Cubs have more runs than the Expos.

11 is greater than 8.

## 11 > 8

The Expos have fewer runs than the Cubs.

8 is less than 11.

## 8 < 11

Which number is less?

1. 8 or 14    2. 17 or 9    3. 11 or 16    4. 18 or 10
5. 7 or 4    6. 19 or 12    7. 13 or 15    8. 6 or 16

Which number is greater?

9. 6 or 13    10. 12 or 7    11. 15 or 10    12. 19 or 8
13. 5 or 9    14. 13 or 18    15. 11 or 4    16. 14 or 19

Give the numbers that are

17. less than 6.
4   9   11   2

18. greater than 8.
9   7   3   5

19. greater than 14.
10   15   19   12

20. less than 13.
18   6   14   12

21. greater than 21.
25   43   39   52

22. less than 32.
17   51   20   40

23. less than 38.
22   17   36   19

24. greater than 26.
18   35   16   48

25. greater than 38.
45   62   59   43

Give two number sentences. Use < and >.

**Here's how**

9 and 7

9 > 7

7 < 9

26. 7 and 6    27. 5 and 9    28. 3 and 8    29. 6 and 14
30. 19 and 4    31. 27 and 34    32. 39 and 67    33. 43 and 27
34. 53 and 36    35. 24 and 58    36. 0 and 29    37. 47 and 19
38. 26 and 49    39. 30 and 10    40. 41 and 38    41. 52 and 54
42. 0 and 31    43. 61 and 53    44. 26 and 47    45. 78 and 96

# Ordering Numbers

4 is one less than 5.

10 is one greater than 9.

14, 15, and 16 are between 13 and 17.

Give the number that is one greater.

1. 8    2. 3    3. 5    4. 2    5. 18    6. 21    7. 39

8. 27    9. 42    10. 79    11. 53    12. 86    13. 0    14. 98

Give the number that is one less.

15. 7    16. 9    17. 14    18. 19    19. 32    20. 40    21. 48

22. 39    23. 57    24. 66    25. 73    26. 80    27. 99    28. 1

Give the missing numbers.

**29.** 9 ▦ ▦ ▦ 13    **30.** 12 ▦ ▦ ▦ 16

**31.** 28 ▦ ▦ ▦ ▦ 33    **32.** 43 ▦ ▦ ▦ ▦ 48

**33.** 31 ▦ ▦ ▦ ▦ ▦ 37    **34.** 39 ▦ ▦ ▦ ▦ ▦ 45

**35.** Between 23 and 29    **36.** Between 26 and 32

**37.** Between 5 and 14    **38.** Between 8 and 15

**39.** Between 17 and 24    **40.** Between 9 and 18

**41.** Between 47 and 59    **42.** Between 56 and 68

Give the numbers in order.
Start with the least number.

**43.** 8  7  9  6      **44.** 12  14  11  13    **45.** 25  27  24  26

**46.** 34  32  35  33    **47.** 44  46  43  45    **48.** 57  55  54  56

Give the numbers in order.
Start with the greatest number.

**49.** 17  19  16  18    **50.** 12  10  13  11    **51.** 23  21  24  22

**52.** 29  31  28  30    **53.** 36  34  35  37    **54.** 48  46  49  47

Use the table to help you find the answer.

| Group | Age |
|-------|---------|
| A | 5–16 |
| B | 17–25 |
| C | over 25 |

**55.** James Big Eagle is 14. Which group should he be in?

**56.** Helen Dwyer is 53. Which group should she be in?

More practice
Set 1, page 354

# Counting

**A.** Alice counted the $10 bills. She counted by tens.

10  20  30  40

There are four $10 bills.

$40

**B.** Eric counted the $5 bills. He counted by fives.

5  10  15  20  25

There are five $5 bills.

$25

**C.** Pat counted the $2 bills. She counted by twos.

2  4  6  8  10

There are five $2 bills.

$10

Count by tens.

**Here's how**

Begin at 40. Count to 70.

*40  50  60  70*

1. Begin at 10. Count to 50.
2. Begin at 40. Count to 80.
3. Begin at 50. Count to 90.
4. Begin at 30. Count to 70.

Count by fives.

5. Begin at 5. Count to 35.
6. Begin at 50. Count to 70.
7. Begin at 20. Count to 40.
8. Begin at 55. Count to 80.

Count by twos.

9. Begin at 2. Count to 18.
10. Begin at 70. Count to 82.
11. Begin at 16. Count to 30.
12. Begin at 58. Count to 70.

Count by fours.

★ 13. Begin at 12. Count to 32.
★ 14. Begin at 70. Count to 98.

## Time Out

On this calendar, which digit occurs most often?

| AUGUST | | | | | | |
|---|---|---|---|---|---|---|
| S | M | T | W | T | F | S |
| | | | | 1 | 2 | 3 | 4 |
| 5 | 6 | 7 | 8 | 9 | 10 | 11 |
| 12 | 13 | 14 | 15 | 16 | 17 | 18 |
| 19 | 20 | 21 | 22 | 23 | 24 | 25 |
| 26 | 27 | 28 | 29 | 30 | 31 | |

Rachel started the table. She has recorded the digits for the 1st through the 10th of the month.

| Digits | Number of times |
|---|---|
| 0 | / |
| 1 | // |
| 2 | / |
| 3 | / |
| 4 | / |
| 5 | |
| 6 | / |
| 7 | / |
| 8 | / |
| 9 | / |

Copy and complete the table to help you decide which digit occurs most often.

# Pictographs

The graph below is called a **pictograph.**
It shows the number of aluminum cans
collected by members of a club.

◌ = 5 cans

| | |
|---|---|
| Milton | ◌ ◌ ◌ ◌ ◌ ◌ ◌ ◌ ◌ |
| Emma | ◌ ◌ ◌ ◌ |
| Terri | ◌ ◌ ◌ ◌ ◌ ◌ ◌ ◌ ◌ ◌ ◌ |
| Jay | ◌ ◌ ◌ ◌ ◌ ◌ |
| Lara | ◌ ◌ ◌ |
| Joshua | ◌ ◌ ◌ ◌ ◌ |

To find how many cans Milton
collected, you count by fives.

5   10   15   20   25   30   35   40   45

45 cans

How many cans did each member collect?

1. Milton   2. Emma   3. Terri   4. Jay   5. Lara   6. Joshua

7. Who collected the fewest?   8. Who collected the most?

9. Put the names in order.   ★ 10. How many cans did the
   Begin with the member           club collect?
   who collected the fewest.

The football teams at King School kept
a record of the touchdowns they scored.

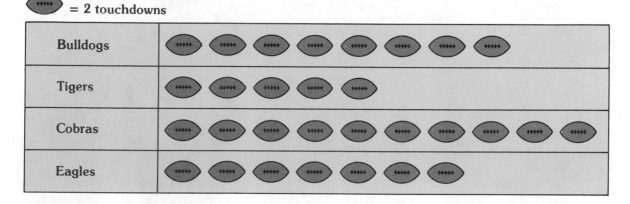

= 2 touchdowns

| | |
|---|---|
| Bulldogs | |
| Tigers | |
| Cobras | |
| Eagles | |

How many touchdowns did each team score?

**11.** Bulldogs    **12.** Tigers    **13.** Cobras    **14.** Eagles

**15.** Which team scored the
fewest touchdowns?

**16.** Which team scored the
most touchdowns?

**17.** Put the teams in order.
Begin with the team that
scored the most touchdowns.

**★18.** How many touchdowns
were scored altogether?

## Keeping Skillful

Give the numbers that are

**1.** greater than 4.
2  7  0  9

**2.** less than 7.
8  14  3  18

**3.** less than 11.
6  10  13  16

**4.** greater than 15.
11  19  12  17

**5.** less than 23.
18  5  25  21

**6.** greater than 35.
39  37  42  53

**7.** greater than 39.
22  38  42  27

**8.** less than 36.
26  21  28  20

**9.** less than 36.
34  30  37  41

# Bar Graphs

Mr. McPike's class made a **bar graph.** They showed how many students had birthdays on each day of the week.

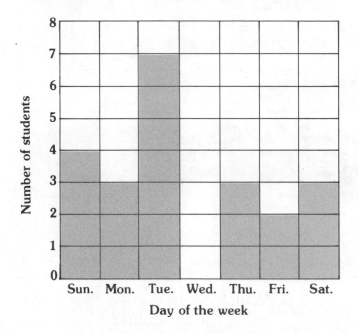

The days are at the bottom of the graph. The number of students are at the left. Four students had birthdays on Sunday.

How many students had birthdays on

1. Monday?  2. Tuesday?  3. Wednesday?  4. Thursday?

5. Friday?  6. Saturday?  7. Sunday?

8. The most birthdays are on which day of the week?

9. The fewest birthdays are on which day of the week?

10. On which days are there fewer than 4 birthdays?

★11. How many students are in Mr. McPike's class?

Ms. Kenagy's class made a bar graph to show the number of letters in each student's last name.

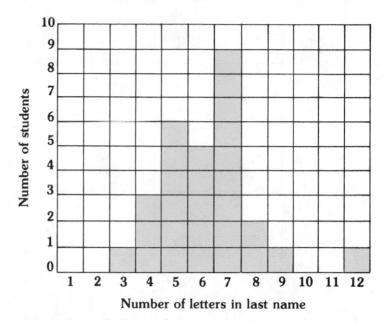

Number of letters in last name

**12.** What do the numbers at the bottom of the graph show?

**13.** What do the numbers at the left of the graph show?

How many students have a last name with

**14.** 8 letters?   **15.** 11 letters?   **16.** 4 letters?

**17.** 10 letters?   **18.** 6 letters?   **19.** 9 letters?

**20.** 5 letters?   **21.** 7 letters?   **22.** 12 letters?

**23.** How many letters are in the longest name in the class?

**24.** How many names have fewer than 7 letters?

**25.** How many names have more than 6 letters?

**★26.** How many students are in Ms. Kenagy's class?

# Number Pairs

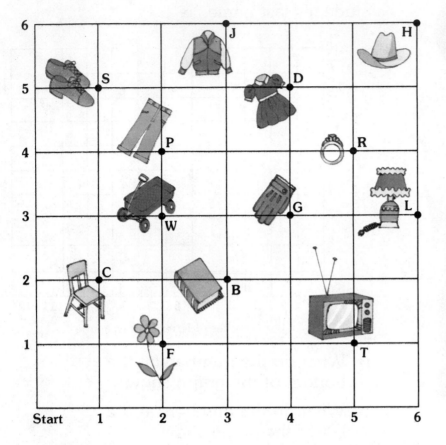

Give the letter
that is at each
point.

1. (2, 3)
2. (4, 5)
3. (3, 6)
4. (6, 3)
5. (6, 6)
6. (2, 4)

Give the number
pair for each
item.

7. Gloves
8. Jackets
9. Books
10. Shoes
11. Flowers
12. Hats

The items in the store are
located by **number pairs.**

The number pair (3, 2) tells
where the books are located.

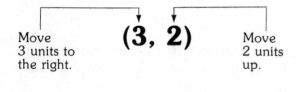

Move
3 units to
the right.

**(3, 2)**

Move
2 units
up.

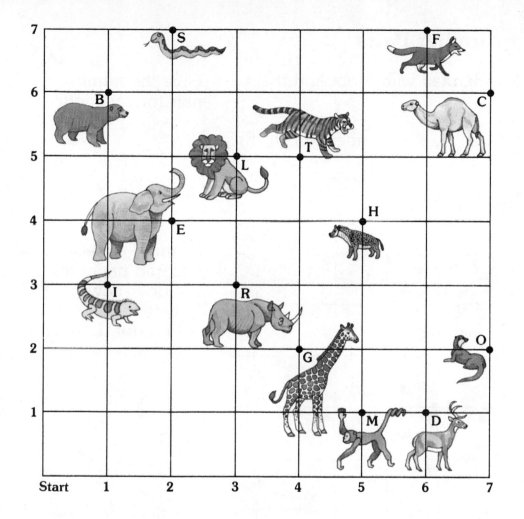

Elie and Steve went to the zoo.
Give the number pair for each animal.

**13.** S  **14.** R  **15.** G  **16.** F  **17.** E  **18.** I  **19.** O  **20.** T

Give the letter for each number pair.

**21.** (1, 6)  **22.** (5, 1)  **23.** (7, 6)  **24.** (3, 5)  **25.** (6, 1)

Give the letter for each location to see what Elie got.

**26.** (2, 7) (7, 2) (3, 3) (2, 4)  **27.** (6, 7) (2, 4) (2, 4) (4, 5)

## Graphing Number Pairs

The point A is marked with a dot and the letter A.

Point A is located by the number pair (4, 2).

4 units to the right  **(4, 2)**  2 units up

Give the number pair for each letter.

1. Q    2. R    3. S

4. U    5. V    6. W

7. X    8. Y    9. Z

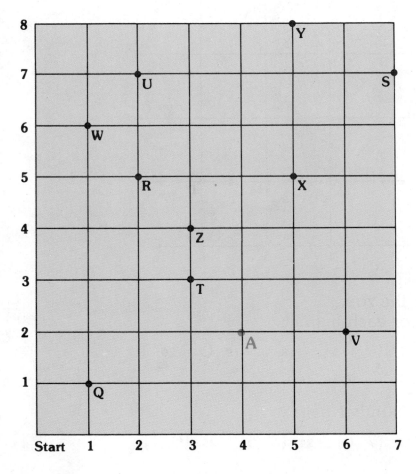

Number a piece of squared paper like the one shown. Locate each point with a dot. Label it with the letter given.

10. B (2, 3)

11. C (3, 4)

12. D (4, 4)

13. E (5, 5)

14. F (4, 6)

15. G (3, 5)

16. H (1, 2)

17. I (2, 1)

18. J (5, 2)

19. K (6, 1)

Number a piece of squared paper like the one on page 18.

20. Locate point B (1, 1).

21. Locate point C (3, 5). Connect B and C.

22. Locate point D (5, 1). Connect C and D.

23. Locate point E (2, 3).

24. Locate point F (4, 3). Connect E and F.

25. What letter have you drawn?

Number another piece of squared paper.

26. Locate point A (2, 1).

27. Locate point B (2, 8). Connect A and B.

28. Locate point C (6, 8).

29. Locate point D (2, 5). Connect C and D.

30. Locate point E (6, 1). Connect D and E.

31. What letter have you drawn?

Number another piece of squared paper.

32. Locate point A (1, 7).

33. Locate point B (6, 1). Connect A and B.

34. Locate point C (1, 1).

35. Locate point D (6, 7). Connect C and D.

36. What letter have you drawn?

Number another piece of squared paper.

37. Locate point P (1, 1).

38. Locate point Q (1, 8). Connect P and Q.

39. Locate point R (5, 8). Connect Q and R.

40. Locate point S (1, 5).

41. Locate point T (4, 5). Connect S and T.

42. Locate point U (5, 1). Connect U and P.

43. What letter have you drawn?

*44. Give directions for drawing the letter W.

### Making a Bar Graph

Ria asked 20 students to choose their favorite sport from this list: softball, ice-skating, swimming, basketball, or hockey.

Then she used the information to make a bar graph.

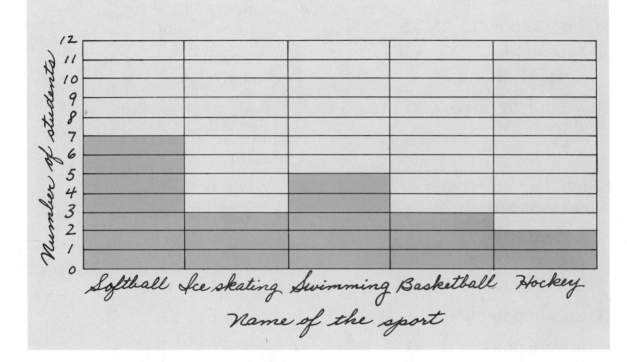

1. Ask 10 students to choose their favorite sport from this list.

   Softball
   Ice-skating
   Swimming
   Basketball
   Hockey

2. Use a piece of squared paper to make a graph.

3. Count how many students chose softball. Color a bar for this number.

4. Do the same for each sport.

5. Compare your graph with others.

# Chapter 1 Test
# Numbers, pages 2-20

1. Give the 5th letter of the alphabet.

2. Joan is twelfth in line. How many are ahead of her?

Which number is less?

3. 15 or 9    4. 17 or 28

Which number is greater?

5. 25 or 52    6. 34 or 86

7. Which numbers are greater than 13?

26  19  8  11

Give two number sentences. Use < and >.

8. 26 and 19    9. 8 and 11

Give the numbers in order. Start with the least number.

10. 15  17  14  16

11. 54  56  53  55

Count

12. from 10 to 60 by tens.

13. from 20 to 45 by fives.

14. from 30 to 44 by twos.

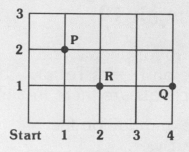

15. What point is at (2, 1)?

16. Give the number pair for Q.

Each  = 5¢ in this pictograph.

| Joel | 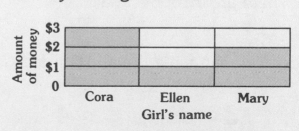 |
| John | |

17. How much money does John have?

18. Who has more money?

This bar graph shows how much money each girl earned.

19. How much did Mary earn?

20. Who earned the most?

# Chapter 2 Addition and Subtraction Facts

## Sums Through 10

There are 4 robot people and
3 robot dogs on Planet Tobor.
How many robots are there in all?

You can use an addition fact
to find this answer.

A. Think of putting the 4 people
with the 3 dogs.

$$3 + 4 = 7$$

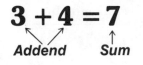

Addend    Sum

B. Or think of putting the 3 dogs
with the 4 people.

$$4 + 3 = 7$$

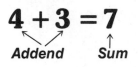

Addend    Sum

There are 7 robots in all.

C. You can write the addition facts
in another way.

$$
\begin{array}{r}
3 \\
+ 4 \\
\hline
7
\end{array}
\begin{array}{l}
\leftarrow \text{ Addend } \rightarrow \\
\leftarrow \text{ Addend } \rightarrow \\
\leftarrow \text{ Sum } \rightarrow
\end{array}
\begin{array}{r}
4 \\
+ 3 \\
\hline
7
\end{array}
$$

Give two addition facts for each picture.

**Here's how**

★ ★ ★ ★    2 + 6 = 8
★ ★ ★ ★    6 + 2 = 8

1. ★ ★    2. ★ ★    3. ★ ★    4. ★ ★
    ★ ★      ★ ★     ★ ★ ★    ★ ★
    ★       ★ ★     ★ ★      ★ ★ ★
                                ★ ★

Give each sum.

5. $\begin{array}{r} 3 \\ +5 \\ \hline \end{array}$    6. $\begin{array}{r} 2 \\ +8 \\ \hline \end{array}$    7. $\begin{array}{r} 7 \\ +2 \\ \hline \end{array}$    8. $\begin{array}{r} 6 \\ +4 \\ \hline \end{array}$    9. $\begin{array}{r} 8 \\ +0 \\ \hline \end{array}$

10. $\begin{array}{r} 4 \\ +1 \\ \hline \end{array}$    11. $\begin{array}{r} 5 \\ +3 \\ \hline \end{array}$    12. $\begin{array}{r} 0 \\ +3 \\ \hline \end{array}$    13. $\begin{array}{r} 2 \\ +7 \\ \hline \end{array}$    14. $\begin{array}{r} 3 \\ +6 \\ \hline \end{array}$

15. $\begin{array}{r} 1 \\ +1 \\ \hline \end{array}$    16. $\begin{array}{r} 8 \\ +2 \\ \hline \end{array}$    17. $\begin{array}{r} 2 \\ +2 \\ \hline \end{array}$    18. $\begin{array}{r} 9 \\ +1 \\ \hline \end{array}$    19. $\begin{array}{r} 4 \\ +4 \\ \hline \end{array}$

20. $\begin{array}{r} 3 \\ +7 \\ \hline \end{array}$    21. $\begin{array}{r} 3 \\ +3 \\ \hline \end{array}$    22. $\begin{array}{r} 7 \\ +3 \\ \hline \end{array}$    23. $\begin{array}{r} 1 \\ +7 \\ \hline \end{array}$    24. $\begin{array}{r} 5 \\ +5 \\ \hline \end{array}$

25. $3 + 2$    26. $4 + 6$    27. $2 + 6$    28. $5 + 0$

29. $5 + 4$    30. $6 + 1$    31. $3 + 4$    32. $1 + 8$

33. $0 + 6$    34. $2 + 5$    35. $4 + 5$    36. $2 + 3$

37. $6 + 2$    38. $4 + 2$    39. $6 + 3$    40. $5 + 2$

More practice
Set 2, page 354

# Sums of 11 Through 18

A. Mr. Greene has 5 red balloons and 8 yellow balloons to sell. How many balloons are there in all?

You can write two addition facts.

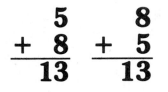

$$5 + 8 = 13 \qquad 8 + 5 = 13$$

There are 13 balloons.

B. You can draw a picture to help you find a sum. Here is a picture for $7 + 8$, or $8 + 7$.

First draw a row of 7 marks.

✓ ✓ ✓ ✓ ✓ ✓ ✓

Next draw a row of 8 marks.

✓ ✓ ✓ ✓ ✓ ✓ ✓

✗ ✗ ✗ ✗ ✗ ✗ ✗ ✗

Count the number of marks to find the answer.

$$7 + 8 = 15$$

$$8 + 7 = 15$$

Draw a picture for each pair of facts.
Then give each sum.

1. $8 + 9$  2. $8 + 6$  3. $9 + 3$  4. $6 + 7$  5. $7 + 9$
   $9 + 8$     $6 + 8$     $3 + 9$     $7 + 6$     $9 + 7$

Give each sum.

6. $6$ $+6$  7. $9$ $+4$  8. $4$ $+9$  9. $9$ $+9$  10. $3$ $+8$  11. $9$ $+6$  12. $7$ $+5$  13. $5$ $+7$

14. $8$ $+3$  15. $9$ $+5$  16. $2$ $+9$  17. $8$ $+9$  18. $9$ $+8$  19. $7$ $+7$  20. $5$ $+9$  21. $8$ $+8$

22. $9$ $+4$  23. $5$ $+8$  24. $9$ $+2$  25. $4$ $+8$  26. $6$ $+9$  27. $8$ $+5$  28. $3$ $+9$  29. $8$ $+4$

• **Discuss**  Does the order in which you add
two numbers change the sum?

**More practice**
**Set 3, page 354**

• **Discuss**  What is the sum when you add
0 and any number?

## Keeping Skillful

Give the numbers in order. Begin with the least number.

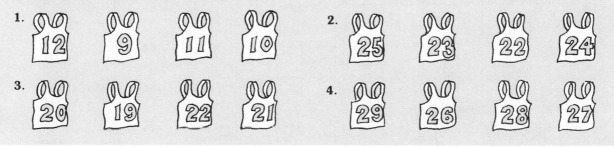

1. 12  9  11  10     2. 25  23  22  24

3. 20  19  22  21     4. 29  26  28  27

# Using Addition Facts

Aponi made a table by using the rule **Add 5.** This rule tells her to add 5 to each number.

| | +5 |
|---|---|
| 3 | 8 |  ← 3 + 5 = 8
| 6 | 11 |  ← 6 + 5 = 11
| 8 | 13 |
| 9 | 14 |

Use the rules. Give each sum.

| | +3 |
|---|---|
| 1. 1 | |
| 2. 2 | |
| 3. 3 | |
| 4. 4 | |

| | +7 |
|---|---|
| 5. 2 | |
| 6. 4 | |
| 7. 6 | |
| 8. 8 | |

| | +4 |
|---|---|
| 9. 1 | |
| 10. 3 | |
| 11. 7 | |
| 12. 9 | |

| | +9 |
|---|---|
| 13. 0 | |
| 14. 4 | |
| 15. 5 | |
| 16. 7 | |

| | +8 |
|---|---|
| 17. 5 | |
| 18. 0 | |
| 19. 7 | |
| 20. 4 | |
| 21. 8 | |

| | +2 |
|---|---|
| 22. 7 | |
| 23. 2 | |
| 24. 5 | |
| 25. 4 | |
| 26. 9 | |

| | +6 |
|---|---|
| 27. 5 | |
| 28. 8 | |
| 29. 2 | |
| 30. 6 | |
| 31. 3 | |

| | +5 |
|---|---|
| 32. 4 | |
| 33. 0 | |
| 34. 7 | |
| 35. 2 | |
| 36. 5 | |

Add.

37. 8   38. 9   39. 3   40. 4   41. 3   42. 6   43. 2   44. 7
+2    +8    +6    +4    +0    +4    +3    +8

45. 3   46. 9   47. 9   48. 7   49. 6   50. 4   51. 8   52. 3
+3    +3    +1    +3    +7    +5    +9    +9

53. 9   54. 0   55. 7   56. 2   57. 4   58. 8   59. 1   60. 6
+9    +5    +5    +6    +7    +3    +7    +9

61. 4   62. 7   63. 3   64. 5   65. 8   66. 4   67. 9   68. 2
+6    +7    +4    +8    +6    +2    +6    +8

For each problem, tell how many animals in all.

69. 6 yellow fish
8 red fish

70. 4 kittens
3 turtles

71. 2 birds
5 rabbits

72. 9 puppies
7 turtles

73. 5 birds
6 fish

74. 9 turtles
2 fish

75. 5 puppies
9 kittens

76. 3 chickens
8 birds

77. 1 rabbit
6 turtles

78. 7 blue birds
1 yellow bird

79. 7 fish
6 kittens

80. 8 puppies
4 chickens

# Minuends Through 10

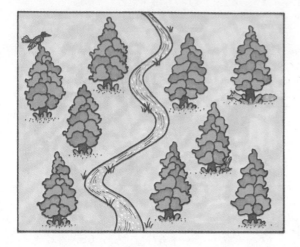

A. There were 9 trees. A clerk sold 5 of them. How many trees were left?

You can use a subtraction fact to find this answer.

Think of taking away 5 of the trees.

$$9 - 5 = 4$$
Difference

There were 4 trees left.

B. There were 8 tractors. 2 of them were red, and the rest were blue. How many were blue?

You can use a subtraction fact to find this answer.

Think of taking away the 2 red tractors.

$$8 - 2 = 6$$

There are 6 blue tractors.

C. You can write subtraction facts in another way.

$$\begin{array}{r} 9 \\ -5 \\ \hline 4 \end{array} \longleftarrow \text{Difference} \longrightarrow \begin{array}{r} 8 \\ -2 \\ \hline 6 \end{array}$$

Give a subtraction fact for each picture.

1. ● ● / ● 2. ● ● / ○ 3. ● ● / ○ ● ● 4. ● ● ● / ● ● ●
   ● ● ● ●     ●     ● ●         ● ● ●

Give each difference.

| 5. | 6. | 7. | 8. | 9. | 10. | 11. |
|---|---|---|---|---|---|---|
| 9<br>−2 | 6<br>−5 | 2<br>−2 | 10<br>− 1 | 7<br>−3 | 3<br>−1 | 9<br>−8 |

| 12. | 13. | 14. | 15. | 16. | 17. | 18. |
|---|---|---|---|---|---|---|
| 5<br>−1 | 10<br>− 9 | 8<br>−2 | 4<br>−0 | 10<br>− 3 | 9<br>−1 | 9<br>−9 |

| 19. | 20. | 21. | 22. | 23. | 24. | 25. |
|---|---|---|---|---|---|---|
| 7<br>−6 | 9<br>−3 | 3<br>−2 | 10<br>− 5 | 7<br>−1 | 5<br>−5 | 8<br>−4 |

| 26. | 27. | 28. | 29. | 30. | 31. | 32. |
|---|---|---|---|---|---|---|
| 10<br>− 2 | 8<br>−0 | 10<br>− 6 | 10<br>− 8 | 5<br>−3 | 9<br>−4 | 7<br>−2 |

| | | | | |
|---|---|---|---|---|
| 33. $10 - 8$ | 34. $9 - 6$ | 35. $7 - 5$ | 36. $10 - 3$ | 37. $9 - 2$ |
| 38. $8 - 6$ | 39. $6 - 3$ | 40. $9 - 0$ | 41. $5 - 2$ | 42. $8 - 1$ |
| 43. $10 - 2$ | 44. $2 - 1$ | 45. $8 - 3$ | 46. $9 - 7$ | 47. $8 - 8$ |
| 48. $6 - 4$ | 49. $4 - 4$ | 50. $9 - 5$ | 51. $6 - 1$ | 52. $10 - 7$ |
| 53. $5 - 4$ | 54. $8 - 4$ | 55. $10 - 4$ | 56. $7 - 2$ | 57. $6 - 0$ |

More practice
Set 4, page 355

● *Discuss*  What is the answer when you
subtract 0 from a number?

● *Discuss*  What is the answer when you
subtract a number from itself?

(twenty-nine) **29**

# Minuends of 11 Through 18

A. A museum has 13 models. 8 are planes, and the rest are cars. How many models are cars?

You can use a subtraction fact to find the answer.

Think of removing the 8 planes.

$$13 - 8 = 5$$

5 of the models are cars.

B. You can draw a picture to help you find the answer to $15 - 6$.

First draw 15 marks.

///// ///// /////

You want to subtract 6, so cross off 6 marks.

///// ///// /////

9 marks are left.

$$15 - 6 = 9$$

• **Discuss** How would you draw a picture to help you find the answer to $16 - 9$?

Draw a picture for each fact.
Give each difference.

1. $11 - 7$   2. $17 - 9$   3. $13 - 6$   4. $16 - 7$   5. $11 - 3$
6. $15 - 8$   7. $12 - 4$   8. $14 - 5$   9. $12 - 7$   10. $15 - 9$

Give each difference.

11. $\begin{array}{r} 12 \\ -\ 6 \\ \hline \end{array}$
12. $\begin{array}{r} 15 \\ -\ 9 \\ \hline \end{array}$
13. $\begin{array}{r} 11 \\ -\ 2 \\ \hline \end{array}$
14. $\begin{array}{r} 18 \\ -\ 9 \\ \hline \end{array}$
15. $\begin{array}{r} 13 \\ -\ 5 \\ \hline \end{array}$
16. $\begin{array}{r} 11 \\ -\ 8 \\ \hline \end{array}$
17. $\begin{array}{r} 14 \\ -\ 7 \\ \hline \end{array}$

18. $\begin{array}{r} 11 \\ -\ 3 \\ \hline \end{array}$
19. $\begin{array}{r} 14 \\ -\ 6 \\ \hline \end{array}$
20. $\begin{array}{r} 13 \\ -\ 8 \\ \hline \end{array}$
21. $\begin{array}{r} 12 \\ -\ 4 \\ \hline \end{array}$
22. $\begin{array}{r} 11 \\ -\ 5 \\ \hline \end{array}$
23. $\begin{array}{r} 13 \\ -\ 9 \\ \hline \end{array}$
24. $\begin{array}{r} 11 \\ -\ 6 \\ \hline \end{array}$

25. $\begin{array}{r} 13 \\ -\ 4 \\ \hline \end{array}$
26. $\begin{array}{r} 17 \\ -\ 9 \\ \hline \end{array}$
27. $\begin{array}{r} 11 \\ -\ 9 \\ \hline \end{array}$
28. $\begin{array}{r} 14 \\ -\ 8 \\ \hline \end{array}$
29. $\begin{array}{r} 15 \\ -\ 6 \\ \hline \end{array}$
30. $\begin{array}{r} 12 \\ -\ 8 \\ \hline \end{array}$
31. $\begin{array}{r} 16 \\ -\ 8 \\ \hline \end{array}$

32. $12 - 3$   33. $13 - 9$   34. $14 - 9$   35. $12 - 5$   36. $15 - 7$
37. $12 - 4$   38. $14 - 5$   39. $15 - 9$   40. $11 - 4$   41. $13 - 6$
42. $17 - 8$   43. $12 - 9$   44. $11 - 7$   45. $13 - 8$   46. $16 - 7$
47. $11 - 6$   48. $14 - 6$   49. $13 - 4$   50. $15 - 8$   51. $12 - 3$
52. $16 - 9$   53. $12 - 7$   54. $13 - 7$   55. $18 - 9$   56. $15 - 6$
57. $13 - 5$   58. $17 - 9$   59. $14 - 8$   60. $16 - 8$   61. $11 - 9$

**More practice
Set 5, page 355**

# Using Subtraction Facts

Gayle made a table by using the rule **Subtract 7.** This rule tells her to subtract 7 from each number.

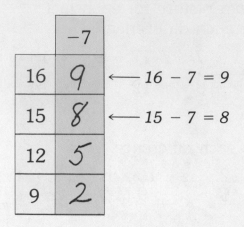

| −7 | |
|---|---|
| 16 | 9 | ← 16 − 7 = 9
| 15 | 8 | ← 15 − 7 = 8
| 12 | 5 |
| 9 | 2 |

Use the rules. Give each difference.

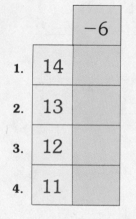

| | −6 | |
|---|---|---|
| 1. | 14 | |
| 2. | 13 | |
| 3. | 12 | |
| 4. | 11 | |

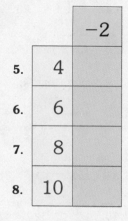

| | −2 | |
|---|---|---|
| 5. | 4 | |
| 6. | 6 | |
| 7. | 8 | |
| 8. | 10 | |

| | −9 | |
|---|---|---|
| 9. | 18 | |
| 10. | 16 | |
| 11. | 13 | |
| 12. | 11 | |

| | −4 | |
|---|---|---|
| 13. | 6 | |
| 14. | 9 | |
| 15. | 10 | |
| 16. | 13 | |

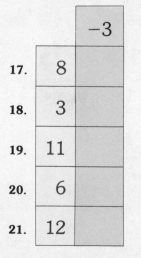

| | −3 | |
|---|---|---|
| 17. | 8 | |
| 18. | 3 | |
| 19. | 11 | |
| 20. | 6 | |
| 21. | 12 | |

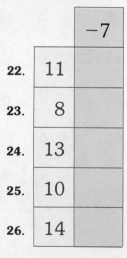

| | −7 | |
|---|---|---|
| 22. | 11 | |
| 23. | 8 | |
| 24. | 13 | |
| 25. | 10 | |
| 26. | 14 | |

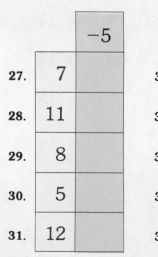

| | −5 | |
|---|---|---|
| 27. | 7 | |
| 28. | 11 | |
| 29. | 8 | |
| 30. | 5 | |
| 31. | 12 | |

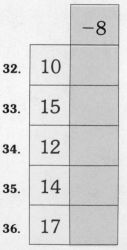

| | −8 | |
|---|---|---|
| 32. | 10 | |
| 33. | 15 | |
| 34. | 12 | |
| 35. | 14 | |
| 36. | 17 | |

Subtract.

37. 10 − 6
38. 12 − 7
39. 8 − 4
40. 17 − 9
41. 14 − 5
42. 7 − 7
43. 11 − 5

44. 9 − 2
45. 15 − 6
46. 10 − 3
47. 13 − 8
48. 4 − 2
49. 16 − 7
50. 12 − 4

51. 11 − 8
52. 5 − 0
53. 12 − 6
54. 16 − 8
55. 10 − 9
56. 9 − 3
57. 15 − 7

58. 10 − 1
59. 14 − 9
60. 8 − 1
61. 15 − 9
62. 11 − 9
63. 7 − 4
64. 13 − 5

For each problem, tell how many were left.

65. 5 tennis balls
Gave away 3

66. 9 football tickets
Sold 5

67. 7 tennis balls in a box
Removed 3

68. 9 soccer tickets
Sold 6

69. 8 baseballs
Used 2

70. 10 footballs
Gave away 4

71. 11 tennis hats
Used 6

72. 12 baseball hats
Sold 9

73. 18 soccer balls in a box
Removed 9

74. 14 baseballs
Gave away 6

75. 13 footballs in a bag
Removed 6

76. 16 baseball bats
Sold 8

77. 13 soccer balls
Gave away 4

78. 15 tennis balls
Used 6

## Subtraction: Comparison

There are 8 boats and 5 cars. There are
how many more boats than cars? There
are how many fewer cars than boats?

Match the cars with the boats.
Write a subtraction sentence.

# 8 – 5 = 3

There are 3 more boats than cars.
There are 3 fewer cars than boats.


There are how many more stars than dots?
Write the subtraction sentence you use.

1. ★ ★ ★ ★ ★   ★ ★
   ● ● ●

2. ● ● ● ● ● ●
   ★ ★ ★ ★ ★   ★ ★ ★

3. ★ ★ ★ ★ ★
   ● ● ●

4. ★ ★ ★ ★ ★   ★ ★ ★ ★ ★
   ● ● ● ● ● ●

5. ● ●
   ★ ★ ★ ★ ★   ★ ★ ★ ★

6. ★ ★ ★ ★ ★   ★ ★ ★ ★ ★ ★
   ● ● ● ●

There are how many fewer dots than stars?
Write the subtraction sentence you use.

7. ★ ★ ★ ★ ★  ★
   ● ● ● ●

8. ● ● ● ● ●
   ★ ★ ★ ★ ★  ★ ★

9. ● ● ● ●
   ★ ★ ★ ★ ★  ★ ★ ★ ★

10. ★ ★ ★ ★ ★  ★ ★ ★
    ● ●

11. ★ ★ ★ ★ ★  ★ ★ ★ ★ ★
    ● ● ● ● ●

12. ● ● ● ● ●
    ★ ★ ★ ★ ★  ★ ★ ★ ★  ★

Write the subtraction sentence for each problem.
Give the answer.

13. There are 3 oranges and 10 apples.
    How many more apples are there?

14. There are 11 cats and
    7 dogs. How many fewer
    dogs are there?

15. There are 7 lions and
    15 tigers. How many more
    tigers are there?

16. There are 13 birds and
    8 fish. How many more
    birds are there?

17. There are 4 turtles and
    12 monkeys. How many
    more monkeys are there?

18. There are 8 ducks and
    17 frogs. How many fewer
    ducks are there?

19. There are 14 elephants and
    5 bears. How many more
    elephants are there?

20. There are 9 squirrels and
    16 rabbits. How many more
    rabbits are there?

21. There are 14 chickens and
    6 turkeys. How many fewer
    turkeys are there?

# Families of Facts

A. You can use one picture to help you find two addition sentences and two subtraction sentences.

Think of putting the 6 zinnias and 7 sunflowers together.

6 + 7 = 13
7 + 6 = 13

Think of separating the 13 flowers into two groups.

13 − 7 = 6
13 − 6 = 7

These four sentences make up a *family of facts.*

  6 + 7 = 13    7 + 6 = 13
13 − 7 = 6    13 − 6 = 7

B. These number sentences also make up a family of facts.

  6 + 6 = 12
12 − 6 = 6

*Discuss* The sentences below make up a family of facts. What do you notice about the numbers in these sentences?

4 + 5 = 9   5 + 4 = 9
9 − 5 = 4   9 − 4 = 5

Copy and give each answer. Tell which fact does not belong to the family.

Here's how     2 + 9       $2 + 9 = 11$

11 − 9       $11 - 9 = 2$

9 − 2       $(9 - 2 = 7)$

9 + 2       $9 + 2 = 11$

11 − 2       $11 - 2 = 9$

1. 4 + 8      2. 9 − 6      3. 9 − 8
7 + 5      3 + 6      9 + 8
12 − 4      6 + 3      17 − 9
12 − 8      9 − 3      8 + 9
8 + 4      3 + 3      17 − 8

4. 12 − 3      5. 8 + 2      6. 7 + 3
12 − 9      10 − 2      3 + 7
3 + 9      6 + 4      10 − 7
12 − 6      10 − 8      10 − 3
9 + 3      2 + 8      10 − 5

7. 18 − 9      8. 4 + 4      9. 6 + 6
8 + 8      8 − 4      7 + 7
9 + 9      3 + 3      14 − 7

Give the sentences that make up
a family of facts.

★10. 4, 6, 10      ★11. 7, 3, 4      ★12. 14, 6, 8

★13. 7, 16, 9      ★14. 11, 7, 4      ★15. 1, 9, 10

| 1 | 8 | 4 |
|---|---|---|
| 5 | 3 | 2 |
| 6 | 7 | 9 |

Give each sentence.

Here's how

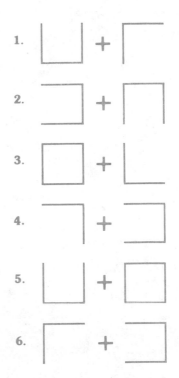

$1 + 2 = 3$

1.

2.

3.

4.

5.

6.

# Using Addition and Subtraction Facts

For each exercise, give a number sentence.
Then write yes or no.

Is this a name for 8?

**Here's how**

| | | |
|---|---|---|
| $5 + 3$ | $5 + 3 = 8$ | *yes* |
| $16 - 9$ | $16 - 9 = 7$ | *no* |
| $13 - 5$ | $13 - 5 = 8$ | *yes* |
| $2 + 7$ | $2 + 7 = 9$ | *no* |
| $9 - 1$ | $9 - 1 = 8$ | *yes* |

Is this a name for 9?

1. $5 + 4$
2. $11 - 2$
3. $10 - 2$
4. $6 + 3$
5. $4 + 6$

Is this a name for 6?

6. $2 + 3$
7. $14 - 8$
8. $12 - 5$
9. $3 + 4$
10. $3 + 3$

Is this a name for 4?

11. $2 + 2$
12. $13 - 8$
13. $10 - 6$
14. $12 - 8$
15. $4 + 0$

Is this a name for 5?

16. $4 + 2$
17. $3 + 2$
18. $16 - 7$
19. $11 - 6$
20. $3 + 1$

Is this a name for 3?

21. $11 - 9$
22. $1 + 1$
23. $10 - 7$
24. $9 - 5$
25. $8 - 4$

Is this a name for 7?

26. $4 + 4$
27. $15 - 8$
28. $2 + 5$
29. $6 + 2$
30. $13 - 6$

**38** (thirty-eight)

Use the rules.
Give each sum or difference.

|      |     | +5 |
|------|-----|----|
| 31.  | 7   |    |
| 32.  | 5   |    |
| 33.  | 3   |    |
| 34.  | 9   |    |
| 35.  | 6   |    |

|      |     | +8 |
|------|-----|----|
| 36.  | 4   |    |
| 37.  | 1   |    |
| 38.  | 8   |    |
| 39.  | 2   |    |
| 40.  | 7   |    |

|      |     | −4 |
|------|-----|----|
| 41.  | 7   |    |
| 42.  | 12  |    |
| 43.  | 6   |    |
| 44.  | 10  |    |
| 45.  | 13  |    |

|      |     | −7 |
|------|-----|----|
| 46.  | 12  |    |
| 47.  | 9   |    |
| 48.  | 15  |    |
| 49.  | 7   |    |
| 50.  | 14  |    |

Give each sum or difference.

51. $\begin{array}{r} 5 \\ +6 \end{array}$   52. $\begin{array}{r} 5 \\ -2 \end{array}$   53. $\begin{array}{r} 12 \\ -\ 3 \end{array}$   54. $\begin{array}{r} 9 \\ +4 \end{array}$   55. $\begin{array}{r} 4 \\ +3 \end{array}$   56. $\begin{array}{r} 9 \\ -3 \end{array}$   57. $\begin{array}{r} 7 \\ +6 \end{array}$

58. $\begin{array}{r} 10 \\ -\ 8 \end{array}$   59. $\begin{array}{r} 18 \\ -\ 9 \end{array}$   60. $\begin{array}{r} 6 \\ +9 \end{array}$   61. $\begin{array}{r} 6 \\ -3 \end{array}$   62. $\begin{array}{r} 14 \\ -\ 6 \end{array}$   63. $\begin{array}{r} 9 \\ +7 \end{array}$   64. $\begin{array}{r} 8 \\ +9 \end{array}$

65. $\begin{array}{r} 8 \\ +4 \end{array}$   66. $\begin{array}{r} 7 \\ -5 \end{array}$   67. $\begin{array}{r} 4 \\ +7 \end{array}$   68. $\begin{array}{r} 17 \\ -\ 8 \end{array}$   69. $\begin{array}{r} 7 \\ +7 \end{array}$   70. $\begin{array}{r} 8 \\ -1 \end{array}$   71. $\begin{array}{r} 15 \\ -\ 9 \end{array}$

Give three addition facts and three subtraction facts
that are names for each number.

★72. 7   ★73. 4   ★74. 9   ★75. 6   ★76. 8   ★77. 5

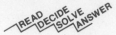

# Problem Solving: Choosing the Operation

| READ | Read the problem.<br>What facts are given?<br>What is the question? | A. Wade had 8 frogs. He caught 7 more. How many frogs did Wade have then? |
|---|---|---|
| DECIDE | What must you do to solve the problem? | Add the number of frogs Wade caught to the number he had. |
| SOLVE | Do the work. | This number sentence shows the work.<br><br>$$8 + 7 = 15$$ |
| ANSWER | Does the answer make sense? | 15 frogs |

READ  B. Mrs. Grey caught 17 fish. She used 9 for supper. How many fish did she have left?

DECIDE  Subtract the number of fish Mrs. Grey used from the number she caught.

SOLVE  $17 - 9 = 8$

ANSWER  8 fish

For each problem, write a
number sentence. Then give
the answer.

1. Kay walked 3 miles before
   lunch and 4 miles after
   lunch. She walked how
   many miles in all?

2. Wade saw 14 robins and
   6 crows. He saw how many
   fewer crows than robins?

3. Mrs. Grey had 12 candles.
   She used 8 of them. How
   many candles were left?

4. Kay found 3 red rocks and
   8 white rocks. She found
   how many rocks in all?

5. The Greys had 9 boxes of
   raisins. They ate 5 of
   them. How many boxes did
   the Greys have left?

6. The Greys had 9 cans of
   orange juice and 5 cans
   of tomato juice. They had
   how many cans of juice?

7. Wade found 13 red rocks.
   He gave away 6. How many
   rocks did he have then?

8. Mr. Grey had 6 fish. He
   caught 9 more. How many
   fish did he have then?

9. Wade counted 8 tents in
   Camp K and 9 in Camp W.
   How many tents were in
   these two camps?

10. Kay had 7 frogs and
    11 fish. She had how many
    more fish than frogs?

## Missing Addends

What number do you add to 9 to get 14? You have to find the **missing addend.**

A. Hilda drew a picture to find the missing addend.

First she drew 9 marks.

///// /////∫

Then she drew more marks to make 14 in all.

///// /////∫/////

Hilda drew 5 more marks. The missing addend is 5.

9 + 5 = 14

B. Mona used subtraction to find the missing addend.

She subtracted 9 from 14.

$$\begin{array}{r} 14 \\ -\ 9 \\ \hline 5 \end{array}$$

The difference is 5, so the missing addend is 5.

9 + 5 = 14

Find each missing addend to complete the sentence.

**Here's how**

? + 7 = 13

6 + 7 = 13

1. 1 + ? = 10
2. ? + 4 = 5
3. ? + 2 = 8
4. 5 + ? = 7
5. 4 + ? = 10
6. 7 + ? = 15
7. ? + 6 = 11
8. ? + 3 = 9
9. 9 + ? = 15
10. ? + 5 = 12
11. ? + 6 = 14
12. ? + 4 = 13
13. 9 + ? = 18
14. ? + 0 = 7
15. 9 + ? = 16
16. ? + 8 = 17
17. 8 + ? = 11
18. 9 + ? = 9

# Chapter 2 Test
## Addition and Subtraction Facts, pages 22–42

Add.

1. 5
   +5

2. 8
   +7

3. 3
   +4

4. 6
   +0

5. 2
   +6

6. 7
   +4

7. 5
   +4

8. 7
   +5

9. 9
   +9

10. 6
    +8

11. 1
    +9

12. 4
    +9

Subtract.

13. 9
    −6

14. 13
    − 7

15. 8
    −3

16. 16
    − 8

17. 6
    −2

18. 11
    − 9

19. 7
    −6

20. 14
    − 7

21. 17
    − 8

22. 15
    − 9

23. 8
    −0

24. 12
    − 6

Which fact does not belong to the family?

25. $14 - 9 = 5$

    $9 + 5 = 14$

    $14 - 5 = 9$

    $14 - 6 = 8$

    $5 + 9 = 14$

26. $16 - 8 = 8$

    $7 + 7 = 14$

    $8 + 8 = 16$

Give the answers.

27. Antonio had 8 rocks. He found 2 more. How many rocks did he have then?

28. Lara had 10 pears and 7 apples. She had how many more pears than apples?

29. Ed had 12 tickets. He sold 4. How many tickets did Ed have then?

30. Kiku counted 8 robins and 5 crows. She counted how many birds in all?

# Chapter 3 Geometry

## Geometric Shapes

Traffic signs have different shapes. Some of these shapes have sides and corners.

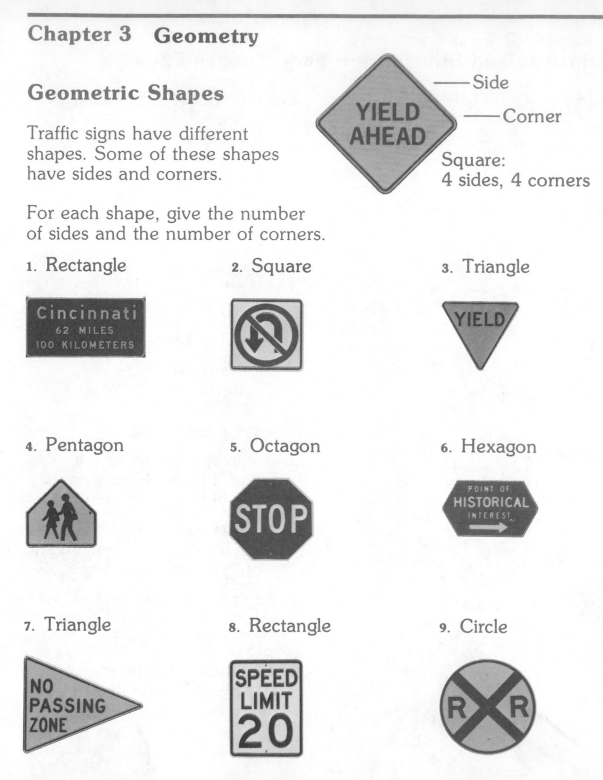

—— Side

—— Corner

Square:
4 sides, 4 corners

For each shape, give the number of sides and the number of corners.

1. Rectangle

2. Square

3. Triangle

4. Pentagon

5. Octagon

6. Hexagon

7. Triangle

8. Rectangle

9. Circle

Give the name for each shape.

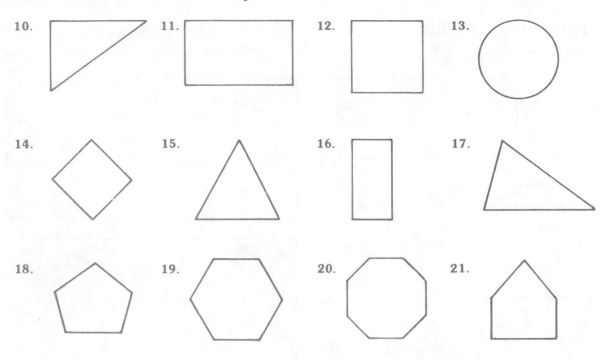

10.

11.

12.

13.

14.

15.

16.

17.

18.

19.

20.

21.

**Discuss** Name some objects that have these shapes.

Give the number of sides and corners for each shape.

22. Triangle

23. Circle

24. Square

25. Rectangle

26. Hexagon

27. Octagon

28. Pentagon

# Meaning of Symmetry

Terry folded a piece of
wax paper.

He traced a pattern with
his pencil by starting and
ending on the fold.

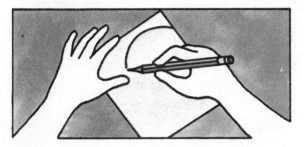

Terry opened the paper. He
had traced a **symmetric figure.**

This figure is **symmetric** because
the two parts match.

Tell if each figure looks
symmetric. Use yes or no.

1.

2.

3.

4.

Trace each figure and cut it out.
Tell if the figure is symmetric.
Use yes or no.

**5.**

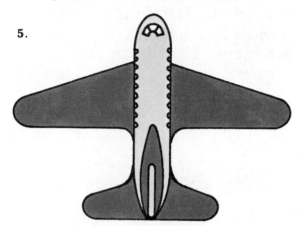

**6.**

**7.**

**8.**

**9.**

**10.**

# Line of Symmetry

You can fold a figure to see if it has a **line of symmetry.** Symmetric figures have a line of symmetry.

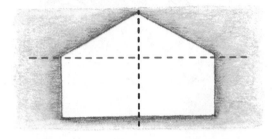

When the figure is folded on the blue line, the two parts do not match. The blue line is not a line of symmetry.

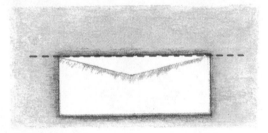

When the figure is folded on the red line, the two parts match. The red line is a line of symmetry.

Trace each figure, cut it out, and fold it. Tell if the broken line is a line of symmetry. Use yes or no.

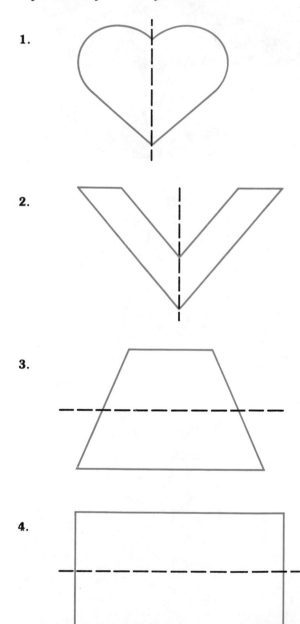

1.

2.

3.

4.

Tell if each figure looks like it has
a line of symmetry. Use yes or no.

Trace and complete each figure.
Use the broken line as a line of symmetry.

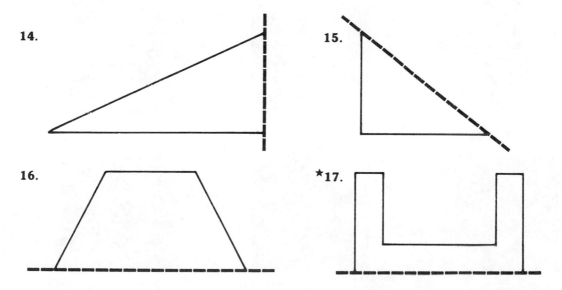

14.

15.

16.

★17.

# Lab Activity

## Geoboards

These figures match.

These figures do not match.

Make a figure on your geoboard to match each of these.

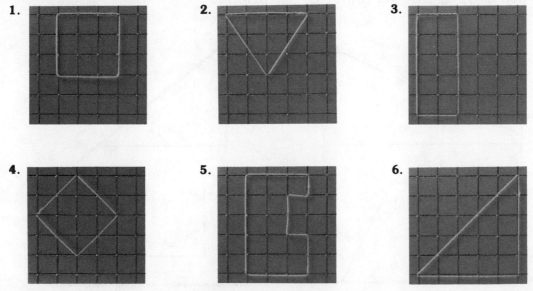

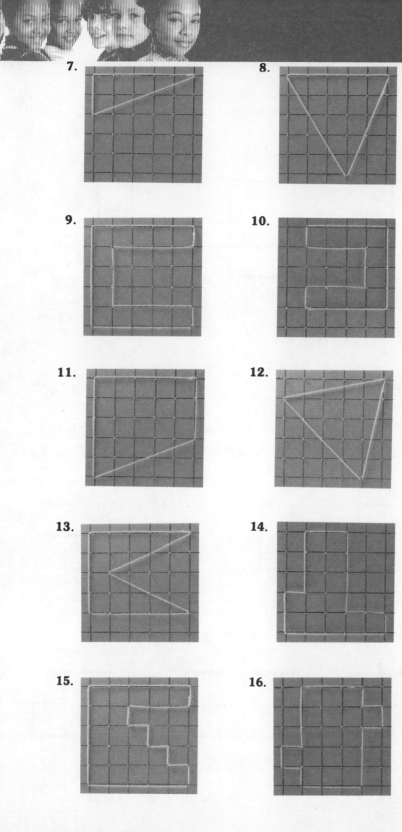

**Keeping Skillful**

1. $2 + 3$

2. $8 - 6$

3. $5 + 4$

4. $11 - 4$

5. $6 - 4$

6. $7 - 5$

7. $7 + 5$

8. $3 + 9$

9. $5 + 4$

10. $5 - 4$

11. $6 + 7$

12. $8 + 6$

13. $15 - 8$

14. $7 + 3$

15. $7 - 3$

16. $17 - 8$

17. $9 + 6$

18. $9 - 6$

19. $8 + 9$

20. $16 - 9$

(fifty-one) **51**

# Congruent Figures

Figures that have the same size and shape are **congruent.**

Tell if each figure is congruent to the blue figure.

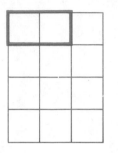 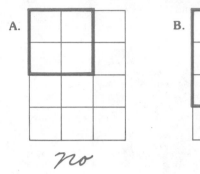 A.  B. 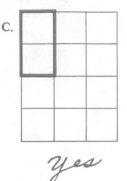 C.

*no*      *no*      *yes*

Figure C is the same size and shape as the blue figure.
Figure C is congruent to the blue figure.

For each exercise, tell if the figure is congruent
to the blue figure in the row. Use yes or no.

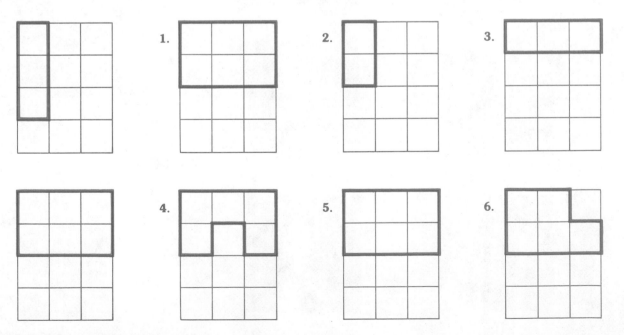

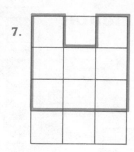 **7.** 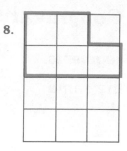 **8.** 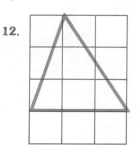 **9.**

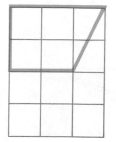 **10.** 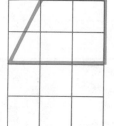 **11.** 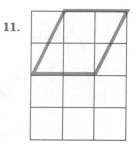 **12.**

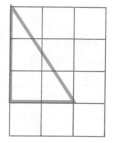 **13.** 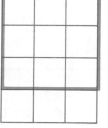 **14.** **15.**

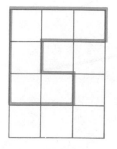 **16.** 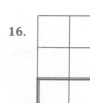 **17.** 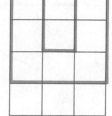 **18.**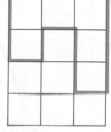

# Segments and Congruent Segments

The picture shows **segments.**

Segments that are the same
length are **congruent.**

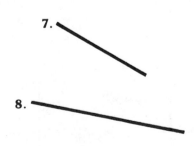

Are the segments in the picture below congruent?
Here is a way to tell.

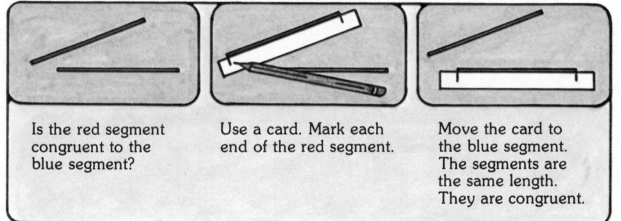

Is the red segment
congruent to the
blue segment?

Use a card. Mark each
end of the red segment.

Move the card to
the blue segment.
The segments are
the same length.
They are congruent.

Is each segment congruent to this segment? —————
Use yes or no.

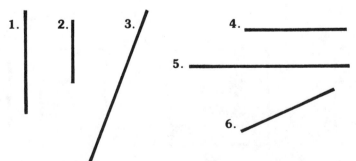

1.

2.

3.

4.

5.

6.

7.

8.

The sides of these figures are segments.
Look at each figure. Tell if the red side
is congruent to the blue side.
Use yes or no.

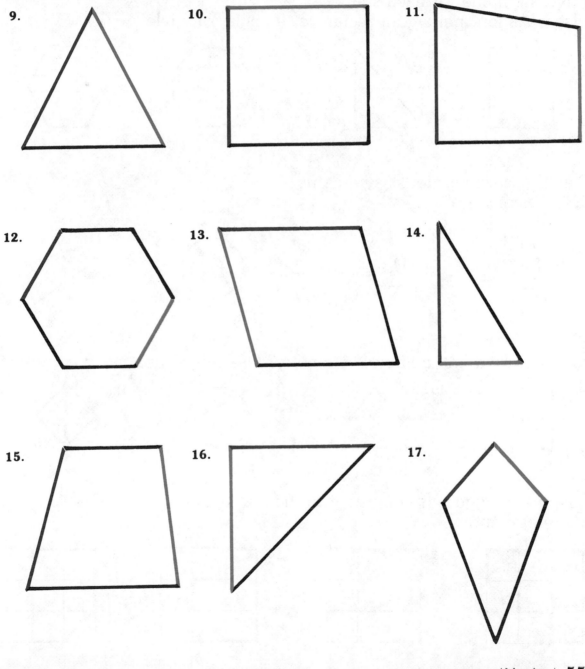

9.

10.

11.

12.

13.

14.

15.

16.

17.

# Chapter 3 Test
## Geometry, pages 44-55

Give the name for each shape.
Use hexagon, pentagon, rectangle, triangle, or circle.

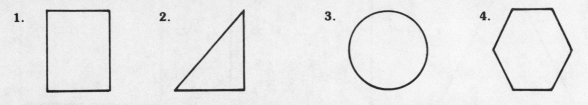

1.   2.   3.   4.

Tell if each figure looks symmetric.
Use yes or no.

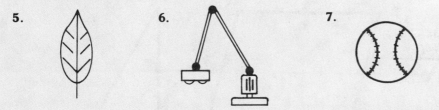

5.   6.   7.   8.

Is the broken line a line of symmetry? Use yes or no.

9.   10.   11.   12.

Tell if each figure is congruent to the first figure.
Use yes or no.

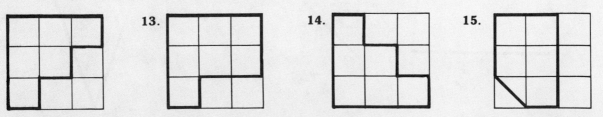

13.   14.   15.

# Problems Around Us

1. How many boats are there in all?

2. There are how many more sailboats than rowboats?

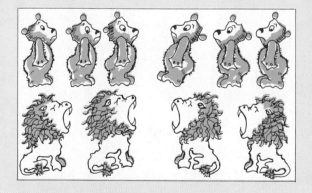

3. How many animals are there in all?

4. There are how many more bears than lions?

5. Jack had 9 marbles. He bought 6 more. How many did he have in all?

6. Lynn had 12 pencils. She gave away 8. How many did she have left?

7. There are 16 cats and 9 dogs. How many more cats are there?

8. Kathy saw 6 sparrows and 8 robins. She saw how many birds in all?

9. Al picked 16 apples. He gave away 7. How many apples did he have left?

10. Sue had 14 cents. She spent 9 cents. She had how much money left?

11. Ed caught 5 fish and Pat caught 8 fish. How many did they catch in all?

12. Ann bought 9 tickets. She used 4 of them. How many did she have left?

13. Don saw 8 white rabbits and 7 brown rabbits. He saw how many in all?

14. There are 15 boys and 9 girls. How many more boys are there?

# Individualized Skills Maintenance

**Diagnose**

A  *pages 22–27*     B  *pages 28–33*

| A | B |
|---|---|
| 9 + 7 | 13 − 8 |
| 8 + 7 | 14 − 6 |
| 5 + 8 | 16 − 7 |

**Practice**

A

| 1. | 2. | 3. | 4. | 5. | 6. | 7. |
|---|---|---|---|---|---|---|
| 4<br>+4 | 3<br>+1 | 2<br>+7 | 2<br>+3 | 4<br>+5 | 1<br>+5 | 4<br>+3 |

| 8. | 9. | 10. | 11. | 12. | 13. | 14. |
|---|---|---|---|---|---|---|
| 6<br>+5 | 5<br>+2 | 6<br>+7 | 5<br>+3 | 9<br>+4 | 6<br>+4 | 3<br>+8 |

| 15. | 16. | 17. | 18. | 19. | 20. | 21. |
|---|---|---|---|---|---|---|
| 9<br>+8 | 6<br>+3 | 7<br>+8 | 3<br>+9 | 8<br>+5 | 4<br>+7 | 8<br>+6 |

B

| 22. | 23. | 24. | 25. | 26. | 27. | 28. |
|---|---|---|---|---|---|---|
| 8<br>−4 | 6<br>−1 | 9<br>−4 | 7<br>−7 | 12<br>− 5 | 9<br>−3 | 11<br>− 3 |

| 29. | 30. | 31. | 32. | 33. | 34. | 35. |
|---|---|---|---|---|---|---|
| 16<br>− 9 | 14<br>− 5 | 17<br>− 8 | 7<br>−5 | 11<br>− 7 | 10<br>− 4 | 15<br>− 6 |

| 36. | 37. | 38. | 39. | 40. | 41. | 42. |
|---|---|---|---|---|---|---|
| 10<br>− 3 | 6<br>−4 | 14<br>− 8 | 13<br>− 5 | 12<br>− 4 | 15<br>− 8 | 13<br>− 4 |

# Unit 1 Review

Chapter 1, pages 2–20

**1.** Pablo is working on his third problem. How many has he worked?

**2.** Which number is less, 16 or 18?

**3.** Which number is greater, 49 or 94?

**4.** Give the numbers in order. Start with the least number.

   19   17   16   18

Count from 10 to 30 by

**5.** fives.   **6.** twos.

This graph shows the number of rocks May and Dan found.

Each $\bigcirc$ = 5 rocks.

| May | $\bigcirc$ $\bigcirc$ $\bigcirc$ $\bigcirc$ $\bigcirc$ |
|-----|-------------------|
| Dan | $\bigcirc$ $\bigcirc$ $\bigcirc$ |

How many rocks were found

**7.** by May?   **8.** by Dan?

Chapter 2, pages 22–42

Add.

**9.** $\begin{array}{r} 4 \\ +7 \end{array}$   **10.** $\begin{array}{r} 4 \\ +3 \end{array}$   **11.** $\begin{array}{r} 8 \\ +6 \end{array}$

Subtract.

**12.** $\begin{array}{r} 11 \\ -\ 6 \end{array}$   **13.** $\begin{array}{r} 15 \\ -\ 8 \end{array}$   **14.** $\begin{array}{r} 16 \\ -\ 7 \end{array}$

**15.** Sharma had 8 fish. She bought 7 more. She had how many in all?

**16.** Yung had 16 pens. He gave away 8. He had how many left?

Chapter 3, pages 44–55

Give the name of each shape.

**17.** 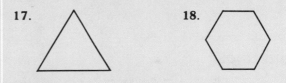   **18.**

Tell if each figure looks symmetric. Use yes or no.

**19.**    **20.**

Tell if the figures are congruent. Use yes or no.

**21.**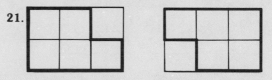

# Unit 1 Test
## Chapters 1-3, pages 2-56

Add.

1. 7
 +2

2. 4
 +3

3. 5
 +1

4. 3
 +2

5. 4
 +6

6. 2
 +8

7. 6
 +5

8. 7
 +9

9. 5
 +4

10. 3
 +8

11. 8
 +7

12. 9
 +8

Subtract.

13. 7
 −2

14. 16
 − 8

15. 10
 − 1

16. 12
 − 6

17. 11
 − 2

18. 12
 − 4

19. 10
 − 4

20. 8
 −3

21. 11
 − 7

22. 16
 − 9

23. 13
 − 5

24. 15
 − 8

25. Sumi is fifth in line. How many are in front of her?

26. Which number is less, 21 or 12?

27. Which number is greater, 38 or 48?

28. Give the numbers in order. Start with the least.

5   7   6   4

Count from 20 to 40 by

29. fives.    30. twos.

31. Eva had 14 pencils. She gave away 6. How many did she have left?

32. Cal saw 2 red cars and 8 blue cars. How many cars did he see in all?

33. Tom saw 7 tigers and 5 lions. He saw how many more tigers than lions?

Give the name of each shape. Use square, triangle, or circle.

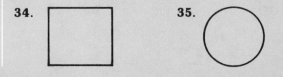

34.    35.

# Unit 2

# Chapter 4   Numeration Through 999

## Hundreds, Tens, and Ones

A.

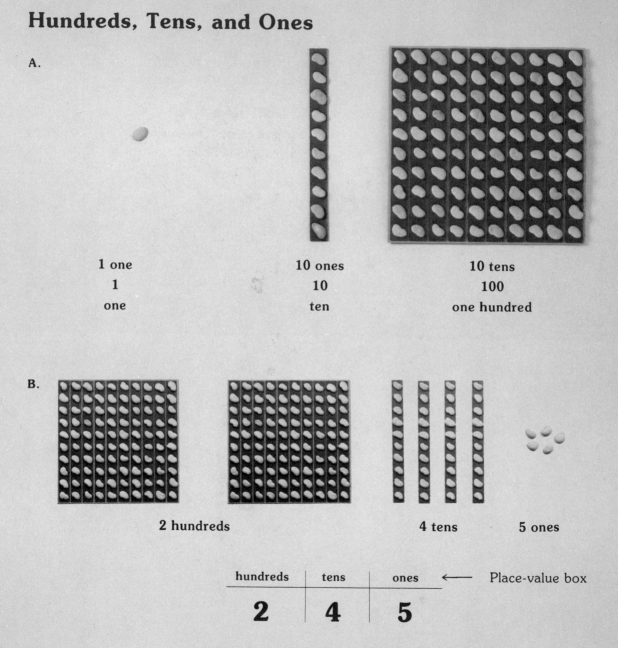

1 one
1
one

10 ones
10
ten

10 tens
100
one hundred

B.

2 hundreds        4 tens        5 ones

| hundreds | tens | ones | ← Place-value box |
|----------|------|------|---|
| **2** | **4** | **5** | |

two hundred forty-five

Give a place-value box for each number.

**Here's how**

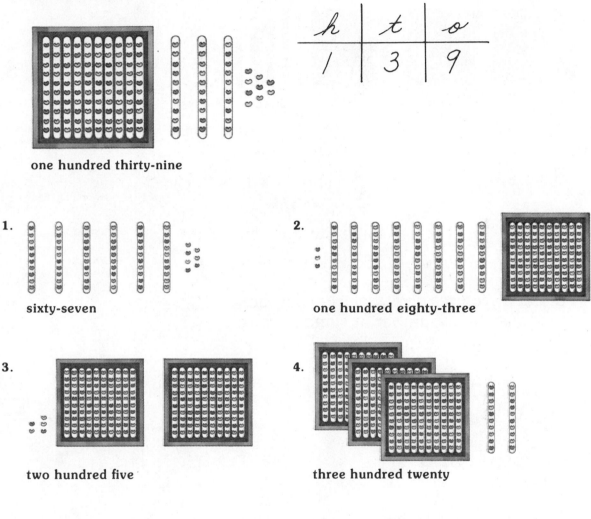

one hundred thirty-nine

| h | t | o |
|---|---|---|
| 1 | 3 | 9 |

1. sixty-seven

2. one hundred eighty-three

3. two hundred five

4. three hundred twenty

5. five hundred thirty-four

6. ninety-one

7. six hundred eighteen

8. two hundred fifty-three

9. three hundred twenty-seven

10. eight hundred sixty-two

11. four hundred eighty-three

12. nine hundred seventy-five

13. seven hundred nine

14. one hundred forty

# Standard Form

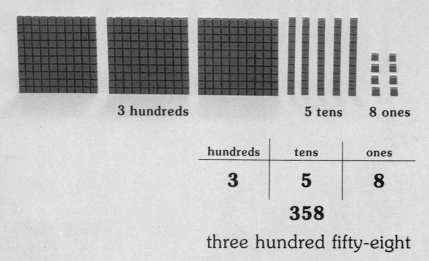

3 hundreds          5 tens    8 ones

| hundreds | tens | ones |
|:---:|:---:|:---:|
| **3** | **5** | **8** |

**358**

three hundred fifty-eight

358 is the *standard form.*

For each picture, give a place-value box.
Then give each number in standard form.

### Here's how

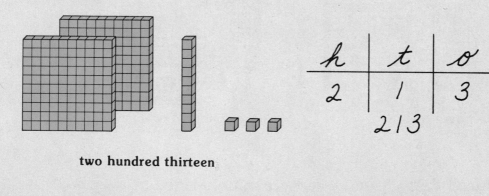

| h | t | o |
|:---:|:---:|:---:|
| 2 | 1 | 3 |

213

two hundred thirteen

**1.**

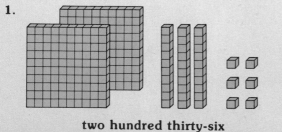

two hundred thirty-six

**2.**

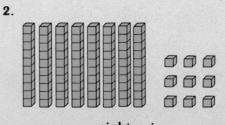

eighty-nine

**3.**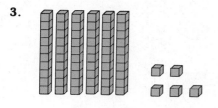

sixty-five

**4.**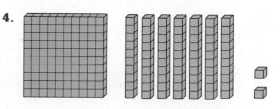

one hundred seventy-two

**5.**

three hundred fifty-four

**6.**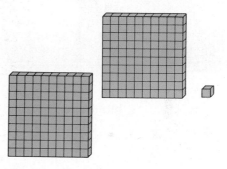

two hundred one

# Give the standard form for each number.

**7.**

| hundreds | tens | ones |
|:---:|:---:|:---:|
| 1 | 5 | 9 |

**8.**

| hundreds | tens | ones |
|:---:|:---:|:---:|
| 2 | 8 | 0 |

**9.**

| hundreds | tens | ones |
|:---:|:---:|:---:|
| 3 | 2 | 4 |

**10.**

| hundreds | tens | ones |
|:---:|:---:|:---:|
|  | 8 | 6 |

**11.**

| hundreds | tens | ones |
|:---:|:---:|:---:|
| 8 | 1 | 3 |

**12.**

| hundreds | tens | ones |
|:---:|:---:|:---:|
| 7 | 0 | 0 |

**13.**

| hundreds | tens | ones |
|:---:|:---:|:---:|
| 9 | 7 | 5 |

**14.**

| hundreds | tens | ones |
|:---:|:---:|:---:|
|  | 4 | 2 |

**15.**

| hundreds | tens | ones |
|:---:|:---:|:---:|
| 6 | 5 | 4 |

**16.**

| hundreds | tens | ones |
|:---:|:---:|:---:|
| 6 | 0 | 8 |

**17.**

| hundreds | tens | ones |
|:---:|:---:|:---:|
| 2 | 5 | 9 |

**18.**

| hundreds | tens | ones |
|:---:|:---:|:---:|
| 8 | 7 | 5 |

# Place Value

Mr. Johnson wrote this assignment on the board.

| hundreds | tens | ones |
|:---:|:---:|:---:|
| **2** | **1** | **5** |

hundreds place     tens place     ones place

**2**     **1**     **5**

**two hundred fifteen**

Is 7 in the hundreds place? Write yes or no.

1. 784    2. 377    3. 407    4. 796    5. 172    6. 700    7. 970

Is 3 in the tens place? Write yes or no.

8. 306    9. 134    10. 635    11. 783    12. 532    13. 343    14. 831

Is 5 in the ones place? Write yes or no.

15. 985    16. 569    17. 550    18. 235    19. 52    20. 485    21. 526

Give the standard form for each number.

**Here's how**

1 ten
8 hundreds
9 ones    $819$

22. 7 hundreds
6 tens
4 ones

23. 5 ones
2 tens
1 hundred

24. 7 tens
4 hundreds
6 ones

25. 3 tens
2 hundreds
8 ones

26. 5 hundreds
1 ten
3 ones

27. 2 ones
4 tens
6 hundreds

28. 4 tens
5 ones

29. 7 hundreds
9 ones

30. 2 hundreds
3 tens

31. 8 tens
6 hundreds

32. 1 one
9 hundreds

33. 8 hundreds
7 ones

34. six hundred forty-five

35. nineteen

36. ninety-seven

37. one hundred seventy-one

38. forty-two

39. five hundred ten

40. five hundred twenty

41. sixty-two

42. seven hundred three

43. three hundred eighty-six

44. fifty-five

45. two hundred fourteen

More practice
Set 6, page 355

# Numbers Through 999

We use ten digits to show numbers.

How many digits does each number have?

1. [7][6]   2. [8][7][6]   3. [5]   4. [3][0][0]   5. [4][7]

What digit is in the ones place?

6. 123   7. 762   8. 304   9. 450   10. 321   11. 267   12. 581

13. 798   14. 590   15. 859   16. 652   17. 106   18. 319   19. 244

What digit is in the tens place?

20. 907   21. 194   22. 371   23. 889   24. 348   25. 567   26. 654

27. 216   28. 430   29. 703   30. 121   31. 492   32. 985   33. 132

What digit is in the hundreds place?

**34.** 789   **35.** 853   **36.** 175   **37.** 458

**38.** 657   **39.** 375   **40.** 206   **41.** 549

For each exercise, write two different numbers that have 2 digits.

**Here's how**

2, 5 *25, 52*

**42.** 1, 9   **43.** 5, 7   **44.** 3, 6   **45.** 7, 8

For each exercise, write three different numbers that have 3 digits.

**Here's how**

3, 1, 8 *318, 183, 831*

**46.** 2, 4, 9   **47.** 6, 3, 7   **48.** 4, 7, 1

**49.** 2, 5, 8   **50.** 6, 1, 2   **51.** 3, 9, 5

For each exercise, write six different numbers that have 3 digits.

**Here's how**

2, 4, 6 *246, 264, 426, 462, 624, 642*

**52.** 8, 3, 5   **53.** 1, 7, 9   **54.** 8, 7, 9

● *Discuss* What number is one greater than 999?

● *Discuss* What is another name for 10 hundreds?

**More practice**
**Set 7, page 356**

Mrs. Earlybird set her alarm clock to ring at 9 o'clock. She went to bed and fell asleep at 8:00 P.M. How many hours did she sleep?

# Comparing Numbers

A. Plane A travels at 568 kilometers per hour.
Plane B travels at 430 kilometers per hour.
Which plane travels faster?

Which is greater, 568 or 430?

568 ● 430   Look at the digits in the hundreds place.
5 is greater than 4.

568 is greater than 430.

568 > 430

Plane A travels faster than Plane B.

B. Plane C travels at 752 kilometers per hour.
Plane D travels at 756 kilometers per hour.
Which plane travels slower?

Which is less, 752 or 756?

752 ● 756   Look at the digits in the hundreds place.
They are the same.

752 ● 756   Look at the digits in the tens place.
They are the same.

752 ● 756   Look at the digits in the ones place.
2 is less than 6.

752 is less than 756.

752 < 756

Plane C travels slower than Plane D.

Replace the ●. Use < or >.

**Here's how**

37 ● 33

# 37 > 33

1. 2 ● 6          2. 6 ● 0

3. 13 ● 7         4. 12 ● 9

5. 33 ● 63        6. 56 ● 26

7. 20 ● 50        8. 30 ● 70

9. 126 ● 926      10. 444 ● 494

11. 823 ● 813     12. 517 ● 515

13. 950 ● 900     14. 774 ● 770

15. 433 ● 473     16. 378 ● 379

17. 119 ● 217     18. 453 ● 463

19. 617 ● 607     20. 890 ● 897

Use 258, 825, 582, 852, and 528 to give the answers.

★21. Which number is greatest?

★22. Which number is least?

★23. Which two numbers have 5 in the tens place? Which is greater?

## Keeping Skillful

| | | | |
|---|---|---|---|
| 1. 6 +8 | 2. 9 +9 | 3. 7 +4 | 4. 9 +2 |
| 5. 0 +6 | 6. 9 +7 | 7. 8 +3 | 8. 6 +5 |
| 9. 9 +8 | 10. 6 +4 | 11. 7 +6 | 12. 1 +8 |
| 13. 4 +8 | 14. 5 +3 | 15. 4 +9 | 16. 2 +7 |
| 17. 5 +8 | 18. 3 +4 | 19. 6 +3 | 20. 4 +5 |
| 21. 3 +7 | 22. 2 +8 | 23. 5 +7 | 24. 8 +8 |
| 25. 2 +3 | 26. 8 +7 | 27. 9 +5 | 28. 6 +2 |
| 29. 6 +9 | 30. 5 +1 | 31. 3 +9 | 32. 7 +7 |

# Ordering Numbers

This number line shows the numbers in order.

346 is one less than 347.     363 is one greater than 362.

321, 322, and 323 are between 320 and 324.

Give the number that is one greater.

1. 332    2. 361    3. 349    4. 354    5. 317    6. 326    7. 370
8. 131    9. 514    10. 642    11. 269    12. 893    13. 475    14. 750

Give the number that is one less.

15. 314    16. 342    17. 368    18. 321    19. 379    20. 335    21. 356
22. 635    23. 240    24. 596    25. 951    26. 469    27. 801    28. 782

Give the numbers between

29. 340 and 347.    30. 355 and 362.    31. 317 and 324.
32. 423 and 431.    33. 681 and 689.    34. 149 and 157.
35. 596 and 607.    36. 104 and 115.    37. 798 and 809.

Are these numbers in order, beginning with the least? Write yes or no.

38. 28  35  46

39. 57  61  74

40. 784  165  237

41. 452  560  453

42. 65  67  64  66

43. 12  21  31  32

Give the numbers in order. Begin with the least number.

44. 67  23  45

45. 46  48  47

46. 512  541  523

47. 147  234  112

48. 23  26  18  29

49. 85  81  57  53

Are these numbers in order, beginning with the greatest? Write yes or no.

50. 42  23  16

51. 24  13  46

52. 367  179  471

53. 932  719  823

54. 56  55  54  52

55. 62  61  27  25

Give the numbers in order. Begin with the greatest number.

56. 15  56  37

57. 68  54  72

58. 228  240  234

59. 150  176  125

60. 31  36  58  49

61. 82  80  81  83

# Counting Numbers

| 160 | 161 | 162 | 163 | 164 | 165 | 166 | 167 | 168 | 169 |
| 170 | 171 | 172 | 173 | 174 | 175 | 176 | 177 | 178 | 179 |
| 180 | 181 | 182 | 183 | 184 | 185 | 186 | 187 | 188 | 189 |
| 190 | 191 | 192 | 193 | 194 | 195 | 196 | 197 | 198 | 199 |
| 200 | 201 | 202 | 203 | 204 | 205 | 206 | 207 | 208 | 209 |
| 210 | 211 | 212 | 213 | 214 | 215 | 216 | 217 | 218 | 219 |
| 220 | 221 | 222 | 223 | 224 | 225 | 226 | 227 | 228 | 229 |
| 230 | 231 | 232 | 233 | 234 | 235 | 236 | 237 | 238 | 239 |
| 240 | 241 | 242 | 243 | 244 | 245 | 246 | 247 | 248 | 249 |

A. The green squares show counting by ones from 223 to 227. Count every number.

223   224   225   226   227

B. The red squares show counting by twos from 236 to 244. Count every second number.

236   238   240   242   244

C. The blue squares show counting by fives from 160 to 180. Count every fifth number.

160   165   170   175   180

D. The yellow squares show counting by tens from 190 to 230. Count every tenth number.

190   200   210   220   230

Count by ones.

1. Begin at 83. Stop at 88.
2. Begin at 183. Stop at 188.
3. Begin at 17. Stop at 23.
4. Begin at 417. Stop at 423.
5. Begin at 946. Stop at 952.
6. Begin at 797. Stop at 803.

Count by twos.

7. Begin at 82. Stop at 92.
8. Begin at 182. Stop at 192.
9. Begin at 46. Stop at 56.
10. Begin at 546. Stop at 556.
11. Begin at 744. Stop at 752.
12. Begin at 420. Stop at 430.

Count by fives.

13. Begin at 65. Stop at 90.
14. Begin at 165. Stop at 190.
15. Begin at 40. Stop at 70.
16. Begin at 340. Stop at 370.
17. Begin at 825. Stop at 860.
18. Begin at 320. Stop at 355.

Count by tens.

19. Begin at 30. Stop at 90.
20. Begin at 130. Stop at 190.
21. Begin at 55. Stop at 95.
22. Begin at 855. Stop at 895.
23. Begin at 415. Stop at 475.
24. Begin at 500. Stop at 580.

Count by threes.

★25. Begin at 12. Stop at 30.
★26. Begin at 212. Stop at 230.

More practice
Set 8, page 356

# Pennies, Dimes, and Dollars

**A.** One penny has a value of 1 cent.

**B.** One dime has a value of 10 cents.

**C.** One dollar has a value of 100 cents.

1¢ or $0.01

10¢ or $0.10

100¢ or $1.00

**D.**

2 dollars

4 dimes

**$2.46**

6 pennies

For each picture, use $ and . to show the value.

**1.**

**2.**

For each exercise, write the amount in two ways.

**Here's how**

3 dollars, 4 dimes, 1 penny

341¢    $3.41

7. 2 dollars, 6 dimes, 3 pennies

8. 4 dimes, 3 pennies

9. 8 dollars, 5 dimes, 5 pennies

10. 6 dollars, 2 dimes

11. 4 dollars, 2 dimes, 1 penny

12. 5 dollars

13. 9 dollars, 3 dimes, 8 pennies

14. 1 dollar, 6 pennies

15. 6 dollars, 1 dime, 9 pennies

16. 7 pennies

# Nickels, Quarters, and Half Dollars

**A.**

One nickel
5¢ or $0.05

**B.**

One quarter
25¢ or $0.25

**C.**

One half-dollar
50¢ or $0.50

For each picture, use $ and . to show value.

**1.**

**2.**

3.

Give the missing number.

4. 1 half-dollar or ▦ dimes

5. 1 quarter or ▦ nickels

6. 50¢ or ▦ nickels

7. $1.00 or ▦ dimes

Sometimes you need nickels, dimes, and quarters when you call from a telephone booth. How many coins of each kind are needed?

**Here's how**

$1.40

5 quarters
1 dime
1 nickel

8. 45¢      9. $1.05      10. $1.25

11. 95¢      12. $0.70      13. $1.60

How many nickels, dimes, or quarters are needed? Use the fewest number of each.

★14. $0.85      ★15. $1.35      ★16. $2.90

**Making Change**

Mr. Sullivan sold a set of pencils for $3.62.
The customer gave him 4 one-dollar bills.

This is how Mr. Sullivan made change.

He started with $3.62.
He picked coins until he reached $4.00.

| $3.62 | $3.63 | $3.64 | $3.65 | $3.75 | $4.00 |

Here is another way he could have made change.

| $3.62 | $3.63 | $3.64 | $3.65 | $3.70 | $3.80 | $3.90 | $4.00 |

• **Discuss**  Are there other ways Mr. Sullivan
could have made change?

For each exercise, show how Mr. Sullivan could give change. Draw a picture of the coins.

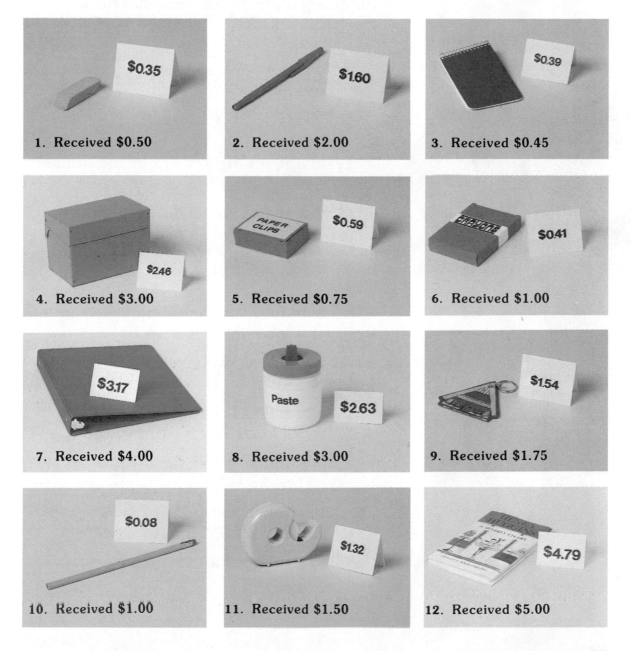

1. Received $0.50 — $0.35

2. Received $2.00 — $1.60

3. Received $0.45 — $0.39

4. Received $3.00 — $2.46

5. Received $0.75 — $0.59

6. Received $1.00 — $0.41

7. Received $4.00 — $3.17

8. Received $3.00 — Paste $2.63

9. Received $1.75 — $1.54

10. Received $1.00 — $0.08

11. Received $1.50 — $1.32

12. Received $5.00 — $4.79

## Giving Sensible Answers

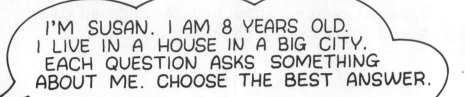

I'M SUSAN. I AM 8 YEARS OLD. I LIVE IN A HOUSE IN A BIG CITY. EACH QUESTION ASKS SOMETHING ABOUT ME. CHOOSE THE BEST ANSWER.

1. How old is my father?   (4, 40, 400)

2. How old is my older brother? (1, 10, 100)

3. How many rooms are in my house? (8, 80, 800)

4. How many meals do I eat each day? (3, 30, 300)

5. How many teachers do I have? (2, 20, 200)

6. How many students are in my room? (3, 30, 300)

7. How many students are in my school?   (7, 70, 700)

8. How many hours do I spend in school each day?   (6, 60, 600)

9. How much did I spend for a pencil? ($0.05, $5.00, $50.00)

10. How much did I spend for an apple? ($0.25, $2.50, $25.00)

11. How many friends came to play? (4, 40, 400)

## Chapter 4 Test
## Numeration Through 999, pages 62–82

Give the standard form for
each number.

1.

| hundreds | tens | ones |
|----------|------|------|
| 4 | 2 | 6 |

2.

| hundreds | tens | ones |
|----------|------|------|
| | 5 | 7 |

What digit is in the ones
place?

3. 367  4. 942  5. 138

What digit is in the tens
place?

6. 523  7. 184  8. 650

What digit is in the hundreds
place?

9. 792  10. 315  11. 490

Replace the ●. Use < or >.

12. 47 ● 56  13. 862 ● 841

14. 26 ● 21  15. 912 ● 714

Give the numbers in order.
Begin with the least number.

16. 96  91  95

17. 472  568  391

18. 28  41  32  50

19. Count by twos. Begin
at 142. Stop at 152.

20. Count by fives. Begin
at 205. Stop at 230.

21. Count by tens. Begin
at 410. Stop at 460.

22. Use $ and . to show
2 dollars, 9 dimes,
4 pennies.

Give the missing number.

23. 1 quarter or ▦ nickels

24. $1.00 or ▦ quarters

Choose the best answer.

25. May is 6 years old. How
old is her younger sister?
(2, 20, 200)

# Chapter 5   Addition Computation

## Addition: No Renaming

A. Jan delivered 54 papers on Monday and 32 papers on Tuesday. How many papers did she deliver in all?

Find 54 + 32.

| Add 54 and 32 to find the sum. | Add the ones. 4 + 2 = 6 | Add the tens. 5 + 3 = 8 |
|---|---|---|
| 54 +32 | 54 +32 ___ 6 | 54 +32 ___ 86 |

Jan delivered 86 papers.

Tell what was done in each example.

B.  23
   + 4
   ____
    27

C.  801
   + 57
   ____
   858

D.  513
   +242
   ____
   755

E.  230
   +  2
   ____
   232

Add.

1. 15
  +50

2. 22
  +21

3. 74
  + 4

4. 31
  + 6

5. 11
  +13

6. 53
  + 3

7. 132
  + 6

8. 505
  + 4

9. 411
  + 64

10. 340
  + 24

11. 712
  +184

12. 326
  +431

13. 30
  + 2

14. 54
  +23

15. 203
  +442

16. 472
  + 5

17. 164
  + 25

18. 45
  + 3

19. 36
  +63

20. 436
  +252

21. 243
  + 4

22. 522
  + 53

23. 50
  +30

24. 782
  +217

25. Joe walked 12 blocks and rode 27 blocks. How many blocks did he travel in all?

26. Ed delivered 103 papers. Sara delivered 40 papers. How many papers were delivered in all?

Fifteen boys delivered 262 papers. Thirteen girls delivered 225 papers.

★27. How many students were there in all?

★28. How many papers were delivered in all?

# Renaming Ones and Tens

A. 2 hundreds   14 tens   5 ones

| hundreds | tens | ones |
|:---:|:---:|:---:|
| 2 | 14 | 5 |

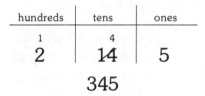

Put 10 tens together to make another hundred. 4 tens are left over.

| hundreds | tens | ones |
|:---:|:---:|:---:|
| 1 | 4 | |
| 2 | 1̶4̶ | 5 |

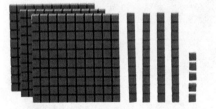

Put the hundreds together.

| hundreds | tens | ones |
|:---:|:---:|:---:|
| 1 | 4 | |
| 2 | 1̶4̶ | 5 |

345

There are 345 blocks.

B. Tell how to rename 3 tens 28 ones.

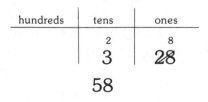

| hundreds | tens | ones |
|:---:|:---:|:---:|
| | 2 | 8 |
| | 3 | 2̶8̶ |

58

Give the standard form for each number.

**Here's how**

| hundreds | tens | ones |
|----------|------|------|
| 3 | 18 | 6 |

| h | t | o |
|---|---|---|
| 3 | 18 | 6 |

486

**1.**

| hundreds | tens | ones |
|----------|------|------|
| | 4 | 13 |

**2.**

| hundreds | tens | ones |
|----------|------|------|
| | 2 | 16 |

**3.**

| hundreds | tens | ones |
|----------|------|------|
| | 1 | 29 |

**4.**

| hundreds | tens | ones |
|----------|------|------|
| | 3 | 24 |

**5.**

| hundreds | tens | ones |
|----------|------|------|
| 8 | 3 | 25 |

**6.**

| hundreds | tens | ones |
|----------|------|------|
| 4 | 6 | 12 |

**7.**

| hundreds | tens | ones |
|----------|------|------|
| 5 | 4 | 28 |

**8.**

| hundreds | tens | ones |
|----------|------|------|
| 2 | 11 | 7 |

**9.**

| hundreds | tens | ones |
|----------|------|------|
| 1 | 16 | 8 |

**10.**

| hundreds | tens | ones |
|----------|------|------|
| 5 | 22 | 5 |

**11.**

| hundreds | tens | ones |
|----------|------|------|
| 4 | 23 | 1 |

**12.**

| hundreds | tens | ones |
|----------|------|------|
| 1 | 15 | 3 |

**13.**

| hundreds | tens | ones |
|----------|------|------|
| 3 | 16 | 8 |

**14.**

| hundreds | tens | ones |
|----------|------|------|
| 2 | 14 | 9 |

**15.**

| hundreds | tens | ones |
|----------|------|------|
| 7 | 10 | 4 |

**★16.**

| hundreds | tens | ones |
|----------|------|------|
| 2 | 6 | 52 |

**★17.**

| hundreds | tens | ones |
|----------|------|------|
| 6 | 7 | 83 |

**★18.**

| hundreds | tens | ones |
|----------|------|------|
| 3 | 8 | 27 |

# Addition: Renaming Ones

A. The giant counted 35 gold coins and 47 silver coins. How many coins did he count?

Find 35 + 47.

Add the ones.
5 + 7 = 12
12 ones =
1 ten 2 ones

Add the tens.
1 + 3 + 4 = 8

$$\begin{array}{r} 1\phantom{0} \\ 35 \\ +47 \\ \hline 2 \end{array} \qquad \begin{array}{r} 1\phantom{0} \\ 35 \\ +47 \\ \hline 82 \end{array}$$

The giant counted 82 coins.

Tell what was done in each example.

B.
$$\begin{array}{r} 1\phantom{0} \\ 74 \\ +\phantom{0}8 \\ \hline 82 \end{array}$$

C.
$$\begin{array}{r} 1\phantom{0} \\ 26 \\ +18 \\ \hline 44 \end{array}$$

Add.

| | | | | | | |
|---|---|---|---|---|---|---|
| 1. $\begin{array}{r}16 \\ +\ 6 \\ \hline\end{array}$ | 2. $\begin{array}{r}32 \\ +\ 8 \\ \hline\end{array}$ | 3. $\begin{array}{r}27 \\ +\ 7 \\ \hline\end{array}$ | 4. $\begin{array}{r}49 \\ +\ 2 \\ \hline\end{array}$ | 5. $\begin{array}{r}67 \\ +\ 3 \\ \hline\end{array}$ | 6. $\begin{array}{r}59 \\ +\ 9 \\ \hline\end{array}$ | 7. $\begin{array}{r}83 \\ +\ 8 \\ \hline\end{array}$ |
| 8. $\begin{array}{r}45 \\ +15 \\ \hline\end{array}$ | 9. $\begin{array}{r}18 \\ +58 \\ \hline\end{array}$ | 10. $\begin{array}{r}25 \\ +16 \\ \hline\end{array}$ | 11. $\begin{array}{r}16 \\ +34 \\ \hline\end{array}$ | 12. $\begin{array}{r}42 \\ +49 \\ \hline\end{array}$ | 13. $\begin{array}{r}34 \\ +38 \\ \hline\end{array}$ | 14. $\begin{array}{r}27 \\ +56 \\ \hline\end{array}$ |
| 15. $\begin{array}{r}57 \\ +\ 5 \\ \hline\end{array}$ | 16. $\begin{array}{r}13 \\ +\ 9 \\ \hline\end{array}$ | 17. $\begin{array}{r}26 \\ +59 \\ \hline\end{array}$ | 18. $\begin{array}{r}49 \\ +25 \\ \hline\end{array}$ | 19. $\begin{array}{r}28 \\ +\ 9 \\ \hline\end{array}$ | 20. $\begin{array}{r}65 \\ +\ 8 \\ \hline\end{array}$ | 21. $\begin{array}{r}57 \\ +39 \\ \hline\end{array}$ |
| 22. $\begin{array}{r}19 \\ +73 \\ \hline\end{array}$ | 23. $\begin{array}{r}36 \\ +27 \\ \hline\end{array}$ | 24. $\begin{array}{r}89 \\ +\ 4 \\ \hline\end{array}$ | 25. $\begin{array}{r}36 \\ +\ 8 \\ \hline\end{array}$ | 26. $\begin{array}{r}38 \\ +47 \\ \hline\end{array}$ | 27. $\begin{array}{r}69 \\ +28 \\ \hline\end{array}$ | 28. $\begin{array}{r}78 \\ +\ 4 \\ \hline\end{array}$ |

29. The giant had 11 golden eggs. The hen laid 9 more. How many eggs did the giant have in all?

30. Jack had 59 beans. He picked 27 more. How many beans did he have in all?

31. Jack had 26 gold coins and 18 silver coins. How many coins did he have in all?

32. The giant climbed 28 steps. Then he climbed 27 steps more. How many steps did he climb in all?

**More practice**
**Set 9, page 356**

# Addition: Renaming Ones

A. The class had 238 leaves and collected 254 more. How many leaves did they have in all?

Find 238 + 254.

Add the ones.
8 + 4 = 12
12 ones =
1 ten 2 ones

Add the tens.
1 + 3 + 5 = 9

Add the hundreds.
2 + 2 = 4

$$\begin{array}{r} 1 \\ 238 \\ +254 \\ \hline 2 \end{array}$$

$$\begin{array}{r} 1 \\ 238 \\ +254 \\ \hline 92 \end{array}$$

$$\begin{array}{r} 1 \\ 238 \\ +254 \\ \hline 492 \end{array}$$

The class had 492 leaves.

Tell what was done in each example.

B.
$$\begin{array}{r} 1 \\ 628 \\ +\phantom{0}25 \\ \hline 653 \end{array}$$

C.
$$\begin{array}{r} 1 \\ 213 \\ +347 \\ \hline 560 \end{array}$$

Add.

1.  719
    + 31

2.  455
    + 15

3.  249
    + 29

4.  618
    + 78

5.  334
    + 37

6.  928
    + 64

7.  156
    +406

8.  507
    +127

9.  324
    +426

10. 362
    +529

11. 428
    +352

12. 636
    +324

13. 127
    + 45

14. 234
    +519

15. 808
    + 39

16. 247
    +346

17. 268
    +415

18. 316
    + 49

19. 719
    + 13

20. 436
    +457

21. 127
    +338

22. 258
    + 26

23. 539
    + 44

24. 357
    +639

25. The class collected
    127 elm leaves and 45 oak
    leaves. How many leaves
    did the class have in all?

Sixteen girls counted
89 trees. Eighteen boys
counted 109 trees.

*26. How many students were
    there?

*27. How many trees were
    counted?

**More practice
Set 10, page 357**

More practice
Set 10, page 357

**Time Out**

What is the name of the
tallest tree in the world?

Use these clues to help you.

The third letter is D.

The sixth letter is O.

The first letter is R.

The fifth letter is O.

The second letter is E.

The seventh letter is D.

The fourth letter is W.

# Addition: Renaming Tens

**A.** One day 183 adults and 274 children went to the aquarium. How many people went to the aquarium?

Find 183 + 274.

Add the ones.
3 + 4 = 7

Add the tens.
8 + 7 = 15
15 tens =
1 hundred 5 tens

Add the hundreds.
1 + 1 + 2 = 4

$$\begin{array}{r} 183 \\ +274 \\ \hline 7 \end{array} \qquad \begin{array}{r} \phantom{0}1\phantom{00} \\ 183 \\ +274 \\ \hline 57 \end{array} \qquad \begin{array}{r} \phantom{0}1\phantom{00} \\ 183 \\ +274 \\ \hline 457 \end{array}$$

457 people went to the aquarium.

Tell what was done in each example.

**B.**
$$\begin{array}{r} 1\phantom{00} \\ 564 \\ +285 \\ \hline 849 \end{array}$$

**C.**
$$\begin{array}{r} 1\phantom{00} \\ 672 \\ +\phantom{0}33 \\ \hline 705 \end{array}$$

Add.

| | | | | | |
|---|---|---|---|---|---|
| 1. 284<br>+ 21 | 2. 662<br>+ 46 | 3. 34<br>+593 | 4. 72<br>+460 | 5. 152<br>+ 91 | 6. 386<br>+ 63 |
| 7. 552<br>+153 | 8. 294<br>+214 | 9. 196<br>+491 | 10. 257<br>+562 | 11. 142<br>+184 | 12. 673<br>+252 |
| 13. 562<br>+277 | 14. 95<br>+423 | 15. 851<br>+ 74 | 16. 283<br>+344 | 17. 394<br>+185 | 18. 96<br>+542 |
| 19. 78<br>+271 | 20. 293<br>+653 | 21. 165<br>+354 | 22. 32<br>+585 | 23. 171<br>+ 85 | 24. 493<br>+275 |

25. Liz sold 267 adult tickets
and 381 student tickets.
How many tickets were
sold in all?

26. 195 fish were in one tank
and 64 fish were in another
tank. There were how many
fish in all?

27. There were 593 tropical
fish and 276 goldfish.
How many fish were there
in all?

**More practice
Set 11, page 357**

# Using Addition

Add.

**Here's how**

573 + 64

$$\begin{array}{r} \overset{1}{5}73 \\ +\ 64 \\ \hline 637 \end{array}$$

1. 13 + 2
2. 36 + 58
3. 148 + 302
4. 452 + 135
5. 226 + 437
6. 532 + 213
7. 74 + 5
8. 19 + 57
9. 84 + 9
10. 48 + 26
11. 966 + 25
12. 274 + 23
13. 427 + 53
14. 147 + 561
15. 53 + 36
16. 38 + 7
17. 32 + 24
18. 27 + 5
19. 738 + 45
20. 417 + 52
21. 578 + 91
22. 446 + 352
23. 354 + 81
24. 529 + 260
25. 234 + 683
26. 324 + 62
27. 406 + 273
28. 382 + 35

|      |     | + 19 |
|------|-----|------|
|      | 8   | 27   |
| 29.  | 56  |      |
| 30.  | 122 |      |
| 31.  | 490 |      |
| 32.  | 45  |      |

|      |     | + 47 |
|------|-----|------|
| 33.  | 31  |      |
| 34.  | 46  |      |
| 35.  | 13  |      |
| 36.  | 9   |      |
| 37.  | 582 |      |

|      |     | + 125 |
|------|-----|-------|
| 38.  | 23  |       |
| 39.  | 162 |       |
| 40.  | 36  |       |
| 41.  | 448 |       |
| 42.  | 194 |       |

Add. Use the code to help you answer the riddle below.

Why do you do your math problem with a pencil?

**Here's how**

$136 + 48 = 184 \, P$

| CODE | |
|------|------|
| 18 A | 123 L |
| 27 B | 146 N |
| 49 C | 168 O |
| 54 D | 184 P |
| 75 E | 225 S |
| 87 H | 256 T |
| 92 I | 319 U |

**Word 1**

43. $19 + 8$

44. $62 + 13$

45. $25 + 24$

46. $10 + 8$

47. $135 + 184$

48. $163 + 62$

49. $24 + 51$

**Word 2**

50. $74 + 182$

51. $24 + 63$

52. $40 + 35$

**Word 3**

53. $119 + 65$

54. $26 + 49$

55. $18 + 128$

56. $3 + 46$

57. $25 + 67$

58. $108 + 15$

**Word 4**

59. $30 + 19$

60. $12 + 6$

61. $109 + 37$

62. $124 + 132$

**Word 5**

63. $27 + 27$

64. $155 + 13$

**Word 6**

65. $31 + 61$

66. $107 + 149$

**Word 7**

67. $15 + 3$

68. $21 + 102$

69. $139 + 29$

70. $114 + 32$

71. $66 + 9$

# Three or More One-Digit Addends

Jeff's spinners landed on 5, 9, and 7.
What is his score?

A. You can add down.

$$\begin{array}{r} 5 \\ 9 \\ + 7 \\ \hline 21 \end{array}$$

5 + 9 = 14
14 + 7 = 21

Jeff's score is 21.

You can add up.

$$\begin{array}{r} 5 \\ 9 \\ + 7 \\ \hline 21 \end{array}$$

16 + 5 = 21
7 + 9 = 16

B. You can add in any order.

7 + 5 + 3 + 5 = 20
7 + 3 + 5 + 5 = 20
5 + 3 + 5 + 7 = 20

Add.

1. 2
   2
   +4

2. 3
   5
   +2

3. 5
   4
   +6

4. 1
   6
   +7

5. 4
   7
   +8

6. 8
   4
   +5

7. 6
   3
   +4

8. 9
   2
   +7

9. 5
   6
   +8

10. 8
    7
    +7

11. 7
    6
    +9

12. 3
    9
    +4

13. 4
    8
    +9

14. 9
    6
    +5

15. 8
    8
    +8

16. 6
    9
    +6

★17. 3
     4
     6
     8
     +2

★18. 2
     7
     3
     5
     +9

★19. 8
     3
     5
     7
     +3

★20. 7
     2
     4
     6
     +5

★21. 5
     9
     7
     4
     +2

★22. 8
     4
     6
     3
     +7

★23. 4
     5
     9
     8
     +9

★24. 9
     8
     7
     6
     +5

25. 7 + 2 + 3     26. 6 + 7 + 4     27. 6 + 3 + 5

28. 5 + 4 + 7     29. 9 + 8 + 6     30. 3 + 7 + 5

31. 2 + 4 + 6 + 8     32. 2 + 5 + 6 + 7     33. 4 + 9 + 7 + 5

34. 8 + 2 + 9 + 4     35. 9 + 6 + 8 + 4     36. 5 + 8 + 3 + 9

These students played the spinner game.
Add to find each score.

|  | Beth | Hugh | Mona | Ian | Viho | Rita |
|---|---|---|---|---|---|---|
| First spinner | 6 | 5 | 2 | 4 | 5 | 6 |
| Second spinner | 3 | 5 | 7 | 3 | 9 | 8 |
| Third spinner | 9 | 2 | 4 | 3 | 6 | 1 |
| Total score | 37. | 38. | 39. | 40. | 41. | 42. |

## More Than Two Addends

A. Hal had 219 stamps, Mary had 107 stamps, and Roy had 58 stamps. How many stamps did they have in all?

Find 219 + 107 + 58.

Add the ones.
9 + 7 + 8 = 24
24 ones =
2 tens 4 ones

$$
\begin{array}{r}
2 \\
219 \\
107 \\
+\ 58 \\
\hline
4
\end{array}
$$

Add the tens.
2 + 1 + 0 + 5 = 8

$$
\begin{array}{r}
2 \\
219 \\
107 \\
+\ 58 \\
\hline
84
\end{array}
$$

Add the hundreds.
2 + 1 = 3

$$
\begin{array}{r}
2 \\
219 \\
107 \\
+\ 58 \\
\hline
384
\end{array}
$$

They had 384 stamps.

Tell what was done in each example.

B. 1
$$
\begin{array}{r}
362 \\
155 \\
+481 \\
\hline
998
\end{array}
$$

C. 2
$$
\begin{array}{r}
17 \\
36 \\
+19 \\
\hline
72
\end{array}
$$

D.
$$
\begin{array}{r}
624 \\
31 \\
+\ \ 2 \\
\hline
657
\end{array}
$$

Add.

1. 18
15
+23

2. 43
21
+ 5

3. 2
22
+13

4. 36
14
+20

5. 122
251
+114

6. 342
323
+131

7. 31
32
+36

8. 25
34
+13

9. 19
43
+24

10. 21
12
+14

11. 232
11
+ 7

12. 153
9
+ 32

13. 116
104
+123

14. 263
252
+181

15. 18
36
+29

16. 39
35
+17

17. 16
119
+227

18. 418
104
+ 57

19. 17
5
+18

20. 19
64
+ 3

21. 242
483
+ 44

22. 386
132
+ 21

23. 127
305
+226

24. 425
339
+222

25. 184
172
+183

26. 275
242
+130

27. 526
9
+ 24

28. 228
4
+ 33

29. 262
30
+592

30. 392
43
+271

31. Raoul had 17 model cars, Amy had 24 cars, and Seth had 5 cars. They had how many cars in all?

32. Maureen had 16 stamps from Spain, 37 stamps from Italy, and 42 stamps from France. How many stamps did she have in all?

Joy has 17 shells and 9 rocks. Vic has 8 shells and 27 rocks. Eva has 35 shells and 6 rocks.

★33. How many shells did they have in all?

★34. How many rocks did they have in all?

**More practice
Set 12, page 357**

# Using Addition

Add.

1. 102
   + 47

2. 420
   + 79

3. 46
   +39

4. 28
   +62

5. 214
   +114

6. 362
   +420

7. 5
   8
   +6

8. 19
   6
   +27

9. 21
   16
   +12

10. 8
    9
    +4

11. 43
    36
    + 7

12. 22
    24
    +23

13. 36
    18
    +45

14. 273
    324
    +191

15. 145
    60
    + 23

16. 14
    15
    +48

17. 190
    532
    +173

18. 156
    71
    + 11

19. 29 + 28 + 19

20. 67 + 408

21. 282 + 64 + 53

22. 145 + 62

23. 42 + 27 + 18

24. 667 + 16

25. 59 + 2 + 33

26. 13 + 30 + 24

27. 68 + 9 + 18

28. 32 + 14 + 43

29. 26 + 45

30. 50 + 15 + 22

31. 226 + 340 + 117

32. 284 + 32 + 31

33. 124 + 348 + 219

34. 185 + 731

35. 3 + 18 + 37

36. 328 + 245

37. 493 + 52 + 24

38. 162 + 31 + 4

39. 83 + 12 + 263

40. 41 + 13 + 5

41. 514 + 202

42. 52 + 33 + 3

43. 341 + 37 + 218

44. 20 + 48 + 15

45. 509 + 46 + 127

46. 183 + 31 + 244

47. 571 + 7 + 280

48. 352 + 31 + 193

# Keeping Skillful

1. $\begin{array}{r} 4 \\ -2 \\ \hline \end{array}$  2. $\begin{array}{r} 8 \\ -4 \\ \hline \end{array}$  3. $\begin{array}{r} 7 \\ -1 \\ \hline \end{array}$  4. $\begin{array}{r} 3 \\ -1 \\ \hline \end{array}$  5. $\begin{array}{r} 6 \\ -0 \\ \hline \end{array}$  6. $\begin{array}{r} 9 \\ -5 \\ \hline \end{array}$  7. $\begin{array}{r} 10 \\ -\ 9 \\ \hline \end{array}$

8. $\begin{array}{r} 12 \\ -\ 8 \\ \hline \end{array}$  9. $\begin{array}{r} 14 \\ -\ 5 \\ \hline \end{array}$  10. $\begin{array}{r} 6 \\ -4 \\ \hline \end{array}$  11. $\begin{array}{r} 8 \\ -5 \\ \hline \end{array}$  12. $\begin{array}{r} 11 \\ -\ 6 \\ \hline \end{array}$  13. $\begin{array}{r} 5 \\ -3 \\ \hline \end{array}$  14. $\begin{array}{r} 9 \\ -2 \\ \hline \end{array}$

15. $\begin{array}{r} 9 \\ -6 \\ \hline \end{array}$  16. $\begin{array}{r} 13 \\ -\ 6 \\ \hline \end{array}$  17. $\begin{array}{r} 14 \\ -\ 9 \\ \hline \end{array}$  18. $\begin{array}{r} 10 \\ -\ 2 \\ \hline \end{array}$  19. $\begin{array}{r} 8 \\ -7 \\ \hline \end{array}$  20. $\begin{array}{r} 4 \\ -4 \\ \hline \end{array}$  21. $\begin{array}{r} 6 \\ -2 \\ \hline \end{array}$

22. $\begin{array}{r} 12 \\ -\ 7 \\ \hline \end{array}$  23. $\begin{array}{r} 14 \\ -\ 6 \\ \hline \end{array}$  24. $\begin{array}{r} 10 \\ -\ 8 \\ \hline \end{array}$  25. $\begin{array}{r} 8 \\ -2 \\ \hline \end{array}$  26. $\begin{array}{r} 7 \\ -4 \\ \hline \end{array}$  27. $\begin{array}{r} 11 \\ -\ 9 \\ \hline \end{array}$  28. $\begin{array}{r} 13 \\ -\ 4 \\ \hline \end{array}$

29. $\begin{array}{r} 9 \\ -1 \\ \hline \end{array}$  30. $\begin{array}{r} 18 \\ -\ 9 \\ \hline \end{array}$  31. $\begin{array}{r} 7 \\ -5 \\ \hline \end{array}$  32. $\begin{array}{r} 15 \\ -\ 7 \\ \hline \end{array}$  33. $\begin{array}{r} 13 \\ -\ 8 \\ \hline \end{array}$  34. $\begin{array}{r} 12 \\ -\ 6 \\ \hline \end{array}$  35. $\begin{array}{r} 5 \\ -4 \\ \hline \end{array}$

36. $7 - 3$   37. $9 - 8$   38. $10 - 3$   39. $13 - 9$   40. $5 - 0$

41. $8 - 8$   42. $15 - 8$   43. $5 - 2$   44. $16 - 8$   45. $11 - 7$

46. $14 - 7$   47. $17 - 8$   48. $12 - 4$   49. $11 - 5$   50. $6 - 3$

51. $10 - 6$   52. $9 - 7$   53. $14 - 8$   54. $12 - 9$   55. $11 - 3$

56. $17 - 9$   57. $16 - 7$   58. $13 - 7$   59. $11 - 4$   60. $10 - 5$

61. $15 - 9$   62. $11 - 8$   63. $12 - 3$   64. $9 - 3$   65. $8 - 6$

66. $12 - 5$   67. $11 - 2$   68. $13 - 5$   69. $16 - 9$   70. $15 - 6$

# Lab Activity

## Possible Sums with Number Cubes

Penny tossed two number cubes. What are the numbers on top? What is their sum?

Penny tossed the number cubes 40 times. She recorded the number of times each sum appeared.

This is the table Penny made.

| Possible sums | Tally | Number of tosses |
|---|---|---|
| 2 | / | 1 |
| 3 | / | 1 |
| 4 | /// | 3 |
| 5 | ⊟ / | 6 |
| 6 | ⊟ /// | 8 |
| 7 | ⊟ | 5 |
| 8 | ⊟ / | 6 |
| 9 | /// | 3 |
| 10 | //// | 4 |
| 11 | // | 2 |
| 12 | / | 1 |

Then she made a bar graph.

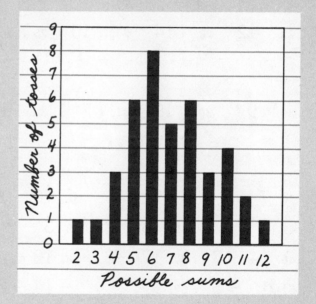

1. Which sum appeared most often?

2. Which sums appeared least often?

3. Toss two number cubes 40 times. Make a table and a graph like the ones Penny made.

# Chapter 5 Test
## Addition Computation, pages 84–102

Give the standard form
for each number.

**1.**

| hundreds | tens | ones |
|----------|------|------|
| | 5 | 26 |

**2.**

| hundreds | tens | ones |
|----------|------|------|
| 2 | 3 | 17 |

**3.**

| hundreds | tens | ones |
|----------|------|------|
| 4 | 28 | 1 |

Add.

**4.**  526
   + 73

**5.**  243
   +102

**6.**  56
   + 6

**7.**  32
   + 8

**8.**  27
   +45

**9.**  58
   +29

**10.**  528
    + 34

**11.**  279
    + 19

**12.**  145
    +126

**13.**  136
    +518

**14.**  723
    +227

**15.**  647
    + 91

**16.**  456
    +350

**17.**  234
    +185

**18.**  782
    + 75

**19.**  391
    +365

**20.**  4
     2
    +5

**21.**  3
     7
    +4

**22.**  8
     7
    +9

**23.**  12
     14
    +21

**24.**  29
     26
    +32

**25.**  142
     253
    +172

# Chapter 6  Subtraction Computation

## Subtraction: No Renaming

A. Jerry collected 75 shells. He gave 43 shells to his brother. How many shells did Jerry have left?

Find 75 − 43.

| Subtract 43 from 75 to find the difference. | Subtract the ones. $5 - 3 = 2$ | Subtract the tens. $7 - 4 = 3$ |
|---|---|---|
| $\begin{array}{r} 75 \\ -43 \\ \hline \end{array}$ | $\begin{array}{r} 75 \\ -43 \\ \hline 2 \end{array}$ | $\begin{array}{r} 75 \\ -43 \\ \hline 32 \end{array}$ |

Jerry had 32 shells left.

Tell what was done in each example.

B. $\begin{array}{r} 389 \\ -149 \\ \hline 240 \end{array}$   C. $\begin{array}{r} 765 \\ -\phantom{0}30 \\ \hline 735 \end{array}$

D. $\begin{array}{r} 48 \\ -\phantom{0}5 \\ \hline 43 \end{array}$   E. $\begin{array}{r} 273 \\ -252 \\ \hline 21 \end{array}$

Subtract.

1.  38
    − 6

2.  27
    − 4

3.  48
    −37

4.  66
    −32

5.  57
    −16

6.  82
    −40

7.  526
    − 5

8.  658
    − 2

9.  341
    − 21

10. 175
    − 40

11. 245
    −112

12. 416
    −210

13. 736
    − 11

14. 928
    − 10

15. 56
    −24

16. 34
    −23

17. 389
    − 4

18. 155
    − 3

19. 98
    −94

20. 38
    −33

21. 833
    −121

22. 797
    −526

23. 845
    − 44

24. 422
    − 11

25. 67
    −24

26. 96
    −65

27. 276
    − 43

28. 999
    − 25

29. 474
    −432

30. 897
    −850

31. 655
    −241

32. 797
    −526

33. 278
    −215

34. 897
    −850

35. 689
    −454

36. 397
    −163

37. There were 29 sailboats and 18 surfboards. How many more sailboats were there?

38. Sandra found 138 shells last year and 115 shells this year. How many more shells did she find last year?

# Renaming Tens or Hundreds

**A.** Rename 236 to show 10 more tens.

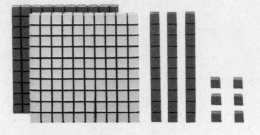

| hundreds | tens | ones |
|:---:|:---:|:---:|
| 2 | 3 | 6 |

Take 1 hundred apart to make 10 tens. Now there are 13 tens.

| hundreds | tens | ones |
|:---:|:---:|:---:|
| 1 | 13 | |
| 2̸ | 3̸ | 6 |

**B.** Rename to show 10 more ones.

| hundreds | tens | ones |
|:---:|:---:|:---:|
| | 3 | 15 |
| | 4̸ | 5̸ |

**C.** Rename to show 10 more tens.

| hundreds | tens | ones |
|:---:|:---:|:---:|
| 6 | 10 | |
| 7̸ | 0̸ | 9 |

**D.** Rename to show 10 more ones.

| hundreds | tens | ones |
|:---:|:---:|:---:|
| | 0 | 14 |
| 3 | 1̸ | 4̸ |

Rename to show 10 more ones.

**Here's how**

| hundreds | tens | ones |
|---|---|---|
| 7 | 5 | 4 |

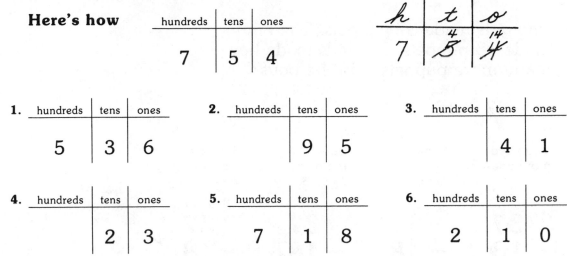

| h | t | o |
|---|---|---|
| 7 | 5⁴ | 4¹⁴ |

**1.**
| hundreds | tens | ones |
|---|---|---|
| 5 | 3 | 6 |

**2.**
| hundreds | tens | ones |
|---|---|---|
|  | 9 | 5 |

**3.**
| hundreds | tens | ones |
|---|---|---|
|  | 4 | 1 |

**4.**
| hundreds | tens | ones |
|---|---|---|
|  | 2 | 3 |

**5.**
| hundreds | tens | ones |
|---|---|---|
| 7 | 1 | 8 |

**6.**
| hundreds | tens | ones |
|---|---|---|
| 2 | 1 | 0 |

Rename to show 10 more tens.

**7.**
| hundreds | tens | ones |
|---|---|---|
| 6 | 1 | 3 |

**8.**
| hundreds | tens | ones |
|---|---|---|
| 3 | 4 | 2 |

**9.**
| hundreds | tens | ones |
|---|---|---|
| 9 | 8 | 5 |

**10.**
| hundreds | tens | ones |
|---|---|---|
| 2 | 5 | 9 |

**11.**
| hundreds | tens | ones |
|---|---|---|
| 4 | 0 | 1 |

**12.**
| hundreds | tens | ones |
|---|---|---|
| 6 | 3 | 2 |

**13.**
| hundreds | tens | ones |
|---|---|---|
| 5 | 3 | 3 |

**14.**
| hundreds | tens | ones |
|---|---|---|
| 3 | 2 | 6 |

**15.**
| hundreds | tens | ones |
|---|---|---|
| 8 | 0 | 0 |

Rename to show 10 more ones.

**★16.**
| hundreds | tens | ones |
|---|---|---|
| 4 | 0 | 8 |

**★17.**
| hundreds | tens | ones |
|---|---|---|
| 7 | 0 | 0 |

**★18.**
| hundreds | tens | ones |
|---|---|---|
| 9 | 0 | 1 |

# Subtraction: Renaming Tens

A. The girls made 37 puppets. The boys made 18 puppets. The girls made how many more puppets than the boys?

Find 37 − 18.

| You need more ones. | Rename 37 to show 10 more ones. | Subtract the ones. 17 − 8 = 9 | Subtract the tens. 2 − 1 = 1 |
|---|---|---|---|
| 37<br>− 18 | 2 17<br>3̶7̶<br>− 18 | 2 17<br>3̶7̶<br>− 18<br>9 | 2 17<br>3̶7̶<br>− 18<br>19 |

The girls made 19 more puppets.

Tell what was done in each example.

B.
5 12
6̶2̶
− 9
53

C.
7 10
8̶0̶
− 54
26

Subtract.

| | | | | | | |
|---|---|---|---|---|---|---|
| 1. 20<br>− 5 | 2. 34<br>− 7 | 3. 40<br>− 8 | 4. 91<br>− 9 | 5. 26<br>− 8 | 6. 51<br>− 2 | 7. 61<br>− 5 |
| 8. 80<br>−32 | 9. 30<br>−25 | 10. 52<br>−46 | 11. 60<br>−11 | 12. 44<br>−37 | 13. 72<br>−26 | 14. 91<br>−33 |
| 15. 48<br>− 9 | 16. 70<br>−67 | 17. 71<br>−35 | 18. 90<br>−44 | 19. 82<br>− 4 | 20. 53<br>− 6 | 21. 74<br>−15 |
| 22. 56<br>−18 | 23. 41<br>−22 | 24. 72<br>− 5 | 25. 67<br>−39 | 26. 80<br>−23 | 27. 78<br>−59 | 28. 25<br>− 7 |
| 29. 22<br>−17 | 30. 54<br>−29 | 31. 93<br>−55 | 32. 33<br>−14 | 33. 85<br>−76 | 34. 64<br>−56 | 35. 96<br>−19 |

36. The class had 23 yards of yarn for the puppets. They used 18 yards. How much yarn was left?

★37. Ninety-three tickets for the puppet show were made. The boys sold 39. The girls sold 49. How many tickets were left to sell?

**More practice
Set 13, page 358**

# Subtraction: Renaming Tens

A. Jack has 393 baseball cards. Sally has 286.
Jack has how many more cards than Sally?

Find 393 − 286.

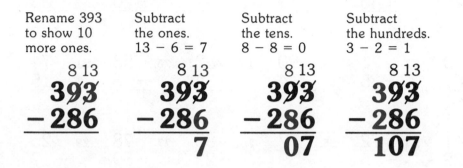

| Rename 393 to show 10 more ones. | Subtract the ones. 13 − 6 = 7 | Subtract the tens. 8 − 8 = 0 | Subtract the hundreds. 3 − 2 = 1 |
|---|---|---|---|
| 8 13 | 8 13 | 8 13 | 8 13 |
| 39̸3̸ | 39̸3̸ | 39̸3̸ | 39̸3̸ |
| −286 | −286 | −286 | −286 |
| | 7 | 07 | 107 |

Jack has 107 more cards than Sally.

Tell what was done in each example.

B.  
2 18  
53̸8̸  
− 19  
519

C.  
6 14  
87̸4̸  
− 8  
866

D.  
4 10  
15̸0̸  
−116  
34

Subtract.

| | | | |
|---|---|---|---|
| 1. 464<br>− 7 | 2. 832<br>− 6 | 3. 251<br>− 2 | 4. 376<br>− 8 |
| 5. 578<br>− 59 | 6. 950<br>− 46 | 7. 452<br>− 38 | 8. 291<br>− 13 |
| 9. 424<br>−116 | 10. 967<br>−108 | 11. 883<br>−235 | 12. 556<br>−439 |
| 13. 365<br>−346 | 14. 763<br>−757 | 15. 287<br>−249 | 16. 955<br>−907 |
| 17. 382<br>− 77 | 18. 861<br>−434 | 19. 495<br>− 9 | 20. 453<br>−216 |
| 21. 674<br>− 49 | 22. 233<br>− 14 | 23. 162<br>−139 | 24. 791<br>−758 |
| 25. 491<br>−429 | 26. 160<br>− 58 | 27. 561<br>− 26 | 28. 250<br>−124 |

29. Jeffrey had 185 baseball cards. He gave away 78 cards. How many cards did he have left?

More practice
Set 14, page 358

## Keeping Skillful

1. 24 + 37
2. 18 + 46
3. 36 + 52
4. 45 + 28
5. 29 + 41
6. 125 + 39
7. 273 + 21
8. 863 + 74
9. 345 + 36
10. 783 + 45
11. 214 + 57
12. 129 + 641
13. 493 + 146
14. 584 + 280
15. 347 + 115
16. 650 + 138
17. 356 + 251
18. 138 + 402
19. 749 + 123
20. 238 + 109
21. 576 + 218
22. 109 + 479
23. 813 + 96

## Subtraction: Renaming Hundreds

A. There were 556 puzzles in the store. 282 were sold. How many were left?

Find 556 − 282.

| Subtract the ones.<br>6 − 2 = 4 | Rename to show 10 more tens. | Subtract the tens.<br>15 − 8 = 7 | Subtract the hundreds.<br>4 − 2 = 2 |
|---|---|---|---|
| $\begin{array}{r} 556 \\ -282 \\ \hline 4 \end{array}$ | $\begin{array}{r} {}^{4\ 15} \\ \cancel{55}6 \\ -282 \\ \hline 4 \end{array}$ | $\begin{array}{r} {}^{4\ 15} \\ \cancel{55}6 \\ -282 \\ \hline 74 \end{array}$ | $\begin{array}{r} {}^{4\ 15} \\ \cancel{55}6 \\ -282 \\ \hline 274 \end{array}$ |

There were 274 puzzles left.

Tell what was done in each example.

B. $\begin{array}{r} {}^{2\ 12} \\ 3\cancel{2}8 \\ -\ 48 \\ \hline 280 \end{array}$
C. $\begin{array}{r} {}^{1\ 10} \\ 2\cancel{0}4 \\ -150 \\ \hline 54 \end{array}$
D. $\begin{array}{r} {}^{17} \\ \cancel{1}73 \\ -\ 92 \\ \hline 81 \end{array}$

Subtract.

1. 629
 &minus; 64

2. 134
 &minus; 41

3. 518
 &minus; 84

4. 729
 &minus; 36

5. 107
 &minus; 24

6. 336
 &minus; 96

7. 156
 &minus; 82

8. 901
 &minus; 90

9. 816
 &minus; 73

10. 204
 &minus; 32

11. 629
 &minus; 43

12. 118
 &minus; 21

13. 216
 &minus;165

14. 679
 &minus;385

15. 529
 &minus;498

16. 344
 &minus;272

17. 607
 &minus;266

18. 746
 &minus;354

19. 338
 &minus;165

20. 407
 &minus;352

21. 967
 &minus;573

22. 425
 &minus;254

23. 863
 &minus;780

24. 635
 &minus;573

25. 253
 &minus; 61

26. 582
 &minus; 91

27. 833
 &minus;362

28. 729
 &minus;579

29. 741
 &minus;690

30. 164
 &minus; 84

31. 109
 &minus; 10

32. 117
 &minus; 91

33. 805
 &minus;342

34. 929
 &minus;382

35. 415
 &minus; 51

36. 875
 &minus; 92

37. Diego's puzzle had 270 pieces. Ann's puzzle had 350 pieces. How many more pieces were in Ann's puzzle?

38. There were 238 puzzles. 146 were round. How many were not round?

39. Shirley's puzzle had 125 pieces. She lost 93 pieces. How many pieces were left?

★40. The colors in the puzzle are green, blue, and red. There are 265 pieces in all. 81 are green. 90 are blue. How many are red?

More practice
Set 15, page 358

(one hundred thirteen) 113

## Using Subtraction

Subtract.

**Here's how**

348 − 172

$$\begin{array}{r} \overset{2\ \ \ 14}{\cancel{3}\ \cancel{4}\ 8} \\ -1\ 7\ 2 \\ \hline 1\ 7\ 6 \end{array}$$

1. 87 − 35
2. 49 − 43
3. 98 − 89
4. 71 − 32
5. 640 − 311
6. 371 − 255
7. 838 − 486
8. 406 − 275
9. 31 − 8
10. 22 − 6
11. 729 − 34
12. 319 − 47
13. 495 − 3
14. 57 − 53
15. 924 − 15
16. 734 − 27
17. 45 − 18
18. 63 − 49
19. 270 − 19
20. 572 − 126
21. 358 − 272
22. 445 − 380
23. 774 − 720
24. 397 − 102
25. 73 − 57
26. 35 − 16
27. 768 − 97
28. 959 − 861

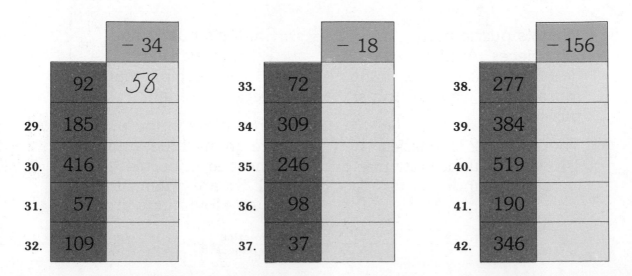

| | − 34 |
|---|---|
| 92 | *58* |
| 29. 185 | |
| 30. 416 | |
| 31. 57 | |
| 32. 109 | |

| | − 18 |
|---|---|
| 33. 72 | |
| 34. 309 | |
| 35. 246 | |
| 36. 98 | |
| 37. 37 | |

| | − 156 |
|---|---|
| 38. 277 | |
| 39. 384 | |
| 40. 519 | |
| 41. 190 | |
| 42. 346 | |

Subtract. Use the code to help you answer the riddle below.

Why is the library the highest building in town?

**Here's how**

$60 - 45 = 15 \quad R$

| CODE | |
|------|---|
| 9 | S |
| 15 | R |
| 18 | E |
| 27 | T |
| 37 | I |
| 62 | O |
| 111 | M |
| 407 | H |
| 454 | A |

**Word 1**

43. $655 - 618$

44. $80 - 53$

**Word 2**

45. $630 - 223$

46. $598 - 144$

47. $357 - 348$

**Word 3**

48. $109 - 82$

49. $542 - 135$

50. $223 - 205$

**Word 4**

51. $408 - 297$

52. $857 - 795$

53. $75 - 66$

54. $108 - 81$

**Word 5**

55. $91 - 82$

56. $419 - 392$

57. $542 - 480$

58. $781 - 766$

59. $108 - 71$

60. $221 - 203$

61. $93 - 84$

## Addition or Subtraction

Tell whether you add
or subtract.

A.
$$\begin{array}{r} {\scriptstyle 1\,10} \\ 2\cancel{0}8 \\ -127 \\ \hline 81 \end{array}$$

B.
$$\begin{array}{r} {\scriptstyle 1} \\ 308 \\ +127 \\ \hline 435 \end{array}$$

C.
$$\begin{array}{r} {\scriptstyle 1} \\ 446 \\ +\phantom{0}81 \\ \hline 527 \end{array}$$

D.
$$\begin{array}{r} {\scriptstyle 8\,14} \\ 99\cancel{4} \\ -\phantom{0}26 \\ \hline 968 \end{array}$$

Add.

1.
$$\begin{array}{r} 23 \\ +45 \\ \hline \end{array}$$

2.
$$\begin{array}{r} 74 \\ +19 \\ \hline \end{array}$$

3.
$$\begin{array}{r} 328 \\ +\phantom{0}66 \\ \hline \end{array}$$

Subtract.

4.
$$\begin{array}{r} 149 \\ -\phantom{0}64 \\ \hline \end{array}$$

5.
$$\begin{array}{r} 515 \\ -\phantom{0}32 \\ \hline \end{array}$$

6.
$$\begin{array}{r} 967 \\ -108 \\ \hline \end{array}$$

Give each answer.
Watch the signs.

7. 39
   + 8

8. 60
   − 54

9. 382
   + 464

10. 836
    − 295

11. 546
    + 407

12. 338
    −   9

13. 843
    + 42

14. 553
    − 21

15. 193
    + 271

16. 365
    − 346

17. 647
    + 15

18. 31
    − 23

19. 386
    + 312

20. 80
    − 37

21. 75
    + 5

22. 409
    − 228

23. 541
    + 67

24. 679
    − 23

25. 651
    + 78

26. 709
    − 256

27. 324
    + 548

28. 920 − 13

29. 483 + 164

30. 362 + 428

31. 176 − 117

32. 746 − 128

33. 245 + 308

How many triangles can you find in each figure?

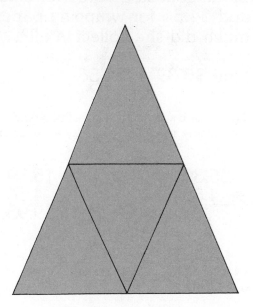

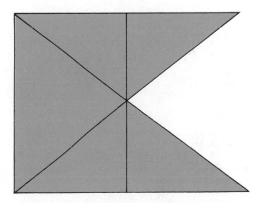

# Addition and Subtraction of Money

A. Maria collected $5.39 for stationery and $4.56 for wrapping paper. How much did she collect in all?

Find $5.39 + $4.56.

Add as you would with whole numbers.

Put $ and . in your answer.

$$\begin{array}{r} \$5.39 \\ +\phantom{\$}4.56 \\ \hline \end{array}$$

$$\begin{array}{r} ^{1}\phantom{0} \\ 539 \\ +456 \\ \hline 995 \end{array}$$

$$\begin{array}{r} \$5.39 \\ +\phantom{\$}4.56 \\ \hline \$9.95 \end{array}$$

Maria collected $9.95 in all.

Tell what was done in each example.

B.
$$\begin{array}{r} ^{8\phantom{0}12}\phantom{0} \\ \$0.\cancel{9}\cancel{2} \\ -\phantom{\$}0.46 \\ \hline \$0.46 \end{array}$$

C.
$$\begin{array}{r} ^{1}\phantom{00} \\ \$1.72 \\ +\phantom{\$}0.95 \\ \hline \$2.67 \end{array}$$

D.
$$\begin{array}{r} ^{4\phantom{0}10}\phantom{0} \\ \$\cancel{5}.\cancel{0}5 \\ -\phantom{\$}2.30 \\ \hline \$2.75 \end{array}$$

Add or subtract. Watch the signs.

1. $1.07
 + 0.88

2. $1.18
 + 2.21

3. $0.80
 + 3.45

4. $4.50
 + 1.63

5. $0.66
 + 0.14

6. $4.25
 + 0.38

7. $5.17
 + 3.59

8. $8.95
 + 0.23

9. $0.38
 + 0.16

10. $0.29
 + 1.39

11. $4.85
 + 2.71

12. $1.75
 + 0.30

13. $0.54
 − 0.28

14. $4.16
 − 4.05

15. $1.15
 − 0.92

16. $3.17
 − 1.40

17. $3.09
 − 2.06

18. $2.50
 −1.49

19. $0.92
 − 0.87

20. $8.56
 − 2.00

21. $0.25
 − 0.19

22. $8.56
 − 6.83

23. $5.06
 − 3.21

24. $9.95
 − 8.49

| Item | Price |
| --- | --- |
| Note cards | $1.50 |
| Flower stationery | $2.50 |
| Thank-you notes | $1.25 |
| Memo pad | $0.95 |
| Birthday cards | $2.60 |
| Gift packet | $3.50 |
| Wrapping paper | $0.75 |

25. Ms. Smith bought one box of note cards and one memo pad. How much did she spend in all?

26. Flower stationery costs how much more than thank-you notes?

27. Ted had $5.25. He bought one gift packet. How much did he have left?

*28. Susan bought two boxes of birthday cards and one package of wrapping paper. She spent how much in all?

**More practice
Set 16, page 359**

More practice
Set 16, page 359

# Using Addition and Subtraction

Add across. Add down.

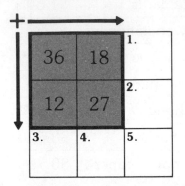

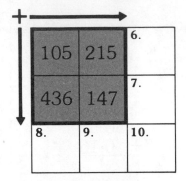

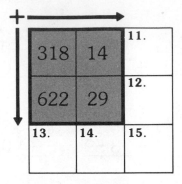

Subtract across. Subtract down.

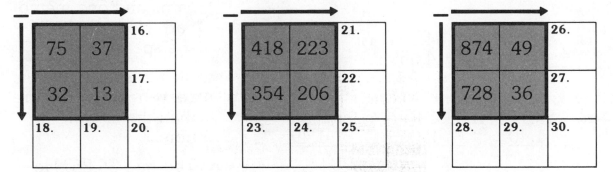

Add or subtract. Watch the signs.

| 31. $\begin{array}{r} 50 \\ -39 \end{array}$ | 32. $\begin{array}{r} 48 \\ +28 \end{array}$ | 33. $\begin{array}{r} 817 \\ -\ 61 \end{array}$ | 34. $\begin{array}{r} 284 \\ +392 \end{array}$ | 35. $\begin{array}{r} 603 \\ -281 \end{array}$ | 36. $\begin{array}{r} 928 \\ +\ 45 \end{array}$ |

| 37. $\begin{array}{r} 781 \\ +166 \end{array}$ | 38. $\begin{array}{r} 456 \\ +\ 29 \end{array}$ | 39. $\begin{array}{r} 591 \\ -548 \end{array}$ | 40. $\begin{array}{r} 167 \\ +216 \end{array}$ | 41. $\begin{array}{r} 705 \\ -152 \end{array}$ | 42. $\begin{array}{r} 365 \\ -346 \end{array}$ |

### Finding Missing Digits

Kim was playing with a paper punch. She found she had been using her math paper by mistake. Help her find the missing digits. Copy and complete each exercise.

1.
```
   4
+ 6 3
─────
  8 7
```

2.
```
  7 6
-   1
─────
    1
```

3.
```
+ 4 6
─────
  9 8
```

4.
```
  5 8
-   1
─────
    7
```

5.
```
  4 2
- 1   3
─────
  3 0 2
```

6.
```
  3 8
-     5
─────
  4 2
```

7.
```
  2 3 5
+     7
─────
  6 5 2
```

8.
```
  1 7
+     5
─────
  9 5
```

9.
```
    3
+ 1
─────
  4 0
```

10.
```
    1
-   3 2
─────
  5 9
```

11.
```
  2 4
+ 2 9
─────
  4   7
```

12.
```
  3   5
- 1 4 6
─────
  2 3
```

13. $1\ \_\ + 9 = 27$

14. $15\ \_\ - 126 = 32$

15. $24 - \_\ = 17$

16. $3\ \_\ + 12 = 55$

17. $2\ \_\ 6 + 23 = 279$

18. $\_\ 8 + 15 = 63$

# Problem Solving: Choosing the Operation

**READ**  A. The school had 325 circus tickets. 183 were sold. How many were left?

**DECIDE**  Subtract the number of tickets sold from the number you had. Use this number sentence.

$$325 - 183 = ?$$

**SOLVE**

$$
\begin{array}{r}
{\scriptstyle 2\ 12} \\
\cancel{3}25 \\
-\ 183 \\
\hline
142
\end{array}
$$

**ANSWER**  142 tickets

**READ**  B. Lynn spent $2.50 for an adult ticket and $2.73 for lunch. How much did she spend in all?

**DECIDE**  Add the amounts spent. Use this number sentence.

$$\$2.50 + \$2.73 = ?$$

**SOLVE**

$$
\begin{array}{r}
{\scriptstyle 1} \\
\$2.50 \\
+\ 2.73 \\
\hline
\$5.23
\end{array}
$$

**ANSWER**  $5.23

Write a number sentence for each problem. Give the answer.

1. The circus had 97 animals last year and 139 animals this year. How many more animals does the circus have this year?

2. There were 15 lions and 8 elephants. How many animals were there in all?

3. The circus traveled 208 kilometers in the morning and 185 kilometers in the afternoon. How many kilometers did the circus travel that day?

4. There were 21 monkeys in the circus. 13 rode bicycles. How many did not ride bicycles?

5. Jason had $3.32. He spent $0.90. How much money did he have left?

6. The school sold 165 student tickets and 132 adult tickets. How many tickets did the school sell in all?

7. Lucy spent $1.75 for a ticket and $0.50 for peanuts. How much did she spend in all?

8. The circus clowns had 350 balloons. They gave away 215 balloons. How many balloons were left?

Nineteen clowns juggled 57 balls. Eight seals juggled 24 balls.

★ 9. How many more clowns than seals were there?

★ 10. There were how many balls in all?

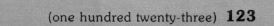

# Chapter 6 Test
## Subtraction Computation, pages 104–123

Rename to show 10 more tens.

1.

| hundreds | tens | ones |
|----------|------|------|
| 3 | 4 | 5 |

2.

| hundreds | tens | ones |
|----------|------|------|
| 2 | 0 | 3 |

Subtract.

3.
$$\begin{array}{r} 19 \\ -\ 6 \\ \hline \end{array}$$

4.
$$\begin{array}{r} 65 \\ -24 \\ \hline \end{array}$$

5.
$$\begin{array}{r} 287 \\ -103 \\ \hline \end{array}$$

6.
$$\begin{array}{r} 81 \\ -\ 2 \\ \hline \end{array}$$

7.
$$\begin{array}{r} 60 \\ -28 \\ \hline \end{array}$$

8.
$$\begin{array}{r} 74 \\ -56 \\ \hline \end{array}$$

9.
$$\begin{array}{r} 190 \\ -\ 24 \\ \hline \end{array}$$

10.
$$\begin{array}{r} 872 \\ -837 \\ \hline \end{array}$$

11.
$$\begin{array}{r} 981 \\ -223 \\ \hline \end{array}$$

12.
$$\begin{array}{r} 546 \\ -\ 75 \\ \hline \end{array}$$

13.
$$\begin{array}{r} 239 \\ -167 \\ \hline \end{array}$$

14.
$$\begin{array}{r} 463 \\ -180 \\ \hline \end{array}$$

Add or subtract.
Watch the signs.

15.
$$\begin{array}{r} 49 \\ +32 \\ \hline \end{array}$$

16.
$$\begin{array}{r} 52 \\ -36 \\ \hline \end{array}$$

17.
$$\begin{array}{r} 742 \\ -423 \\ \hline \end{array}$$

18.
$$\begin{array}{r} 146 \\ +263 \\ \hline \end{array}$$

19.
$$\begin{array}{r} \$1.45 \\ +\ 0.25 \\ \hline \end{array}$$

20.
$$\begin{array}{r} \$8.19 \\ +\ 1.79 \\ \hline \end{array}$$

21.
$$\begin{array}{r} \$5.74 \\ -\ 2.49 \\ \hline \end{array}$$

22.
$$\begin{array}{r} \$2.41 \\ -\ 1.37 \\ \hline \end{array}$$

23. There were 25 cats and 33 dogs. There were how many more dogs than cats?

24. Doug rode 237 blocks in the morning and 314 blocks in the afternoon. How many blocks did he ride in all?

25. Judy had 115 pennies. She spent 35 pennies. How many pennies did she have left?

# Problems Around Us

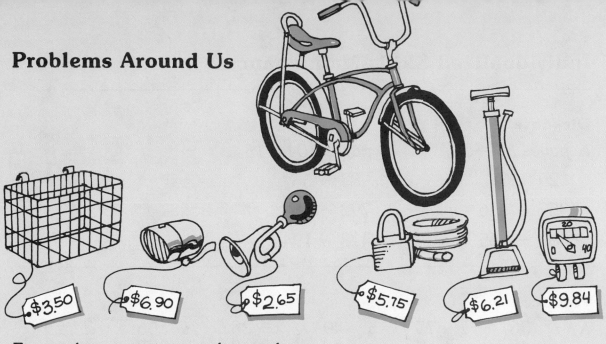

$3.50    $6.90    $2.65    $5.75    $6.21    $9.84

For each exercise, give the total cost.

1. Tire pump
   Horn

2. Basket
   Bike lock

3. Horn
   Basket

4. Light
   Horn

How much more does the speedometer cost than the

5. tire pump?

6. light?

7. horn?

8. bike lock?

Find the answer.

9. There were 47 daisies and 38 dandelions. How many were there in all?

10. There were 789 books in the library. 195 were checked out. How many were left?

11. There were 396 girls and 378 boys. There were how many more girls than boys?

12. Bob had 126 mushrooms. He found 39 more. How many did he have in all?

13. There were 550 packages of seeds. 49 packages were sold. How many were left?

14. There were 43 students on the first bus and 47 on the second bus. How many students were there in all?

# Individualized Skills Maintenance

## Diagnose

**A** *pages 84–95*

    29 + 38

  357 + 126

  582 + 265

**B** *pages 104–115*

    83 − 56

  792 − 563

  418 − 194

## Practice

**A**

1. $36 + 49$
2. $75 + 17$
3. $49 + 28$
4. $38 + 42$
5. $56 + 25$
6. $29 + 67$

7. $128 + 217$
8. $247 + 519$
9. $128 + 364$
10. $426 + 156$
11. $517 + 476$
12. $108 + 536$

13. $495 + 194$
14. $371 + 248$
15. $182 + 235$
16. $250 + 654$
17. $542 + 396$
18. $421 + 193$

**B**

19. $72 - 38$
20. $46 - 19$
21. $95 - 76$
22. $58 - 29$
23. $80 - 58$
24. $67 - 28$

25. $696 - 218$
26. $390 - 165$
27. $854 - 526$
28. $781 - 354$
29. $943 - 728$
30. $415 - 208$

31. $917 - 384$
32. $803 - 562$
33. $627 - 475$
34. $405 - 132$
35. $743 - 271$
36. $948 - 295$

# Unit 2 Review

Chapter 4, pages 62–82
Give the number.

1.

| hundreds | tens | ones |
|----------|------|------|
|          | 1    | 8    |

2.

| hundreds | tens | ones |
|----------|------|------|
| 9        | 6    | 2    |

What digit is in the

3. ones place of 762?

4. tens place of 438?

5. hundreds place of 975?

Replace the ●. Use < or >.

6. 38 ● 83    7. 913 ● 319

Give the numbers in order.
Begin with the least number.

8. 713    137    371

9. 13    65    48    84

10. Use $ and . to show the
amount for *4 dollars,
6 dimes,* and *8 pennies.*

Chapter 5, pages 84–102
Add.

11. 18
   + 75

12. 249
   + 348

13. 532
   + 164

14. 468
   + 391

15. 235
     17
   + 318

16. 164
    783
   + 52

Chapter 6, pages 104–123
Subtract.

17. 38
   − 19

18. 419
   − 276

19. 387
   − 165

20. 725
   − 394

21. 704
   − 582

22. 435
   − 126

Add or subtract. Watch the signs.

23. $6.37
   + 1.58

24. $0.75
   + 2.31

25. $8.05
   − 3.64

26. $0.95
   − 0.76

27. Tomah had $5.75. He spent
$1.39. How much money did
he have left?

# Unit 2 Test
## Chapters 4–6, pages 62–124

What digit is in the

1. tens place of 896?

2. ones place of 127?

3. hundreds place of 265?

Replace the ●. Use < and >.

4. 21 ● 12    5. 136 ● 163

Give the numbers in order.
Begin with the least number.

6. 19  94  56

7. 32  58  79  15

8. Give the missing number.
   $1.00 or ▦ dimes

Add.

9. 6 + 3 + 9

10. 28    11. 45
    +16        +29

12. 136    13. 572
    +512        +184

14. 625    15. 342
    +138        +564

Subtract.

16. 57    17. 25    18. 385
    −28        −16        −124

19. 867    20. 725    21. 508
    −492        −316        −167

Add or subtract.
Watch the signs.

22. $0.25    23. $0.65
    + 0.52        + 0.26

24. $0.48    25. $0.57
    − 0.36        − 0.39

26. $7.28    27. $9.36
    + 1.35        − 4.65

28. There were 49 girls and
    36 boys. There were how
    many students in all?

29. Jim had 65 newspapers. He
    sold 26. How many did he
    have left?

30. Kate had $1.35. She earned
    $2.48. How much did she
    have in all?

# Unit 3

# Chapter 7  Measurement

## Time: 5-Minute Intervals

**A.** The short hand is called the **hour hand.** It moves from one number to the next in 60 minutes, or 1 hour.

**B.** The long hand is called the **minute hand.** It moves from one number to the next in 5 minutes.

2:00

3:00

6:05

6:10

**C.**

8:00

**D.**

9:20

**E.**

3:40

**F.**

7:45

**G.**

11:15

**H.**

2:30

# What time is shown?

**1.**

**2.**

**3.**

**4.**

**5.**

**6.**

**7.**

**8.**

**9.**

**10.**

**11.**

**12.**

How many minutes will it take for the
minute hand to move from

★**13.** 12 to 1?  ★**14.** 8 to 10?  ★**15.** 6 to 12?

# Time: 1-Minute Intervals

A. The first digital clock shows that the time is 12:15.
The second clock shows the time 1 minute later.

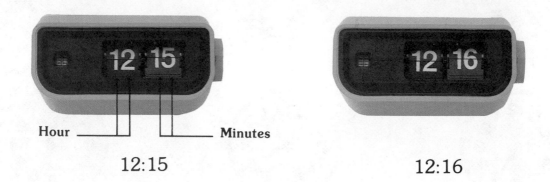

Hour _____ _____ Minutes

12:15                              12:16

B. The minute hand moves from one mark to the next
in 1 minute.

12:15                  12:16                  12:17

Give the time for each clock.
What will the time be 1 minute later?

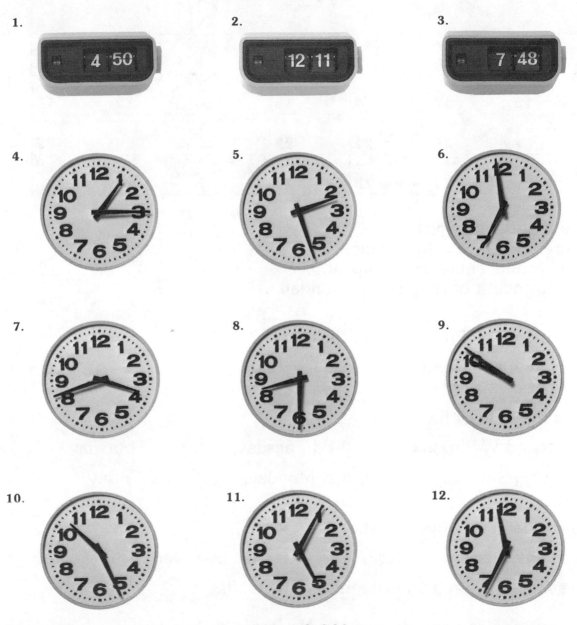

1.
4 50

2.
12 11

3.
7 48

4.

5.

6.

7.

8.

9.

10.

11.

12.

How many minutes are there until 9:00?

*13. It is 8:35.     *14. It is 8:45.     *15. It is 8:27.

# The Calendar

## AUGUST

| Sunday | Monday | Tuesday | Wednesday | Thursday | Friday | Saturday |
|--------|--------|---------|-----------|----------|--------|----------|
|  |  |  | 1 | 2 | 3 | 4 |
| 5 | 6 | 7 | 8 | 9 | *Mr. Rataj's birthday* 10 | 11 |
| 12 | 13 | 14 | 15 | 16 | 17 | 18 |
| 19 | 20 | 21 | 22 | 23 | 24 | 25 |
| 26 | 27 | *Ms. Newton's birthday* 28 | 29 | 30 | 31 |  |

The month is August.
There are 31 days in this month.
The second Thursday is August 9.
The twentieth of August is a Monday.

1. How many Fridays are in this month?

2. How many Sundays are in this month?

Give the date of the

3. second Wednesday.   4. third Tuesday.   5. fifth Thursday.

6. fourth Saturday.   7. first Monday.   8. third Friday.

Which day of the week is the

9. twenty-first?   10. fourth?   11. twenty-seventh?

12. sixteenth?   13. nineteenth?   14. tenth?

15. Give the day and date of Ms. Newton's birthday.

16. Give the day and date of Mr. Rataj's birthday.

| JANUARY | FEBRUARY | MARCH | APRIL |
|---|---|---|---|
| S M T W T F S | S M T W T F S | S M T W T F S | S M T W T F S |
|    1  2  3  4  5  6 |          1  2  3 |          1  2  3 | 1  2  3  4  5  6  7 |
| 7  8  9 10 11 12 13 | 4  5  6  7  8  9 10 | 4  5  6  7  8  9 10 | 8  9 10 11 12 13 14 |
| 14 15 16 17 18 19 20 | 11 12 13 14 15 16 17 | 11 12 13 14 15 16 17 | 15 16 17 18 19 20 21 |
| 21 22 23 24 25 26 27 | 18 19 20 21 22 23 24 | 18 19 20 21 22 23 24 | 22 23 24 25 26 27 28 |
| 28 29 30 31 | 25 26 27 28 | 25 26 27 28 29 30 31 | 29 30 |

| MAY | JUNE | JULY | AUGUST |
|---|---|---|---|
| S M T W T F S | S M T W T F S | S M T W T F S | S M T W T F S |
|     1  2  3  4  5 |            1  2 | 1  2  3  4  5  6  7 |         1  2  3  4 |
| 6  7  8  9 10 11 12 | 3  4  5  6  7  8  9 | 8  9 10 11 12 13 14 | 5  6  7  8  9 10 11 |
| 13 14 15 16 17 18 19 | 10 11 12 13 14 15 16 | 15 16 17 18 19 20 21 | 12 13 14 15 16 17 18 |
| 20 21 22 23 24 25 26 | 17 18 19 20 21 22 23 | 22 23 24 25 26 27 28 | 19 20 21 22 23 24 25 |
| 27 28 29 30 31 | 24 25 26 27 28 29 30 | 29 30 31 | 26 27 28 29 30 31 |

| SEPTEMBER | OCTOBER | NOVEMBER | DECEMBER |
|---|---|---|---|
| S M T W T F S | S M T W T F S | S M T W T F S | S M T W T F S |
|              1 | 1  2  3  4  5  6 |          1  2  3 |              1 |
| 2  3  4  5  6  7  8 | 7  8  9 10 11 12 13 | 4  5  6  7  8  9 10 | 2  3  4  5  6  7  8 |
| 9 10 11 12 13 14 15 | 14 15 16 17 18 19 20 | 11 12 13 14 15 16 17 | 9 10 11 12 13 14 15 |
| 16 17 18 19 20 21 22 | 21 22 23 24 25 26 27 | 18 19 20 21 22 23 24 | 16 17 18 19 20 21 22 |
| 23/30 24 25 26 27 28 29 | 28 29 30 31 | 25 26 27 28 29 30 | 23/30 24/31 25 26 27 28 29 |

17. Give the months in order.

Which months have only

18. 31 days?    19. 30 days?    20. 28 days?

Give the day of the week.

21. March 4    22. January 15    23. July 12

24. September 9    25. May 30    26. November 21

Which months have

★27. five Saturdays?    ★28. five Wednesdays?    ★29. five Sundays?

Give each date.

★30. Second Tuesday in June    ★31. Last Friday in December

# Centimeter

A **centimeter** (cm) is a metric unit of length. The width of your thumbnail is about 1 centimeter.

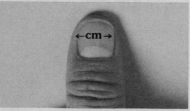

actual size

This bolt is about 10 cm long.

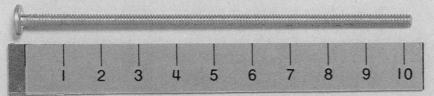

actual size

Measure each object to the nearest centimeter.

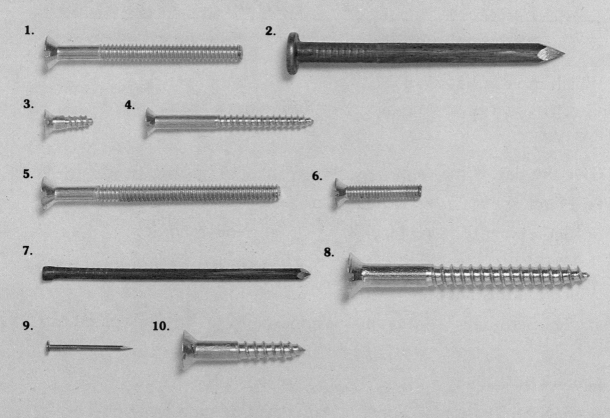

1.

2.

3.

4.

5.

6.

7.

8.

9.

10.

Measure Happy the Clown.

11. About how long is his foot?

12. About how tall is Happy?

13. About how long is his tie?

14. About how wide is his tie?

15. About how long is the stick on the sign?

Measure Happy's dog.

16. About how long is its nose?

17. About how long is its ear?

18. About how long is its tail?

19. About how long is its body?

20. About how long is its back leg?

Use your ruler to draw these lines.

21. 11 cm    22. 9 cm    23. 3 cm

24. 15 cm    25. 6 cm    26. 8 cm

# Meter and Kilometer

The **meter** (m) and **kilometer** (km) are metric units of length. These units are used to measure longer distances.

A. A baseball bat is about 1 meter long.

B. One thousand baseball bats put end-to-end measure about 1 kilometer.

Give the most sensible unit of measure.
Use centimeter, meter, or kilometer.

1.

2.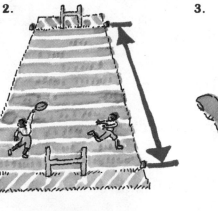

3.

4.

5.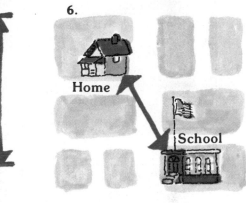

6.

7. Width of a piece of tape

8. Length of a bike trip

9. Length of a pen

10. Height of a door

11. Height of a flagpole

12. Length of a shoe

13. Length of a book

14. Height of a building

15. Height of a table

16. Length of a car

17. Length of a bus trip

18. Height of a person

19. Distance from New York City to Washington, D.C.

20. Distance from the moon to the earth

21. Length of a sheet of notebook paper

22. Distance from Kansas City to San Francisco

# Perimeter

The distance around a figure is called its **perimeter.** You can add to find the perimeter of this rectangle.

$5 + 3 + 5 + 3 = 16$

The perimeter is 16 centimeters.

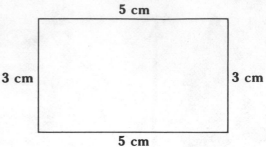

5 cm

3 cm      3 cm

5 cm

Find the perimeter of each figure.

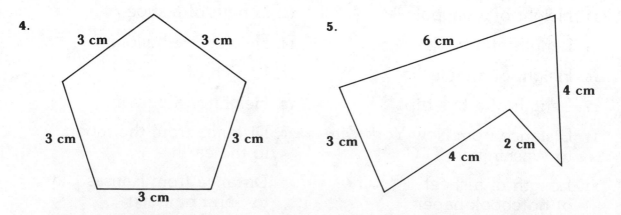

1.

4 cm

4 cm      4 cm

4 cm

2.

2 cm

5 cm      5 cm

2 cm

3.

5 cm      4 cm

3 cm

4.

3 cm      3 cm

3 cm      3 cm

3 cm

5.

6 cm

4 cm

3 cm      2 cm

4 cm

Measure each side to the nearest centimeter. Find the perimeter of each figure.

6.

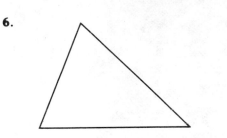

7.

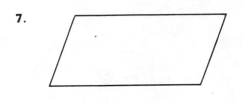

8.

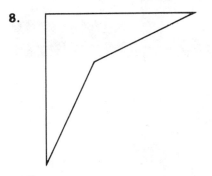

*9.

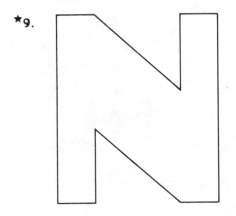

**My Metric Measures**

Measure the distance around your

1. wrist.    2. ankle.

3. neck.    4. head.

5. waist.    6. arm.

Measure your

7. height.        8. arm span.

9. arm length.    10. shoe length.

# Liter

The *liter* (L) is a metric unit for measuring how much a container holds.

Tell if the object holds more than or less than a liter.

1.

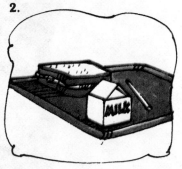

2.

3.

4. A bathtub

5. A little glass

6. A spoon

7. An eye dropper

8. A kitchen sink

9. A cereal bowl

# Gram and Kilogram

The **gram** (g) and **kilogram** (kg) are metric units for measuring weight or mass.

**A.** A dollar bill weighs about 1 gram.

**B.** A brick weighs about 1 kilogram.
1 kilogram = 1000 grams

Which unit would you use to measure each object?
Use grams or kilograms.

1.

2.

3.

4.

5.

6.

7. A nickel    8. A cat    9. An apple

10. A car    11. A spoon    12. A lion

# Inch, Foot, Yard, and Mile

The **inch** (in.), **foot** (ft.), **yard** (yd.), and **mile** (mi.) are customary units of length.

**A.** The distance from your knuckle to the end of your thumb is about 1 inch.

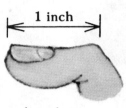

1 inch

Actual size.

**B.** The width of your hands spread is about 1 foot.
1 ft. = 12 in.

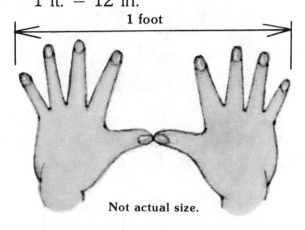

1 foot

Not actual size.

**C.** The distance from the tip of the nose to the finger tip is about 1 yard.
1 yd. = 3 ft.

1 yard

Not actual size.

**D.** The students below made a chain that was about 1 mile long. It took 1200 students.
1 mi. = 5280 ft.

1 mile          Not actual size.

Which unit would you use?

1. Inches or miles

2. Inches or miles

It takes 3 chipmunks 3 minutes to eat 3 acorns. How long will it take 100 chipmunks to eat 100 acorns?

3. Length of a pencil: inches or feet

4. Width of a desk: feet or miles

5. Length of a room: inches or feet

6. Height of a mountain: inches or miles

7. Width of a book: inches or feet

8. Length of a car: feet or miles

Give each answer.
Use inch, foot, yard, or mile.

9. An earthworm is about 4 (?).

10. A football field is about 100 (?) long.

11. The height of a student is about 5 (?).

12. Tampa is about 250 (?) from Miami.

Give each answer.

*13. Estimate in feet the length of the chalkboard in your room.

*14. Measure its length to the nearest foot.

# Cup, Pint, Quart, and Gallon

The **cup** (c.), **pint** (pt.), **quart** (qt.),
and **gallon** (gal.) are customary units of measure.
These units are used to measure liquids.

**A.** 1 cup

**B.** 1 pint = 2 cups

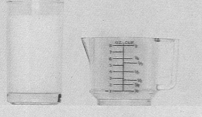

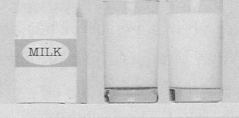

**C.** 1 quart = 2 pints

**D.** 1 gallon = 4 quarts

Which unit would you use?

1. Cup or gallon

2. Cup or gallon

3. Quart or gallon

4. Cup or quart

5. Pint or gallon

6. Cup or gallon

7. Milk in a glass: cup or quart

8. Water in a pond: pint or gallon

9. Cocoa in a mug: cup or quart

10. Water in a sink: cup or gallon

11. Cream in a pitcher: pint or gallon

12. Milk in a cake recipe: cup or quart

13. Water in a water tower: cup or gallon

## Temperature

The **Celsius** (°C) thermometer is used
to measure temperature.

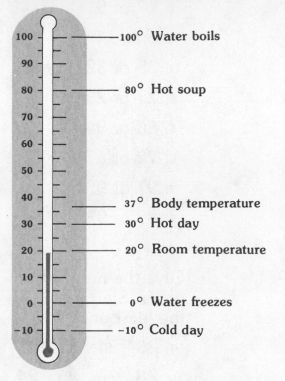

| | |
|---|---|
| 100° | Water boils |
| 80° | Hot soup |
| 37° | Body temperature |
| 30° | Hot day |
| 20° | Room temperature |
| 0° | Water freezes |
| −10° | Cold day |

Use the thermometer to give these temperatures.

1. Body temperature  2. A hot day  3. Room temperature

4. Water freezes  5. A cold day  6. Hot soup

Choose the more sensible temperature for each activity.

7. Make a snow fort:
   −5°C or 10°C

8. Football game:
   75°C or 15°C

9. Have a picnic:
   25°C or 50°C

10. Swim in a lake:
    0°C or 35°C

11. Row a boat:
    30°C or 55°C

12. Shovel snow:
    −10°C or 10°C

# Chapter 7 Test
## Measurement, pages 130–148

What time is shown on each clock?

1.

2.

Which unit would you use?

3. Length of an eraser:
   centimeter or meter

4. Height of a flagpole:
   meter or kilometer

5. Weight of an egg:
   gram or kilogram

6. Weight of a chicken:
   gram or kilogram

7. Height of a building:
   inches or feet

8. Length of a pencil:
   inches or miles

9. Juice in a glass:
   cup or gallon

10. Would a bathtub hold more
    than or less than a liter?

Use the calendar.

| September | | | | | | |
|---|---|---|---|---|---|---|
| S | M | T | W | T | F | S |
| | | | 1 | 2 | 3 | 4 |
| 5 | 6 | 7 | 8 | 9 | 10 | 11 |
| 12 | 13 | 14 | 15 | 16 | 17 | 18 |
| 19 | 20 | 21 | 22 | 23 | 24 | 25 |
| 26 | 27 | 28 | 29 | 30 | | |

11. Which day of the week
    is September 17?

12. What is the date of
    the second Thursday?

13. How many Wednesdays
    are in the month?

14. What is the date of
    the first Saturday?

15. Find the perimeter.

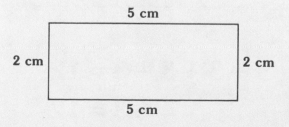

# Chapter 8  Multiplication Facts: 2, 3, 4, or 5

## Meaning of Multiplication

You can use an addition sentence or
a multiplication sentence for each picture.

A. 4 groups of 3                                    B. 2 groups of 4

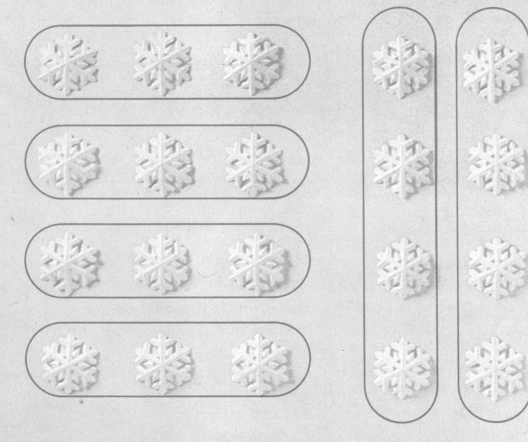

$$3 + 3 + 3 + 3 = 12$$
$$4 \times 3 = 12$$

4 times 3 equals 12

$$4 + 4 = 8$$
$$2 \times 4 = 8$$

2 times 4 equals 8

# Copy and complete each sentence.

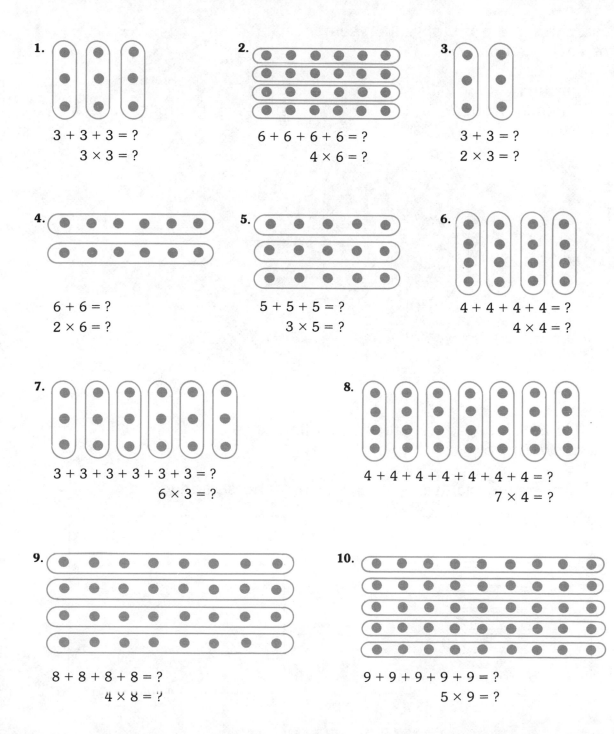

**1.**
3 + 3 + 3 = ?
3 × 3 = ?

**2.**
6 + 6 + 6 + 6 = ?
4 × 6 = ?

**3.**
3 + 3 = ?
2 × 3 = ?

**4.**
6 + 6 = ?
2 × 6 = ?

**5.**
5 + 5 + 5 = ?
3 × 5 = ?

**6.**
4 + 4 + 4 + 4 = ?
4 × 4 = ?

**7.**
3 + 3 + 3 + 3 + 3 + 3 = ?
6 × 3 = ?

**8.**
4 + 4 + 4 + 4 + 4 + 4 + 4 = ?
7 × 4 = ?

**9.**
8 + 8 + 8 + 8 = ?
4 × 8 = ?

**10.**
9 + 9 + 9 + 9 + 9 = ?
5 × 9 = ?

# 2 in Multiplication

You can write a multiplication sentence for each picture.

A. 4 groups
   2 in each group

B. 2 groups
   4 in each group

$$4 \times 2 = 8$$

$$2 \times 4 = 8$$

Mr. Compton asked the students to find the answer to $6 \times 2$.

C. John drew a picture.

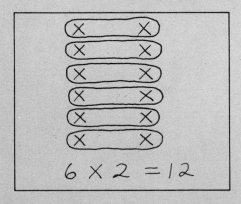

$$6 \times 2 = 12$$

D. Vanessa added.

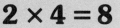

$$2$$
$$2$$
$$2$$
$$2$$
$$2$$
$$+2$$
$$\overline{12}$$

$$6 \times 2 = 12$$

Copy and complete each sentence.

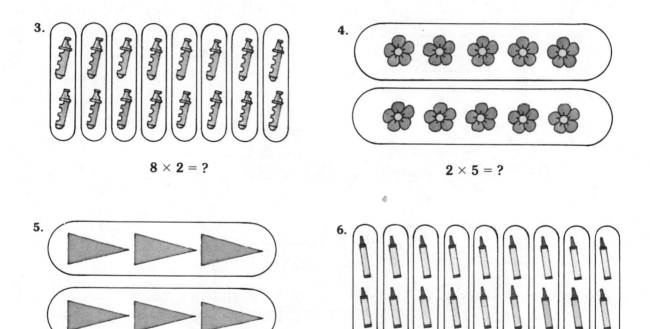

1. $2 \times 7 = ?$

2. $2 \times 2 = ?$

3. $8 \times 2 = ?$

4. $2 \times 5 = ?$

5. $2 \times 3 = ?$

6. $9 \times 2 = ?$

Give each answer.

7. $2 \times 2$   8. $3 \times 2$   9. $4 \times 2$   10. $5 \times 2$   11. $6 \times 2$

12. $7 \times 2$   13. $8 \times 2$   14. $9 \times 2$   15. $2 \times 3$   16. $2 \times 4$

17. $2 \times 5$   18. $2 \times 6$   19. $2 \times 7$   20. $2 \times 8$   21. $2 \times 9$

# 3 in Multiplication

You can write a multiplication sentence
for each picture. 3 and 5 are *factors*.
15 is the *product*.

**A.** 3 groups
5 in each group

**B.** 5 groups
3 in each group

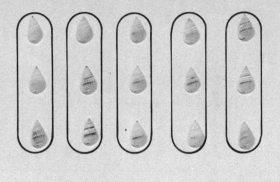

$$3 \times 5 = 15$$

Factor —————— Product

$$5 \times 3 = 15$$

Factor —————— Product

**C.** How many groups? 7
How many in each group? 3

**D.** How many groups? 3
How many in each group? 7

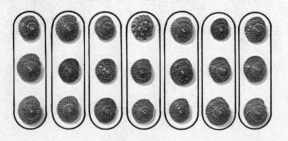

$$7 \times 3 = 21$$

$$3 \times 7 = 21$$

**154** (one hundred fifty-four)

Copy and complete each sentence.

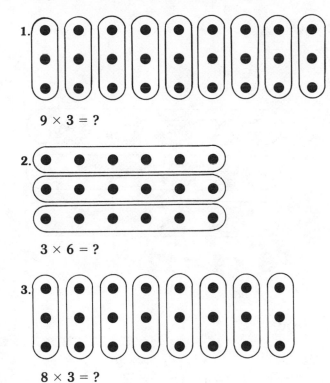

1. $9 \times 3 = ?$

2. $3 \times 6 = ?$

3. $8 \times 3 = ?$

Give each product.

4. $2 \times 3$    5. $3 \times 3$    6. $4 \times 3$

7. $5 \times 3$    8. $6 \times 3$    9. $7 \times 3$

10. $8 \times 3$    11. $9 \times 3$    12. $3 \times 2$

13. $3 \times 4$    14. $3 \times 5$    15. $3 \times 6$

16. $3 \times 7$    17. $3 \times 8$    18. $3 \times 9$

19. $2 \times 4$    20. $4 \times 3$    21. $8 \times 2$

22. $9 \times 3$    23. $2 \times 7$    24. $3 \times 6$

25. $5 \times 2$    26. $3 \times 8$    27. $2 \times 3$

More practice
Set 17, page 360

## Keeping Skillful

Add.

1. $13 + 85$

2. $56 + 37$

3. $123 + 54$

4. $344 + 263$

5. $557 + 415$

6. $47 + 15 + 29$

Subtract.

7. $57 - 32$

8. $86 - 23$

9. $94 - 16$

10. $129 - 60$

11. $462 - 271$

12. $809 - 333$

Add or subtract.

13. $386 + 18$

14. $65 - 28$

15. $684 + 92$

16. $437 + 125$

17. $713 - 281$

18. $580 - 73$

(one hundred fifty-five) **155**

# Order in Multiplication

A. You can use one picture to show
   one multiplication fact.

4 groups of 3                          3 groups of 4

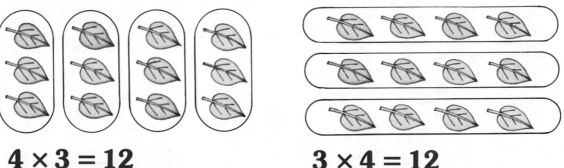

**4 × 3 = 12**                         **3 × 4 = 12**

B. Or you can use one picture to show
   two multiplication facts.

Think of 4 groups of 3.
   4 × 3 = 12

Think of 3 groups of 4.
   3 × 4 = 12

C. You can use this picture for 3 × 7 or 7 × 3.
   There is another way to write multiplication facts.

$$
\begin{array}{r}
7 \\
\times\ 3 \\
\hline
21
\end{array}
\begin{array}{l}
\longleftarrow \text{Factor} \longrightarrow \\
\longleftarrow \text{Factor} \longrightarrow \\
\longleftarrow \text{Product} \longrightarrow
\end{array}
\begin{array}{r}
3 \\
\times\ 7 \\
\hline
21
\end{array}
$$

Give two multiplication sentences for each picture.

**Here's how**

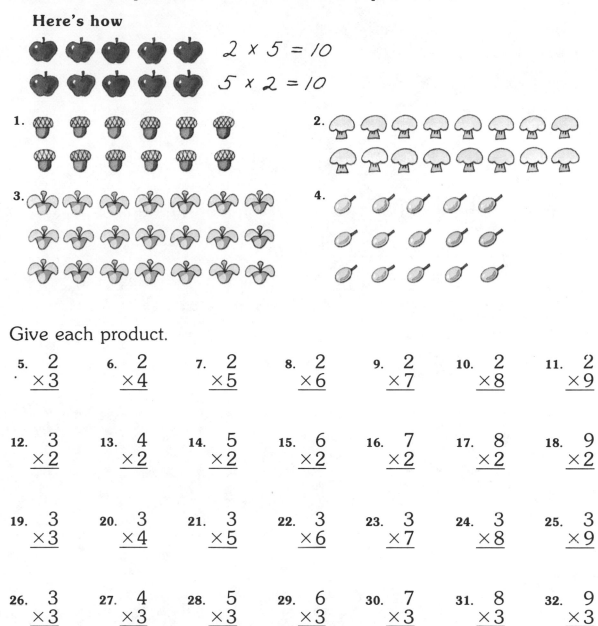

2 x 5 = 10

5 x 2 = 10

1.

2.

3.

4.

Give each product.

| 5. 2<br>×3 | 6. 2<br>×4 | 7. 2<br>×5 | 8. 2<br>×6 | 9. 2<br>×7 | 10. 2<br>×8 | 11. 2<br>×9 |
|---|---|---|---|---|---|---|
| 12. 3<br>×2 | 13. 4<br>×2 | 14. 5<br>×2 | 15. 6<br>×2 | 16. 7<br>×2 | 17. 8<br>×2 | 18. 9<br>×2 |
| 19. 3<br>×3 | 20. 3<br>×4 | 21. 3<br>×5 | 22. 3<br>×6 | 23. 3<br>×7 | 24. 3<br>×8 | 25. 3<br>×9 |
| 26. 3<br>×3 | 27. 4<br>×3 | 28. 5<br>×3 | 29. 6<br>×3 | 30. 7<br>×3 | 31. 8<br>×3 | 32. 9<br>×3 |

• **Discuss**  Does the order in which you multiply two numbers change the answer?

# 4 in Multiplication

There are two multiplication sentences
for the picture in each example.

A.

Think of 4 groups of 8.
### $4 \times 8 = 32$

Think of 8 groups of 4.
### $8 \times 4 = 32$

B.

Think of 4 groups of 5.
### $4 \times 5 = 20$

Think of 5 groups of 4.
### $5 \times 4 = 20$

Copy and complete each sentence.

1.

$4 \times 6 = ?$

$6 \times 4 = ?$

2.

$4 \times 9 = ?$

$9 \times 4 = ?$

3.

$4 \times 4 = ?$

4.

$4 \times 7 = ?$

$7 \times 4 = ?$

Give each answer.

5. 2 ×4   6. 3 ×4   7. 4 ×4   8. 5 ×4   9. 6 ×4   10. 7 ×4   11. 8 ×4   12. 9 ×4

13. 4 ×2   14. 4 ×3   15. 4 ×4   16. 4 ×5   17. 4 ×6   18. 4 ×7   19. 4 ×8   20. 4 ×9

21. 8 ×3   22. 5 ×4   23. 2 ×6   24. 4 ×3   25. 4 ×7   26. 2 ×8   27. 7 ×3   28. 8 ×4

29. There were 4 buses. 7 people were on each bus. How many people were there in all?

30. There were 6 trucks. 4 logs were on each truck. How many logs were there in all?

31. There were 4 trucks. Each truck had 8 wheels. How many wheels were there in all?

32. There were 4 cars. 4 people were in each car. How many people were there in all?

# 5 in Multiplication

Think of 6 groups of 5.

**6 × 5 = 30**

Think of 5 groups of 6.

**5 × 6 = 30**

Copy and complete each sentence.

1.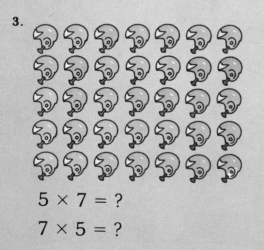

$5 \times 8 = ?$

$8 \times 5 = ?$

2.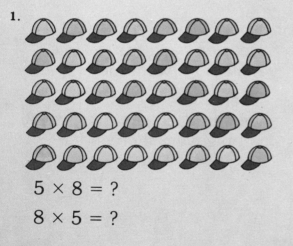

$5 \times 5 = ?$

3.

$5 \times 7 = ?$

$7 \times 5 = ?$

4.

$5 \times 9 = ?$

$9 \times 5 = ?$

Give each answer.

5. $\begin{array}{r} 2 \\ \times 5 \end{array}$  6. $\begin{array}{r} 3 \\ \times 5 \end{array}$  7. $\begin{array}{r} 4 \\ \times 5 \end{array}$  8. $\begin{array}{r} 5 \\ \times 5 \end{array}$  9. $\begin{array}{r} 6 \\ \times 5 \end{array}$  10. $\begin{array}{r} 7 \\ \times 5 \end{array}$  11. $\begin{array}{r} 8 \\ \times 5 \end{array}$  12. $\begin{array}{r} 9 \\ \times 5 \end{array}$

13. $\begin{array}{r} 5 \\ \times 2 \end{array}$  14. $\begin{array}{r} 5 \\ \times 3 \end{array}$  15. $\begin{array}{r} 5 \\ \times 4 \end{array}$  16. $\begin{array}{r} 5 \\ \times 5 \end{array}$  17. $\begin{array}{r} 5 \\ \times 6 \end{array}$  18. $\begin{array}{r} 5 \\ \times 7 \end{array}$  19. $\begin{array}{r} 5 \\ \times 8 \end{array}$  20. $\begin{array}{r} 5 \\ \times 9 \end{array}$

21. $\begin{array}{r} 3 \\ \times 5 \end{array}$  22. $\begin{array}{r} 3 \\ \times 3 \end{array}$  23. $\begin{array}{r} 5 \\ \times 8 \end{array}$  24. $\begin{array}{r} 4 \\ \times 6 \end{array}$  25. $\begin{array}{r} 9 \\ \times 2 \end{array}$  26. $\begin{array}{r} 5 \\ \times 4 \end{array}$  27. $\begin{array}{r} 6 \\ \times 3 \end{array}$  28. $\begin{array}{r} 5 \\ \times 5 \end{array}$

29. There were 5 dragons. Each dragon had 2 wings. How many wings were there in all?

30. There were 5 dragons. Each dragon had 4 legs. How many legs were there in all?

31. There were 5 dragons. Each dragon had 5 teeth. How many teeth were there in all?

More practice
Set 18, page 359

## Time Out

Which of these amounts could you pay with exactly three coins?

7¢     16¢

30¢     24¢

14¢     12¢

# Using Multiplication Facts

Give each product. Use the code to find the words. Can you read them without twisting your tongue?

**CODE**

| | | | |
|---|---|---|---|
| 8 | R | 24 | S |
| 9 | G | 25 | O |
| 12 | I | 27 | P |
| 14 | X | 30 | A |
| 16 | E | 35 | H |
| 18 | L | 36 | N |
| 20 | T | 45 | Y |

**Word 1**

1. $3 \times 8$
2. $4 \times 3$
3. $2 \times 7$

**Word 2**

4. $6 \times 4$
5. $2 \times 9$
6. $6 \times 2$
7. $9 \times 3$
8. $3 \times 9$
9. $2 \times 8$
10. $4 \times 2$
11. $9 \times 5$

**Word 3**

12. $8 \times 3$
13. $4 \times 4$
14. $5 \times 6$
15. $6 \times 3$
16. $4 \times 6$

**Word 4**

17. $3 \times 8$
18. $9 \times 2$
19. $3 \times 4$
20. $3 \times 9$
21. $9 \times 3$
22. $2 \times 6$
23. $4 \times 9$
24. $3 \times 3$

**Word 5**

25. $6 \times 4$
26. $2 \times 6$
27. $3 \times 6$
28. $8 \times 2$
29. $9 \times 4$
30. $4 \times 5$
31. $2 \times 9$
32. $5 \times 9$

**Word 6**

33. $6 \times 5$
34. $8 \times 3$
35. $5 \times 7$
36. $5 \times 5$
37. $2 \times 4$
38. $2 \times 8$

Use the rule.
Give each product.

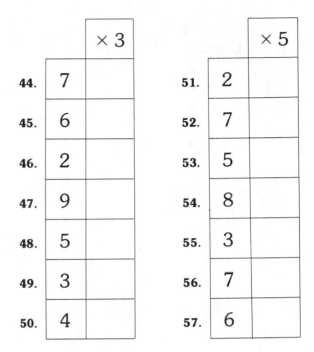

|   | × 4 |
|---|---|
| 9 | 36 | ← 9 × 4 = 36 |
| 4 | 16 | ← 4 × 4 = 16 |
| **39.** 7 | |
| **40.** 5 | |
| **41.** 2 | |
| **42.** 8 | |
| **43.** 6 | |

|   | × 3 |
|---|---|
| **44.** 7 | |
| **45.** 6 | |
| **46.** 2 | |
| **47.** 9 | |
| **48.** 5 | |
| **49.** 3 | |
| **50.** 4 | |

|   | × 5 |
|---|---|
| **51.** 2 | |
| **52.** 7 | |
| **53.** 5 | |
| **54.** 8 | |
| **55.** 3 | |
| **56.** 7 | |
| **57.** 6 | |

For each exercise, tell how many in all.

**58.** 7 oranges were in each box.
There were 3 boxes.

**59.** There were 4 stems.
8 grapes were on each stem.

**60.** 2 bananas were in each box.
There were 3 boxes.

**61.** There were 5 boxes.
8 apples were in each box.

**62.** There were 2 bags.
2 lemons were in each bag.

**63.** 7 peaches were in each jar.
There were 4 jars.

**64.** There were 7 bags.
2 pears were in each bag.

**65.** 6 plums were in each bag.
There were 2 bags.

## Count the Vowels

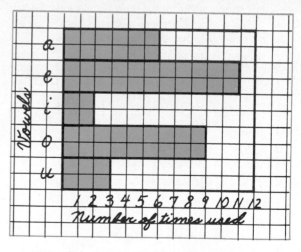

> Dear Desma,
>     Meet Coral and me at the clubhouse after school. Bring your secret code book.
>             Mio

Mio counted the number of times the vowels a, e, i, o, and u were used in her note.

Then she made a bar graph.

| Vowel | Tally | Number of times used |
|-------|-------|----------------------|
| a | ⵜⵜⵜ I | 6 |
| e | ⵜⵜⵜ ⵜⵜⵜ I | 11 |
| i | II | 2 |
| o | ⵜⵜⵜ IIII | 9 |
| u | III | 3 |
| | | |
| | | |

1. Which vowel was used most?

2. Which vowel was used least?

3. Write a note to a friend. Make a table and a graph like the one Mio made.

# Chapter 8 Test
# Multiplication Facts, pages 150-164

Copy and complete
each sentence.

1.
● ● ● ● ●
● ● ● ●
● ● ● ●

$6 + 6 + 6 = ?$

$3 \times 6 = ?$

2.
● ● ● ● ● ● ● ●
● ● ● ● ● ●

$8 + 8 = ?$

$2 \times 8 = ?$

3.
● ● ● ● ● ● ●
● ● ● ● ● ● ●
● ● ● ● ● ● ●
● ● ● ● ● ● ●

$7 + 7 + 7 + 7 = ?$

$4 \times 7 = ?$

4.
● ● ● ● ● ● ● ●
● ● ● ● ● ● ● ●
● ● ● ● ● ● ● ●
● ● ● ● ● ● ● ●
● ● ● ● ● ● ● ●

$8 + 8 + 8 + 8 + 8 = ?$

$5 \times 8 = ?$

Give each answer.

5. $\begin{array}{r} 2 \\ \times 9 \\ \hline \end{array}$

6. $\begin{array}{r} 9 \\ \times 2 \\ \hline \end{array}$

7. $\begin{array}{r} 6 \\ \times 2 \\ \hline \end{array}$

8. $\begin{array}{r} 4 \\ \times 3 \\ \hline \end{array}$

9. $\begin{array}{r} 2 \\ \times 2 \\ \hline \end{array}$

10. $\begin{array}{r} 7 \\ \times 3 \\ \hline \end{array}$

11. $\begin{array}{r} 5 \\ \times 4 \\ \hline \end{array}$

12. $\begin{array}{r} 9 \\ \times 4 \\ \hline \end{array}$

13. $\begin{array}{r} 5 \\ \times 5 \\ \hline \end{array}$

14. $\begin{array}{r} 5 \\ \times 2 \\ \hline \end{array}$

15. $\begin{array}{r} 6 \\ \times 5 \\ \hline \end{array}$

16. $\begin{array}{r} 4 \\ \times 8 \\ \hline \end{array}$

17. $\begin{array}{r} 3 \\ \times 2 \\ \hline \end{array}$

18. $\begin{array}{r} 4 \\ \times 4 \\ \hline \end{array}$

19. $\begin{array}{r} 5 \\ \times 9 \\ \hline \end{array}$

20. $\begin{array}{r} 3 \\ \times 3 \\ \hline \end{array}$

21. $\begin{array}{r} 9 \\ \times 3 \\ \hline \end{array}$

22. $\begin{array}{r} 6 \\ \times 4 \\ \hline \end{array}$

23. $\begin{array}{r} 7 \\ \times 2 \\ \hline \end{array}$

24. $\begin{array}{r} 6 \\ \times 3 \\ \hline \end{array}$

25. $\begin{array}{r} 5 \\ \times 7 \\ \hline \end{array}$

# Chapter 9   Multiplication Facts: 0, 1, 6, 7, 8, or 9

## 0 and 1 in Multiplication

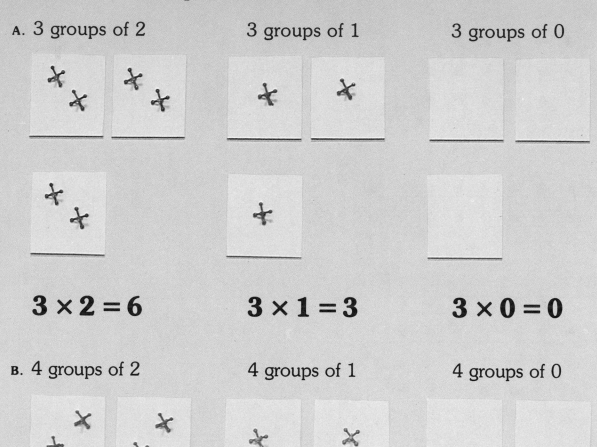

A. 3 groups of 2          3 groups of 1          3 groups of 0

$$3 \times 2 = 6 \qquad 3 \times 1 = 3 \qquad 3 \times 0 = 0$$

B. 4 groups of 2          4 groups of 1          4 groups of 0

$$4 \times 2 = 8 \qquad 4 \times 1 = 4 \qquad 4 \times 0 = 0$$

Give each answer.

1. $4 \times 0$     2. $9 \times 0$     3. $5 \times 0$     4. $6 \times 0$
$0 \times 4$        $0 \times 9$        $0 \times 5$        $0 \times 6$

5. $8 \times 0$     6. $7 \times 0$     7. $3 \times 0$     8. $2 \times 0$
$0 \times 8$        $0 \times 7$        $0 \times 3$        $0 \times 2$

9. $3 \times 1$     10. $7 \times 1$     11. $2 \times 1$     12. $4 \times 1$
$1 \times 3$        $1 \times 7$        $1 \times 2$        $1 \times 4$

13. $9 \times 1$     14. $8 \times 1$     15. $6 \times 1$     16. $5 \times 1$
$1 \times 9$        $1 \times 8$        $1 \times 6$        $1 \times 5$

17. $5 \times 2$     18. $4 \times 4$     19. $0 \times 0$     20. $3 \times 2$

21. $3 \times 5$     22. $1 \times 1$     23. $6 \times 4$     24. $2 \times 4$

25. $7 \times 5$     26. $2 \times 3$     27. $3 \times 6$     28. $4 \times 3$

29. $8 \times 3$     30. $7 \times 4$     31. $5 \times 8$     32. $0 \times 1$

33. $4 \times 7$     34. $2 \times 5$     35. $9 \times 4$     36. $5 \times 4$

37. $3 \times 3$     38. $3 \times 4$     39. $2 \times 2$     40. $6 \times 5$

41. $8 \times 2$     42. $6 \times 3$     43. $9 \times 2$     44. $4 \times 5$

45. $4 \times 9$     46. $3 \times 7$     47. $2 \times 8$     48. $2 \times 6$

49. $5 \times 5$     50. $9 \times 5$     51. $1 \times 0$     52. $8 \times 4$

53. $7 \times 3$     54. $9 \times 3$     55. $7 \times 2$     56. $5 \times 3$

• **Discuss** When you multiply 1 and a number, what is the answer?

• **Discuss** When you multiply 0 and a number, what is the answer?

## Time Out

Which of these shapes can you copy without lifting your pencil from the paper? You can not go over any line more than once.

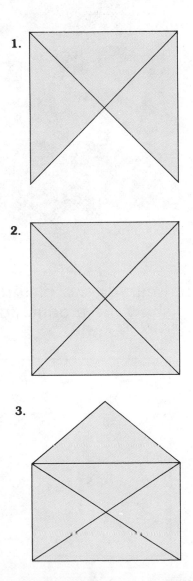

1.

2.

3.

# 6 in Multiplication

A.

Think of 6 groups of 8.
## $6 \times 8 = 48$

Think of 8 groups of 6.
## $8 \times 6 = 48$

B. Keith drew a picture to show the product for $6 \times 9$ and $9 \times 6$.

```
X X X X X X X X X
X X X X X X X X X
X X X X X X X X X
X X X X X X X X X
X X X X X X X X X
X X X X X X X X X

   6 × 9 = 54
   9 × 6 = 54
```

C. Anita drew a picture to show the product for $7 \times 6$ and $6 \times 7$.

```
✓ ✓ ✓ ✓ ✓ ✓ ✓
✓ ✓ ✓ ✓ ✓ ✓ ✓
✓ ✓ ✓ ✓ ✓ ✓ ✓
✓ ✓ ✓ ✓ ✓ ✓ ✓
✓ ✓ ✓ ✓ ✓ ✓ ✓
✓ ✓ ✓ ✓ ✓ ✓ ✓

   7 × 6 = 42
   6 × 7 = 42
```

Copy and complete each sentence.

1. ★ ★ ★ ★ ★ ★
★ ★ ★ ★ ★ ★
★ ★ ★ ★ ★ ★
★ ★ ★ ★ ★ ★
★ ★ ★ ★ ★ ★
★ ★ ★ ★ ★ ★

$6 \times 6 = ?$

2. ★ ★ ★ ★ ★
★ ★ ★ ★ ★
★ ★ ★ ★ ★
★ ★ ★ ★ ★
★ ★ ★ ★ ★
★ ★ ★ ★ ★

$6 \times 5 = ?$
$5 \times 6 = ?$

Give each answer.

| | | | | | | | |
|---|---|---|---|---|---|---|---|
| 3. $\begin{array}{r}2\\ \times 6\\ \hline\end{array}$ | 4. $\begin{array}{r}3\\ \times 6\\ \hline\end{array}$ | 5. $\begin{array}{r}4\\ \times 6\\ \hline\end{array}$ | 6. $\begin{array}{r}5\\ \times 6\\ \hline\end{array}$ | 7. $\begin{array}{r}6\\ \times 6\\ \hline\end{array}$ | 8. $\begin{array}{r}7\\ \times 6\\ \hline\end{array}$ | 9. $\begin{array}{r}8\\ \times 6\\ \hline\end{array}$ | 10. $\begin{array}{r}9\\ \times 6\\ \hline\end{array}$ |
| 11. $\begin{array}{r}6\\ \times 2\\ \hline\end{array}$ | 12. $\begin{array}{r}6\\ \times 3\\ \hline\end{array}$ | 13. $\begin{array}{r}6\\ \times 4\\ \hline\end{array}$ | 14. $\begin{array}{r}6\\ \times 5\\ \hline\end{array}$ | 15. $\begin{array}{r}6\\ \times 6\\ \hline\end{array}$ | 16. $\begin{array}{r}6\\ \times 7\\ \hline\end{array}$ | 17. $\begin{array}{r}6\\ \times 8\\ \hline\end{array}$ | 18. $\begin{array}{r}6\\ \times 9\\ \hline\end{array}$ |
| 19. $\begin{array}{r}9\\ \times 6\\ \hline\end{array}$ | 20. $\begin{array}{r}5\\ \times 4\\ \hline\end{array}$ | 21. $\begin{array}{r}6\\ \times 0\\ \hline\end{array}$ | 22. $\begin{array}{r}6\\ \times 4\\ \hline\end{array}$ | 23. $\begin{array}{r}4\\ \times 8\\ \hline\end{array}$ | 24. $\begin{array}{r}1\\ \times 6\\ \hline\end{array}$ | 25. $\begin{array}{r}6\\ \times 7\\ \hline\end{array}$ | 26. $\begin{array}{r}7\\ \times 3\\ \hline\end{array}$ |
| 27. $\begin{array}{r}6\\ \times 6\\ \hline\end{array}$ | 28. $\begin{array}{r}3\\ \times 9\\ \hline\end{array}$ | 29. $\begin{array}{r}6\\ \times 2\\ \hline\end{array}$ | 30. $\begin{array}{r}8\\ \times 6\\ \hline\end{array}$ | 31. $\begin{array}{r}6\\ \times 3\\ \hline\end{array}$ | 32. $\begin{array}{r}4\\ \times 7\\ \hline\end{array}$ | 33. $\begin{array}{r}5\\ \times 6\\ \hline\end{array}$ | 34. $\begin{array}{r}9\\ \times 4\\ \hline\end{array}$ |

35. 2 peanuts were in each shell. There were 6 shells. How many peanuts were there in all?

36. There were 7 pods. 6 peas were in each pod. How many peas were there in all?

More practice
Set 19, page 360

# 7 in Multiplication

**A.**

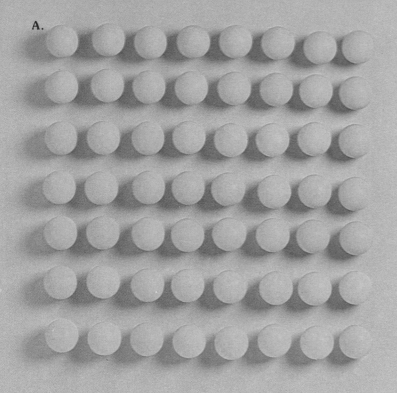

Think of 7 groups of 8.
**$7 \times 8 = 56$**

Think of 8 groups of 7.
**$8 \times 7 = 56$**

**B.** Scott drew a picture to show the product for $7 \times 9$ and $9 \times 7$.

```
/ / / / / / / / /
/ / / / / / / / /
/ / / / / / / / /
/ / / / / / / / /
/ / / / / / / / /
/ / / / / / / / /
/ / / / / / / / /
7 × 9 = 63
9 × 7 = 63
```

**C.** Kathy drew a picture to show the product for $7 \times 7$.

```
X X X X X X X
X X X X X X X
X X X X X X X
X X X X X X X
X X X X X X X
X X X X X X X
X X X X X X X
7 × 7 = 49
```

Give each answer.

1. $\begin{array}{r} 2 \\ \times 7 \\ \hline \end{array}$
2. $\begin{array}{r} 3 \\ \times 7 \\ \hline \end{array}$
3. $\begin{array}{r} 4 \\ \times 7 \\ \hline \end{array}$
4. $\begin{array}{r} 5 \\ \times 7 \\ \hline \end{array}$
5. $\begin{array}{r} 6 \\ \times 7 \\ \hline \end{array}$
6. $\begin{array}{r} 7 \\ \times 7 \\ \hline \end{array}$
7. $\begin{array}{r} 8 \\ \times 7 \\ \hline \end{array}$
8. $\begin{array}{r} 9 \\ \times 7 \\ \hline \end{array}$

9. $\begin{array}{r} 7 \\ \times 2 \\ \hline \end{array}$
10. $\begin{array}{r} 7 \\ \times 3 \\ \hline \end{array}$
11. $\begin{array}{r} 7 \\ \times 4 \\ \hline \end{array}$
12. $\begin{array}{r} 7 \\ \times 5 \\ \hline \end{array}$
13. $\begin{array}{r} 7 \\ \times 6 \\ \hline \end{array}$
14. $\begin{array}{r} 7 \\ \times 7 \\ \hline \end{array}$
15. $\begin{array}{r} 7 \\ \times 8 \\ \hline \end{array}$
16. $\begin{array}{r} 7 \\ \times 9 \\ \hline \end{array}$

17. $\begin{array}{r} 3 \\ \times 7 \\ \hline \end{array}$
18. $\begin{array}{r} 1 \\ \times 7 \\ \hline \end{array}$
19. $\begin{array}{r} 4 \\ \times 6 \\ \hline \end{array}$
20. $\begin{array}{r} 5 \\ \times 7 \\ \hline \end{array}$
21. $\begin{array}{r} 8 \\ \times 7 \\ \hline \end{array}$
22. $\begin{array}{r} 6 \\ \times 3 \\ \hline \end{array}$
23. $\begin{array}{r} 7 \\ \times 4 \\ \hline \end{array}$
24. $\begin{array}{r} 8 \\ \times 5 \\ \hline \end{array}$

25. $\begin{array}{r} 6 \\ \times 5 \\ \hline \end{array}$
26. $\begin{array}{r} 7 \\ \times 9 \\ \hline \end{array}$
27. $\begin{array}{r} 6 \\ \times 6 \\ \hline \end{array}$
28. $\begin{array}{r} 6 \\ \times 7 \\ \hline \end{array}$
29. $\begin{array}{r} 9 \\ \times 6 \\ \hline \end{array}$
30. $\begin{array}{r} 7 \\ \times 0 \\ \hline \end{array}$
31. $\begin{array}{r} 7 \\ \times 7 \\ \hline \end{array}$
32. $\begin{array}{r} 5 \\ \times 4 \\ \hline \end{array}$

33. There were 9 rows of apple trees. 7 apple trees were in each row. How many apple trees were there in all?

34. 7 cornstalks were in each row. There were 7 rows of corn. How many cornstalks were there in all?

35. There were 7 rows of sunflowers. 6 sunflowers were in each row. How many sunflowers were there in all?

36. 5 tomato plants were in each row. There were 7 rows of tomato plants. How many tomato plants were there in all?

(one hundred seventy-one) **171**

# Using Multiplication Facts

For each exercise, give a number sentence.
Then write yes or no.

Is this a name for 36?

**Here's how**

| | | |
|---|---|---|
| $9 \times 4$ | $9 \times 4 = 36$ | *yes* |
| $7 \times 5$ | $7 \times 5 = 35$ | *no* |
| $8 \times 4$ | $8 \times 4 = 32$ | *no* |
| $4 \times 9$ | $4 \times 9 = 36$ | *yes* |
| $6 \times 6$ | $6 \times 6 = 36$ | *yes* |

Is this a name for 24?

1. $6 \times 4$
2. $7 \times 3$
3. $8 \times 3$
4. $4 \times 6$
5. $3 \times 8$

Is this a name for 54?

6. $9 \times 9$
7. $7 \times 7$
8. $6 \times 9$
9. $7 \times 8$
10. $7 \times 9$

Is this a name for 30?

11. $4 \times 8$
12. $6 \times 5$
13. $7 \times 4$
14. $3 \times 9$
15. $5 \times 6$

Is this a name for 42?

16. $6 \times 7$
17. $8 \times 5$
18. $5 \times 9$
19. $7 \times 6$
20. $6 \times 8$

Is this a name for 18?

21. $9 \times 2$
22. $6 \times 3$
23. $4 \times 4$
24. $4 \times 5$
25. $2 \times 9$

Is this a name for 10?

26. $3 \times 3$
27. $5 \times 2$
28. $2 \times 6$
29. $2 \times 4$
30. $2 \times 7$

Use the rule.
Give each product.

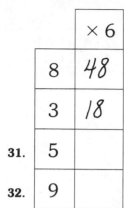

| | × 6 |
|---|---|
| 8 | 48 |
| 3 | 18 |
| 31. 5 | |
| 32. 9 | |

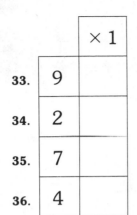

| | × 1 |
|---|---|
| 33. 9 | |
| 34. 2 | |
| 35. 7 | |
| 36. 4 | |

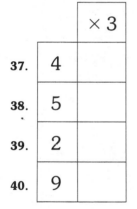

| | × 3 |
|---|---|
| 37. 4 | |
| 38. 5 | |
| 39. 2 | |
| 40. 9 | |

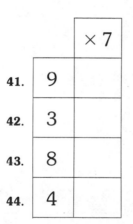

| | × 7 |
|---|---|
| 41. 9 | |
| 42. 3 | |
| 43. 8 | |
| 44. 4 | |

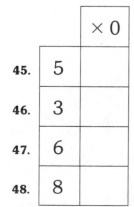

| | × 0 |
|---|---|
| 45. 5 | |
| 46. 3 | |
| 47. 6 | |
| 48. 8 | |

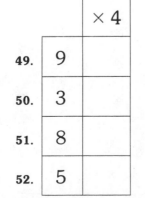

| | × 4 |
|---|---|
| 49. 9 | |
| 50. 3 | |
| 51. 8 | |
| 52. 5 | |

## Time Out

Use the table. Add to find the number for your name.

This is the way Jess found his number.

$$J \quad E \quad S \quad S$$
$$\downarrow \quad \downarrow \quad \downarrow \quad \downarrow$$
$$3 + 1 + 5 + 5 = 14$$

| | | | |
|---|---|---|---|
| **A** | 1 | **N** | 7 |
| **B** | 3 | **O** | 1 |
| **C** | 4 | **P** | 3 |
| **D** | 5 | **Q** | 9 |
| **E** | 1 | **R** | 4 |
| **F** | 6 | **S** | 5 |
| **G** | 7 | **T** | 6 |
| **H** | 8 | **U** | 2 |
| **I** | 2 | **V** | 8 |
| **J** | 3 | **W** | 7 |
| **K** | 4 | **X** | 9 |
| **L** | 5 | **Y** | 8 |
| **M** | 6 | **Z** | 9 |

# 8 and 9 in Multiplication

**A.**

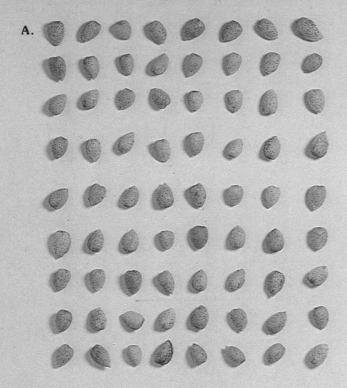

Think of 8 groups of 9.

**8 × 9 = 72**

Think of 9 groups of 8.

**9 × 8 = 72**

**B.** Eric drew a picture to show the product for 8 × 8.

**C.** Jane drew a picture to show the product for 9 × 9.

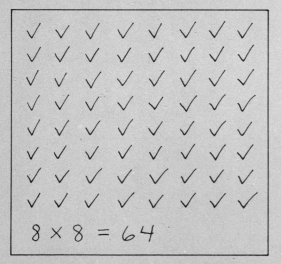

$8 \times 8 = 64$

$9 \times 9 = 81$

Give each answer.

1. 2
×8

2. 3
×8

3. 4
×8

4. 5
×8

5. 6
×8

6. 7
×8

7. 8
×8

8. 9
×8

9. 8
×2

10. 8
×3

11. 8
×4

12. 8
×5

13. 8
×6

14. 8
×7

15. 8
×8

16. 8
×9

17. 2
×9

18. 3
×9

19. 4
×9

20. 5
×9

21. 6
×9

22. 7
×9

23. 8
×9

24. 9
×9

25. 9
×2

26. 9
×3

27. 9
×4

28. 9
×5

29. 9
×6

30. 9
×7

31. 9
×8

32. 9
×9

33. 1
×8

34. 0
×9

35. 8
×6

36. 8
×0

37. 9
×9

38. 9
×1

39. 9
×8

40. 8
×8

41. There were 8 softball teams. Each team had 9 members. How many members were there in all?

42. There were 9 basketball teams. 5 players were on each team. How many players were there in all?

43. There were 4 track teams. Each team had 8 members. How many members were there in all?

44. There were 2 baseball teams. Each team had 9 players. How many players were there in all?

45. There were 8 hockey teams. Each team had 6 members. How many members were there in all?

46. There were 9 volleyball teams. 6 players were on each team. How many players were there in all?

More practice
Set 20, page 360

# Using Multiplication Facts

Find each product. Use the code to help you find the answer to the riddle.

When can your pocket be empty and still have something in it?

| CODE | |
|------|---|
| 24 | I |
| 32 | W |
| 36 | H |
| 40 | S |
| 45 | A |
| 54 | T |
| 63 | N |
| 64 | O |
| 72 | E |
| 81 | L |

**Word 1**

1. $4 \times 8$
2. $9 \times 4$
3. $9 \times 8$
4. $7 \times 9$

**Word 2**

5. $4 \times 6$
6. $9 \times 6$

**Word 3**

7. $6 \times 6$
8. $5 \times 9$
9. $8 \times 5$

**Word 4**

10. $9 \times 5$

**Word 5**

11. $4 \times 9$
12. $8 \times 8$
13. $9 \times 9$
14. $8 \times 9$

**Word 6**

15. $3 \times 8$
16. $9 \times 7$

**Word 7**

17. $8 \times 3$
18. $6 \times 9$

Give each product.

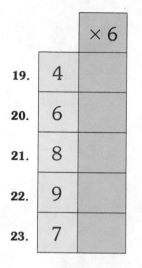

| | ×6 |
|---|---|
| 19. 4 | |
| 20. 6 | |
| 21. 8 | |
| 22. 9 | |
| 23. 7 | |

| | ×7 |
|---|---|
| 24. 7 | |
| 25. 9 | |
| 26. 6 | |
| 27. 5 | |
| 28. 8 | |

| | ×8 |
|---|---|
| 29. 6 | |
| 30. 7 | |
| 31. 8 | |
| 32. 5 | |
| 33. 9 | |

| | ×9 |
|---|---|
| 34. 7 | |
| 35. 8 | |
| 36. 1 | |
| 37. 6 | |
| 38. 9 | |

39. 4 × 3   40. 6 × 5   41. 8 × 9

42. 9 × 5   43. 4 × 8   44. 7 × 0

45. 8 × 8   46. 7 × 3   47. 2 × 9

48. 1 × 6   49. 9 × 4   50. 7 × 7

51. 6 × 4   52. 9 × 9   53. 3 × 8

## Keeping Skillful

What digit is in the ones place?

1. 643     2. 471     3. 316
4. 957     5. 280     6. 108

What digit is in the tens place?

7. 795     8. 214     9. 528
10. 106    11. 847    12. 352

What digit is in the hundreds place?

13. 602    14. 267    15. 510
16. 194    17. 983    18. 325

Give the numbers in order. Begin with the least number.

19. 43   49   47   52

20. 89   98   92   88

21. 136   138   134

22. 429   317   548

23. 314   413   134

24. 298   301   300

25. 756   732   748

# Problem Solving: Choosing the Operation

**READ**  There were 5 boxes of toy cars.
4 toy cars were in each box. How
many toy cars were there in all?

**DECIDE**  Multiply the number of cars in each
box by the number of boxes. Use
this number sentence.

5 × 4 = ?

**SOLVE**
$$\begin{array}{r} 4 \\ \times\ 5 \\ \hline 20 \end{array}$$

**ANSWER**  20 toy cars

For each problem, write a number sentence.
Then give the answer.

1. Tiana had $6.58. She spent $4.39.
   How much did she have left?

   $6.58 − $4.39 = ?

2. Craig bought a game for $5.90 and
   a puzzle for $1.45. How much did
   he spend in all?

   $5.90 + $1.45 = ?

3. There were 6 boxes of balloons. 8 balloons were in each box. How many balloons were there in all?

4. There were 7 bags of tops. 5 tops were in each bag. How many tops were there in all?

5. There were 3 boxes of whistles. 8 whistles were in each box. How many whistles were there in all?

6. There were 48 dolls. 19 dolls were sold. How many dolls were left?

7. There were 9 drum sets. 4 drums were in each set. How many drums were there in all?

8. There were 8 tool sets. 6 tools were in each set. How many tools were there in all?

9. There were 28 large stuffed animals and 57 small stuffed animals. How many animals were there in all?

10. There were 7 model planes on each shelf. There were 9 shelves. How many model planes were there in all?

# Side Trip

## Using a Number Line

A. You can use a number line to help you add.
The first arrow shows 7. The second arrow shows 8 more.
Together, the two arrows show $7 + 8 = 15$.

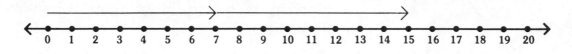

B. You can use a number line to help you multiply.
The number of arrows is 6. The length of each arrow is 3.
These arrows show $6 \times 3 = 18$.

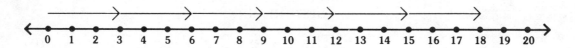

For each exercise, write a number sentence that shows addition.

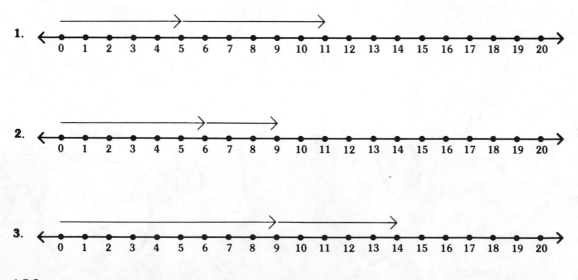

1.

2.

3.

For each exercise, write a number sentence
that shows multiplication.

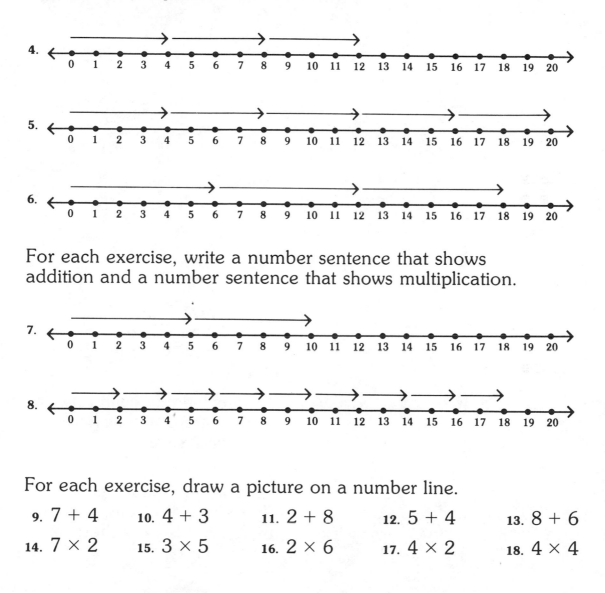

**4.**

0 1 2 3 4 5 6 7 8 9 10 11 12 13 14 15 16 17 18 19 20

**5.**

0 1 2 3 4 5 6 7 8 9 10 11 12 13 14 15 16 17 18 19 20

**6.**

0 1 2 3 4 5 6 7 8 9 10 11 12 13 14 15 16 17 18 19 20

For each exercise, write a number sentence that shows
addition and a number sentence that shows multiplication.

**7.**

0 1 2 3 4 5 6 7 8 9 10 11 12 13 14 15 16 17 18 19 20

**8.**

0 1 2 3 4 5 6 7 8 9 10 11 12 13 14 15 16 17 18 19 20

For each exercise, draw a picture on a number line.

**9.** $7 + 4$    **10.** $4 + 3$    **11.** $2 + 8$    **12.** $5 + 4$    **13.** $8 + 6$

**14.** $7 \times 2$    **15.** $3 \times 5$    **16.** $2 \times 6$    **17.** $4 \times 2$    **18.** $4 \times 4$

Use the number line to show

**★19.** $9 - 5$.    **★20.** $10 - 2$.    **★21.** $16 - 8$.    **★22.** $13 - 6$.    **★23.** $15 - 9$.

# Chapter 9 Test
# Multiplication Facts, pages 166–181

Give each answer.

1. 6
   ×1

2. 8
   ×1

3. 1
   ×7

4. 0
   ×3

5. 4
   ×0

6. 0
   ×6

7. 6
   ×4

8. 6
   ×6

9. 8
   ×6

10. 7
    ×7

11. 9
    ×7

12. 7
    ×5

13. 7
    ×8

14. 8
    ×5

15. 3
    ×8

16. 9
    ×9

17. 4
    ×9

18. 9
    ×8

19. 7
    ×6

20. 4
    ×8

21. 6
    ×3

22. 9
    ×3

23. 8
    ×8

24. 6
    ×9

25. 3
    ×7

26. 5
    ×9

27. 5
    ×6

28. There were 7 students. Each student had 4 books. How many books were there in all?

29. 8 chairs were in each row. There were 6 rows. How many chairs were there in all?

30. Each student had 3 pencils. There were 9 students. How many pencils were there in all?

# Problems Around Us

1. There were 5 pairs of shoes. 2 shoes were in each pair. How many shoes were there in all?

2. There were 3 flowers. Each flower had 6 petals. How many petals were there in all?

3. There were 45 students and 6 adults. How many people were there in all?

4. Vicki had $5.60. She spent $4.35. How much did she have left?

5. There were 6 oranges. Each orange had 7 seeds. How many seeds were there in all?

6. Neal had 45 stamps. He bought 38 more. How many stamps did he have then?

7. There were 9 boxes. 3 jars were in each box. How many jars were there in all?

8. There were 7 classes. 8 students were in each class. How many students were there in all?

9. Isaac had 215 baseball cards. He bought 179 more. How many cards did he have in all?

10. There were 6 packages of balloons. Each package had 8 balloons. How many balloons were there in all?

11. Eva had 416 tickets. She sold 273 tickets. How many tickets were left?

# Individualized Skills Maintenance

## Diagnose

A *pages 84–95*    B *pages 104–115*    C *pages 150–163; 166–179*

| | | |
|---|---|---|
| 634 + 128 | 743 − 581 | 8 × 7 |
| 472 + 386 | 652 − 327 | 9 × 6 |
| 435 + 215 | 240 − 128 | 7 × 9 |

## Practice

**A**

1.  257
    + 138

2.  725
    + 194

3.  182
    + 496

4.  614
    + 137

5.  129
    + 690

6.  372
    + 546

7.  205
    + 438

8.  218
    + 391

9.  372
    + 193

10. 485
    + 214

11. 729
    + 156

12. 581
    + 134

**B**

13. 417
    − 384

14. 752
    − 216

15. 590
    − 138

16. 132
    −  28

17. 219
    − 174

18. 926
    − 384

19. 380
    − 167

20. 926
    − 732

21. 561
    − 238

22. 847
    − 395

23. 678
    − 382

24. 570
    − 246

**C**

25. 9
    × 6

26. 4
    × 7

27. 8
    × 6

28. 7
    × 9

29. 3
    × 8

30. 9
    × 4

31. 8
    × 7

32. 9
    × 9

33. 6
    × 7

34. 8
    × 4

35. 5
    × 6

36. 8
    × 9

37. 7
    × 7

38. 8
    × 8

# Unit 3   Review

Chapter 7, pages 130–148
## What time is shown on each clock?

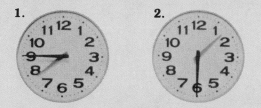

**1.**            **2.**

## Which unit would you use?

**3.** Distance around a baseball: centimeters or meters

**4.** Weight of a tire: grams or kilograms

**5.** Width of your book: inches or miles

**6.** Water in a flower vase: cups or gallons

**7.** Does a kitchen sink hold more than or less than a liter?

## Find the perimeter.

**8.**

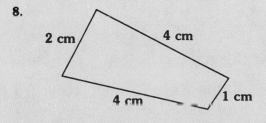

2 cm     4 cm

4 cm     1 cm

Chapter 8, pages 150–164
## Multiply.

**9.** $\begin{array}{r} 3 \\ \times 7 \\ \hline \end{array}$    **10.** $\begin{array}{r} 2 \\ \times 8 \\ \hline \end{array}$    **11.** $\begin{array}{r} 9 \\ \times 3 \\ \hline \end{array}$

**12.** $\begin{array}{r} 4 \\ \times 6 \\ \hline \end{array}$    **13.** $\begin{array}{r} 5 \\ \times 7 \\ \hline \end{array}$    **14.** $\begin{array}{r} 8 \\ \times 4 \\ \hline \end{array}$

Chapter 9, pages 166–181
## Multiply.

**15.** $\begin{array}{r} 0 \\ \times 8 \\ \hline \end{array}$    **16.** $\begin{array}{r} 4 \\ \times 1 \\ \hline \end{array}$    **17.** $\begin{array}{r} 6 \\ \times 8 \\ \hline \end{array}$

**18.** $\begin{array}{r} 7 \\ \times 5 \\ \hline \end{array}$    **19.** $\begin{array}{r} 8 \\ \times 3 \\ \hline \end{array}$    **20.** $\begin{array}{r} 9 \\ \times 7 \\ \hline \end{array}$

## Give each answer.

**21.** There were 9 rows of shells. 4 shells were in each row. How many shells were there in all?

**22.** Sheldon collected 73 leaves. He gave 28 leaves away. How many leaves did he have left?

**23.** Monica read 67 books in one year. The next year she read 82 books. How many books did she read in all?

# Unit 3 Test
## Chapters, 7-9, pages 130-182

What time is shown on each clock?

1.

2.

Which unit would you use?

3. Width of a room:
   meters or kilometers

4. Weight of a dog:
   grams or kilograms

5. Length of a canoe:
   feet or miles

6. Water in a large aquarium:
   cups or gallons

Find the perimeter.

7.

2 cm   2 cm

2 cm   2 cm

8.

3 cm   4 cm

2 cm

Multiply.

9.  $\begin{array}{r} 1 \\ \times 3 \\ \hline \end{array}$
10. $\begin{array}{r} 9 \\ \times 1 \\ \hline \end{array}$
11. $\begin{array}{r} 0 \\ \times 8 \\ \hline \end{array}$

12. $\begin{array}{r} 6 \\ \times 0 \\ \hline \end{array}$
13. $\begin{array}{r} 2 \\ \times 4 \\ \hline \end{array}$
14. $\begin{array}{r} 7 \\ \times 2 \\ \hline \end{array}$

15. $\begin{array}{r} 8 \\ \times 3 \\ \hline \end{array}$
16. $\begin{array}{r} 3 \\ \times 6 \\ \hline \end{array}$
17. $\begin{array}{r} 4 \\ \times 7 \\ \hline \end{array}$

18. $\begin{array}{r} 9 \\ \times 4 \\ \hline \end{array}$
19. $\begin{array}{r} 5 \\ \times 6 \\ \hline \end{array}$
20. $\begin{array}{r} 3 \\ \times 5 \\ \hline \end{array}$

21. $\begin{array}{r} 6 \\ \times 8 \\ \hline \end{array}$
22. $\begin{array}{r} 6 \\ \times 7 \\ \hline \end{array}$
23. $\begin{array}{r} 7 \\ \times 5 \\ \hline \end{array}$

24. $\begin{array}{r} 3 \\ \times 7 \\ \hline \end{array}$
25. $\begin{array}{r} 8 \\ \times 6 \\ \hline \end{array}$
26. $\begin{array}{r} 4 \\ \times 8 \\ \hline \end{array}$

27. $\begin{array}{r} 7 \\ \times 9 \\ \hline \end{array}$
28. $\begin{array}{r} 9 \\ \times 8 \\ \hline \end{array}$
29. $\begin{array}{r} 8 \\ \times 7 \\ \hline \end{array}$

Give the answer.

30. 8 plants were in each row.
    There were 5 rows. How
    many plants were there in all?

# Unit 4

# Chapter 10   Numeration Through 999,999

## Thousands, Hundreds, Tens, and Ones

**A.**

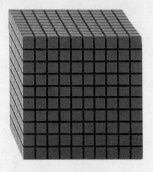

10 hundreds

1 thousand
1000

**10 hundreds = 1 thousand**

Show each number in a place-value box.

**B.**

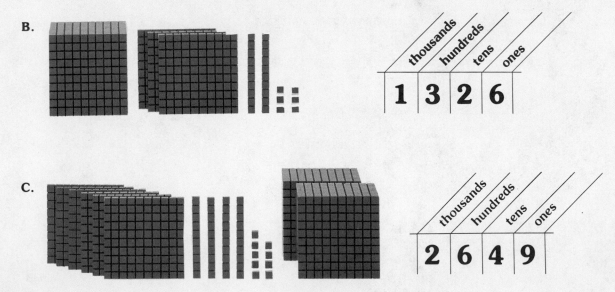

| thousands | hundreds | tens | ones |
|:---:|:---:|:---:|:---:|
| **1** | **3** | **2** | **6** |

**C.**

| thousands | hundreds | tens | ones |
|:---:|:---:|:---:|:---:|
| **2** | **6** | **4** | **9** |

# Show each number in a place-value box.

**Here's how**

| th | h | t | o |
|----|---|---|---|
| 2  | 3 | 0 | 6 |

1.

2.

3.

4.

5.

6.

7.

8.

9.

10.

# Standard Form

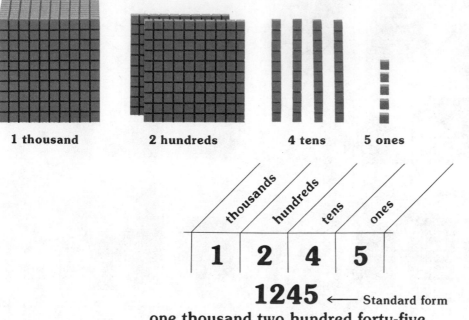

1 thousand    2 hundreds    4 tens    5 ones

| thousands | hundreds | tens | ones |
|:---:|:---:|:---:|:---:|
| **1** | **2** | **4** | **5** |

**1245** ⟵ Standard form

**one thousand two hundred forty-five**

Show each number in a place-value box.
Give the standard form.

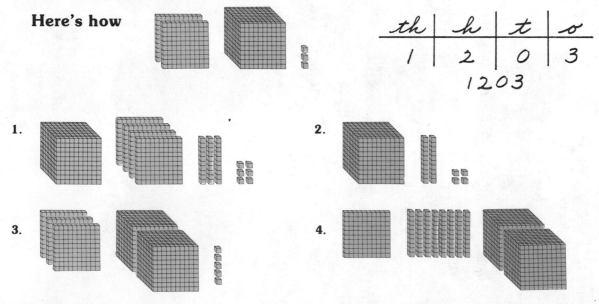

**Here's how**

| th | h | t | o |
|:---:|:---:|:---:|:---:|
| 1 | 2 | 0 | 3 |

1203

1.

2.

3.

4.

Give the standard form for each number.

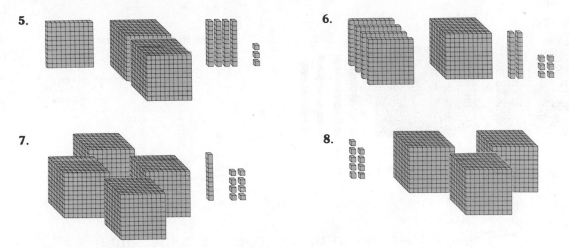

Give the standard form for each number.

**Here's how**

three thousand seventy-five  *3075*

9. two thousand four hundred sixty-eight
10. one thousand nine hundred fifty-three
11. eight thousand six hundred forty-two
12. five hundred eighty-six
13. four thousand five hundred
14. seven thousand thirty-four
15. six hundred ninety
16. nine thousand four hundred two
17. three thousand seventy
18. seven thousand three

Give the word name for each number.

19. 6437    20. 2581    21. 9847    22. 3052    23. 1609

# Place Value

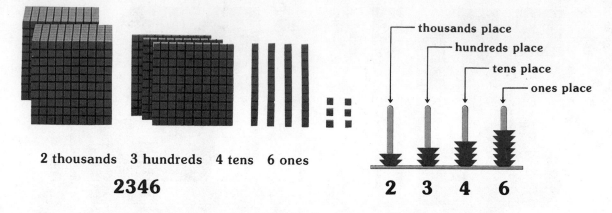

2 thousands   3 hundreds   4 tens   6 ones

**2346**

thousands place
hundreds place
tens place
ones place

**2    3    4    6**

The number shown on the counter is the same as the number shown by the blocks.

Give the standard form for each number.

**Here's how**

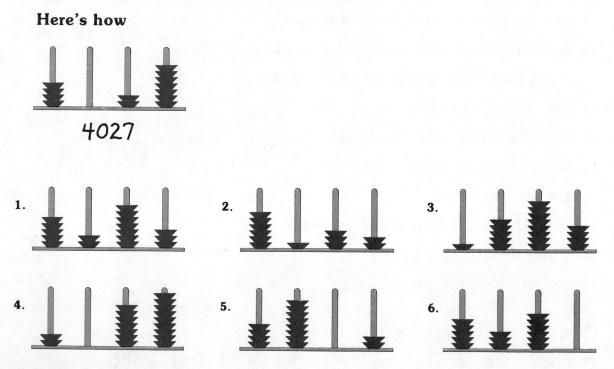

4027

1.

2.

3.

4.

5.

6.

Is 4 in the thousands place? Write yes or no.

7. 4123    8. 5467    9. 4089    10. 4612    11. 435    12. 3004

Is 5 in the hundreds place? Write yes or no.

13. 5134    14. 9578    15. 2569    16. 9052    17. 537    18. 1345

Is 6 in the tens place? Write yes or no.

19. 2659    20. 4361    21. 7856    22. 1164    23. 267    24. 6000

Give the standard form for each number.

**Here's how**

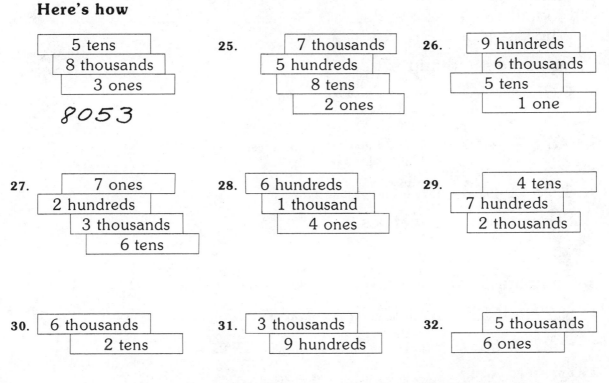

|  | 5 tens |
|  | 8 thousands |
|  | 3 ones |

_8053_

25.
| 7 thousands |
| 5 hundreds |
| 8 tens |
| 2 ones |

26.
| 9 hundreds |
| 6 thousands |
| 5 tens |
| 1 one |

27.
| 7 ones |
| 2 hundreds |
| 3 thousands |
| 6 tens |

28.
| 6 hundreds |
| 1 thousand |
| 4 ones |

29.
| 4 tens |
| 7 hundreds |
| 2 thousands |

30.
| 6 thousands |
| 2 tens |

31.
| 3 thousands |
| 9 hundreds |

32.
| 5 thousands |
| 6 ones |

**More practice
Set 21, page 360**

# Comparing Numbers

A. Shawn has 4978 marbles.
Freddie has 4762 marbles.
Who has more?

Compare 4978 and 4762.

4978 ● 4762   Look at the digits in the thousands place. They are the same.

4978 ● 4762   Look at the digits in the hundreds place. 9 is greater than 7.

4978 > 4762   4978 is greater than 4762.

Shawn has more marbles.

B. Compare 6527 and 6537.

6527 ● 6537   The digits in the thousands place are the same.

6527 ● 6537   The digits in the hundreds place are the same.

6527 ● 6537   Look at the digits in the tens place. 2 is less than 3.

6527 < 6537   6527 is less than 6537.

Which number is greater?

1. 3867 or 3992
2. 5362 or 2784
3. 9116 or 9106
4. 7453 or 7491
5. 6378 or 6375
6. 4125 or 4126

Which number is less?

7. 5652 or 5734
8. 8100 or 7999
9. 3610 or 3578
10. 1468 or 1273
11. 2711 or 2714
12. 9042 or 9046

Replace the ●. Use < or >.

13. 8234 ● 6234
14. 1687 ● 1787
15. 5419 ● 5462
16. 2049 ● 2046
17. 329 ● 239
18. 5237 ● 6894
19. 4627 ● 4618
20. 999 ● 1001
21. 7832 ● 7932
22. 1983 ● 1982
23. 684 ● 687
24. 987 ● 1111
25. 1453 ● 1435
26. 2457 ● 2417
27. 8307 ● 3870
28. 568 ● 528
29. 3598 ● 3594
30. 6001 ● 6021
31. 7054 ● 4056
32. 4827 ● 2475
33. 2983 ● 2980
34. 6504 ● 6501
35. 5136 ● 6135
36. 1730 ● 1940
37. 1852 ● 1843
38. 254 ● 234
39. 9163 ● 9161
40. 8604 ● 8607

## Keeping Skillful

1.  45
   +52

2.  37
   +48

3.  22
    43
   +14

4.  68
     9
   +21

5.  429
   +359

6.  156
   +672

7.  334
    103
   +272

8.  87
    632
   +250

9.  176
   +362

10. 389
   +206

11. 63 + 32
12. 52 + 19
13. 204 + 168
14. 286 + 306
15. 225 + 15 + 738
16. 16 + 48 + 25
17. 472 + 363
18. 792 + 75

# Ordering Numbers

A. Give 3246, 2972, and 3642 in order from least to greatest.

| Write the thousands digits in order. | When the thousands digits are the same, write the hundreds digits in order. | Complete each number. Now the numbers are in order. |
|---|---|---|
| **2** ▦ ▦ ▦ | **2 9** ▦ ▦ | **2 9 7 2** |
| **3** ▦ ▦ ▦ | **3 2** ▦ ▦ | **3 2 4 6** |
| **3** ▦ ▦ ▦ | **3 6** ▦ ▦ | **3 6 4 2** |

B. Study these patterns.

| Each number is 10 greater than the number before it. | Each number is 100 greater than the number before it. | Each number is 1000 greater than the number before it. |
|---|---|---|
| 870 | 971 | 836 |
| 880 | 1071 | 1836 |
| 890 | 1171 | 2836 |
| 900 | 1271 | 3836 |
| 910 | 1371 | 4836 |
| 920 | 1471 | 5836 |

Give the numbers in order from least to greatest.

1. 5000   7000   6000
2. 3700   3500   3600
3. 6780   6800   6790
4. 4998   4997   4999
5. 7624   7316   7532
6. 1209   1243   1215
7. 5627   2413   8345
8. 9380   9375   9328
9. 2500   3500   1500

Give the number that is 10 greater.

10. 640   11. 2400   12. 1375
13. 2813   14. 3557   15. 1890

Give the number that is 100 greater.

16. 1700   17. 2000   18. 4310
19. 8524   20. 5900   21. 945

Give the number that is 1000 greater.

22. 5000   23. 3427   24. 7800
25. 900   26. 23   27. 9000

**Expanded Form**

A. How many nails?

3 hundreds + 2 tens + 4 ones
300 + 20 + 4 = 324

B. 67 ←—— Standard form
6 tens + 7 ones
60 + 7 ←—— Expanded form

C. 502 ←—— Standard form
5 hundreds + 2 ones
500 + 2 ←—— Expanded form

Give the expanded form for each number.

1. 852   2. 94   3. 783
4. 707   5. 620   6. 444

Give the standard form for each number.

7. 200 + 80 + 5   8. 30 + 7
9. 700 + 50   10. 400 + 7

# Ten-Thousands and Hundred-Thousands

**A.** This sign shows the number of people living in Hannibal, Missouri.

**B.** This sign shows the number of people living in El Paso, Texas.

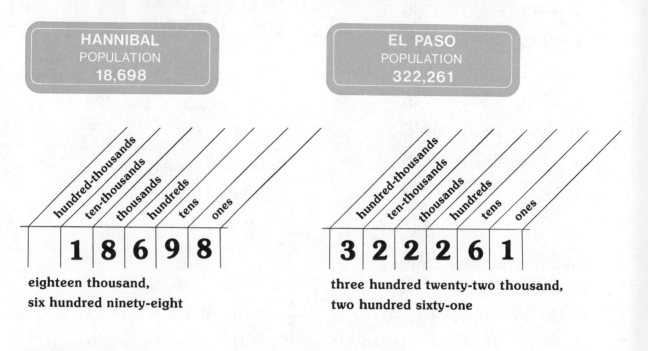

HANNIBAL
POPULATION
18,698

EL PASO
POPULATION
322,261

eighteen thousand,
six hundred ninety-eight

three hundred twenty-two thousand,
two hundred sixty-one

**c.** Read the number on each sign.

CHARLOTTE
241,178

ANN ARBOR
99,797

ALBANY
115,781

SANTA FE
41,167

SAN DIEGO
697,027

BILLINGS
61,581

FORT WAYNE
178,021

WALLA WALLA
23,619

NEW ORLEANS
593,471

Tell what the 8 means in each number.

**Here's how**

82,734    *8 ten-thousands*

846,910    *8 hundred-thousands*

1. 68,142
2. 4807
3. 85,903
4. 134,582
5. 800,612
6. 789
7. 5128
8. 348,290
9. 187,600
10. 98,045
11. 834,601
12. 680,124
13. 84,720
14. 6843
15. 42,586
16. 800,999
17. 3648
18. 92,815

Give the standard form for each number.

19. forty-one thousand, two hundred sixty-three
20. two hundred thirty-four thousand, three hundred fifteen
21. five hundred fifty-two thousand, seven hundred nineteen
22. seventeen thousand, six hundred twelve
23. ten thousand, five hundred thirteen
24. eight thousand, nine hundred ninety-nine
★25. six hundred one thousand, two hundred
★26. one hundred twelve thousand
★27. sixty-two thousand, nine
★28. four hundred thousand, six

Find the least number of colors that can be used for each map.

The same color may be used more than once, but touching shapes must be different colors.

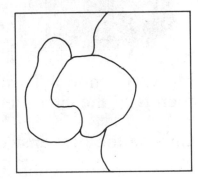

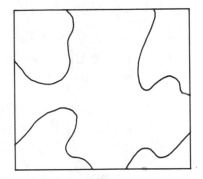

# Giving Sensible Answers

Mr. Graham took Pernell and some of his friends to the circus in the family car.

Choose the best answer.

1. How many elephants were in the circus?
(12   1200   12,000)

2. How many people went to the circus in a week?
(8   80   8000)

3. How much did Pernell's lunch cost at the circus?
($1.50   $15.00   $150.00)

4. How many balloons were sold in a week?
(9   900   900,000)

5. How many cents did a balloon cost?
(50   500   5000)

6. How many friends went to the circus with Pernell?
(3   30   300)

7. How many sandwiches did Pernell eat for lunch?
(2   20   200)

8. How many clowns were in the circus?
(10   100   1000)

9. How many people would the circus tent hold?
(3   30   3000)

10. How much did one circus ticket cost?
($2.50   $250.00   $2500.00)

**Millions**

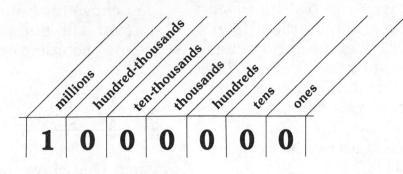

one million

How big is a million?

There are about 1,000,000 minutes in two years.

The weight of 250 full-size cars is about 1,000,000 pounds.

You can count to 1,000,000 in about 11 days and 11 nights.

In 40 days, you breathe about 1,000,000 times.

Which digit is in the millions place?

1. 2,000,000    2. 9,682,340    3. 5,191,112    4. 4,888,888

5. 1,234,567    6. 7,654,321    7. 3,004,605    8. 6,154,328

Give the standard form for each number.

9. four million    10. three million    11. seven million

12. nine million    13. six million    14. eight million

Give the missing number.

★15. 1,000,000 = ▦ thousands    ★16. 1,000,000 = ▦ ten-thousands

# Lab Activity

## Bean Counter

Jay Redsky and his sister Dee made up a game called Bean Counter. They used 36 beans and an empty egg carton. The sections on both sides of the egg carton were labeled:

ones, tens, hundreds, thousands, ten-thousands and hundred-thousands.

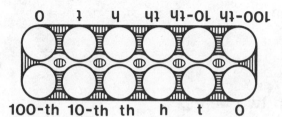

Jay and Dee made these rules for the game.

1. Put 3 beans into each section.

2. When it is your turn, choose any section on your side.

3. Take all the beans from that section and drop them one by one into as many sections as possible. Go around the carton to the right. Do not skip any section.

4. Continue until each player has had 4 turns.

5. Give the number shown by the beans on each side. The player with the greater number wins.

Jay chose his hundreds section to start with and dropped the beans according to the rules.

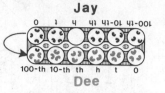

Then Dee chose her ones section and dropped those beans according to the rules.

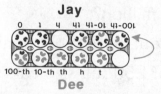

Jay and Dee each took 3 more turns. Then each wrote the number that told how many beans were in each section.

Jay's number was 611,507.

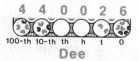

Dee's number was 440,026.

Jay won because he had the greater number. Choose a friend and play this game. Start with any section on your side.

# Chapter 10 Test
## Numeration Through 999,999, pages 188–202

Is 4 in the hundreds place?
Write yes or no.

1. 4128      2. 23,460

Is 2 in the thousands place?
Write yes or no.

3. 2560      4. 15,281

Is 8 in the hundred-thousands
place? Write yes or no.

5. 800,000      6. 238,116

Is 5 in the ten-thousands
place? Write yes or no.

7. 152,100      8. 56,483

Give the standard form for
each number.

9. six thousand, forty-three

10. three thousand, five hundred
seventy-one

11. sixty-two thousand,
nine hundred

12. four hundred twenty-one
thousand, seven hundred
ninety-two

13.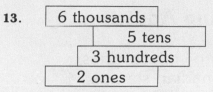

6 thousands
5 tens
3 hundreds
2 ones

14.

7 tens
3 thousands
9 ones

Replace the ●. Use < or >.

15. 6743 ● 6843

16. 9529 ● 9538

17. 8564 ● 7645

Give the numbers in order
from least to greatest.

18. 4532   6532   1532

19. 5618   5345   5427

Choose the best answer.

20. Yuki worked how many
hours last week?

(40   4000   400,000)

# Chapter 11    Addition Computation

## Checking Addition

A. A stamp collector has
45 Canadian stamps,
826 United States stamps,
and 19 European stamps.
How many stamps does she
have in all?

Find 45 + 826 + 19.

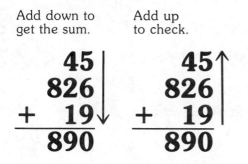

Add down to      Add up
get the sum.      to check.

$$\begin{array}{r} 45 \\ 826 \\ +\ 19 \\ \hline 890 \end{array} \qquad \begin{array}{r} 45 \\ 826 \\ +\ 19 \\ \hline 890 \end{array}$$

She has 890 stamps in all.

Tell how you would check the
addition in each example.

B.
$$\begin{array}{r} 853 \\ 524 \\ +\ 341 \\ \hline 1718 \end{array}$$

C.
$$\begin{array}{r} \$\ 7.28 \\ 6.13 \\ +\ 2.35 \\ \hline \$15.76 \end{array}$$

Check each answer. If it is correct, write
yes. If it is wrong, find the correct answer.

1.
```
   46
   28
 + 15
 ----
   79
```

2.
```
   31
   56
 + 45
 ----
  132
```

3.
```
   24
   43
 + 72
 ----
  148
```

4.
```
  153
  254
 +302
 ----
  609
```

5.
```
  $0.64
   0.51
 + 0.22
 ------
  $1.37
```

6.
```
  $3.20
   9.25
 + 4.36
 ------
 $16.81
```

7.
```
   57
   24
 + 43
 ----
  124
```

8.
```
   84
   73
 + 36
 ----
  183
```

9.
```
   25
   31
 +42
 ----
   88
```

10.
```
   38
   71
 + 65
 ----
  174
```

11.
```
  $0.25
   0.32
 + 0.37
 ------
  $0.84
```

12.
```
  $5.43
   7.62
 + 3.24
 ------
 $16.29
```

Add and check.

13.
```
  561
  293
 +165
```

14.
```
  844
  293
 +321
```

15.
```
  768
  219
 +405
```

16.
```
  926
  834
 +621
```

17.
```
  $5.43
   0.24
 + 2.16
```

18.
```
  $7.83
   4.02
 + 8.23
```

19.
```
   46
   87
 + 20
```

20.
```
   36
    5
 +244
```

21.
```
  782
   53
 +804
```

22.
```
  663
   19
 +710
```

23.
```
  $6.15
   8.42
 + 0.33
```

24.
```
  $3.25
   0.14
 + 1.42
```

25. Anna saved $1.90 in dimes,
$8.05 in nickels, and $0.43
in pennies to buy stamps.
How much did she save in all?

26. Juan had 312 airmail and
709 regular stamps. He then
bought 73 post-card stamps.
How many did he have in all?

★27. Show how to use subtraction
to check 708 + 531 = 1239.

# Addition: Four-Digit Numbers

A. A pirate ship sailed 3563 kilometers in May and 4261 kilometers in June. How many kilometers did the ship sail?

Find 3563 + 4261.

| Add the ones.<br>3 + 1 = 4 | Add the tens.<br>6 + 6 = 12<br>12 tens =<br>1 hundred 2 tens | Add the<br>hundreds.<br>1 + 5 + 2 = 8 | Add the<br>thousands.<br>3 + 4 = 7 |
|---|---|---|---|
| $$\begin{array}{r} 3563 \\ +\,4261 \\ \hline 4 \end{array}$$ | $$\begin{array}{r} {\scriptstyle 1} \\ 3563 \\ +\,4261 \\ \hline 24 \end{array}$$ | $$\begin{array}{r} {\scriptstyle 1} \\ 3563 \\ +\,4261 \\ \hline 824 \end{array}$$ | $$\begin{array}{r} {\scriptstyle 1} \\ 3563 \\ +\,4261 \\ \hline 7824 \end{array}$$ |

The ship sailed 7824 kilometers.

Tell what was done in each example.

B.
$$\begin{array}{r} {\scriptstyle 1} \\ 4926 \\ +\,\,\,801 \\ \hline 5727 \end{array}$$

C.
$$\begin{array}{r} 2035 \\ +\,6243 \\ \hline 8278 \end{array}$$

D.
$$\begin{array}{r} {\scriptstyle 1} \\ \$71.39 \\ +\,\,\,8.26 \\ \hline \$79.65 \end{array}$$

E.
$$\begin{array}{r} {\scriptstyle 1} \\ 1263 \\ 401 \\ +\,\,\,118 \\ \hline 1782 \end{array}$$

Add.

| | | | | | | | | | |
|---|---|---|---|---|---|---|---|---|---|
| 1. | 1726<br>+3413 | 2. | 4088<br>+1704 | 3. | 2813<br>+4016 | 4. | 3145<br>+2806 | 5. | $61.56<br>+ 32.81 |
| 6. | 6513<br>+ 458 | 7. | 2073<br>+ 153 | 8. | 4272<br>+ 685 | 9. | 5620<br>+ 817 | 10. | $52.81<br>+ 1.23 |
| 11. | 2843<br>+1325 | 12. | 6732<br>+ 755 | 13. | 3763<br>+2018 | 14. | 3835<br>+ 900 | 15. | $60.51<br>+ 24.68 |
| 16. | 4801<br>305<br>+ 61 | 17. | 5204<br>453<br>+ 152 | 18. | 2342<br>1056<br>+ 161 | 19. | 4870<br>613<br>+ 915 | 20. | $54.20<br>2.34<br>+ 0.18 |
| 21. | 5693<br>+3234 | 22. | 5736<br>+1653 | 23. | 4583<br>+2170 | ★24. | 3476<br>+8393 | ★25. | $84.86<br>+ 75.08 |

26. The pirates must travel 1048 kilometers to the Indian Ocean and then 932 kilometers to the treasure. How far must they travel?

27. They found 2296 pearls, 451 diamonds, and 232 rubies. How many jewels did they find in all?

More practice
Set 22, page 361

# Using Addition

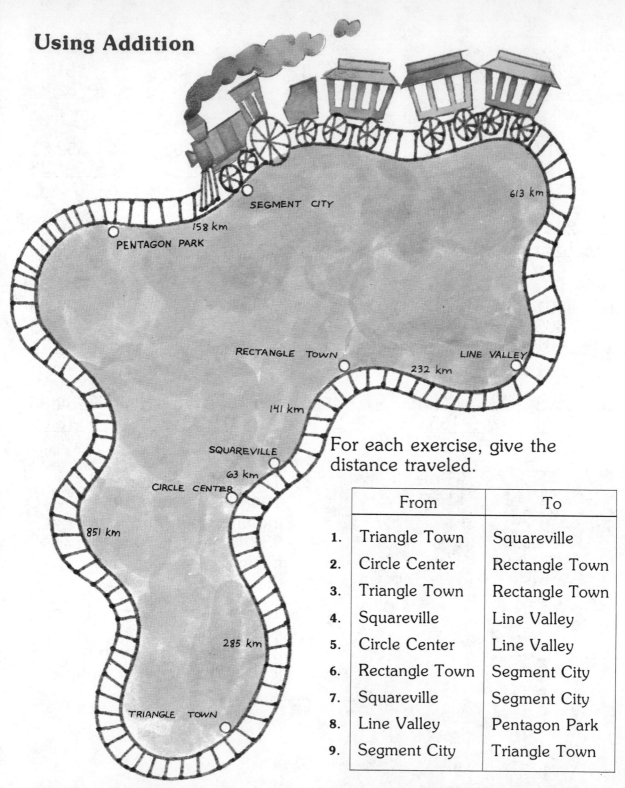

SEGMENT CITY

613 km

158 km

PENTAGON PARK

RECTANGLE TOWN

LINE VALLEY

232 km

141 km

SQUAREVILLE

63 km

CIRCLE CENTER

851 km

285 km

TRIANGLE TOWN

For each exercise, give the distance traveled.

| | From | To |
|---|---|---|
| 1. | Triangle Town | Squareville |
| 2. | Circle Center | Rectangle Town |
| 3. | Triangle Town | Rectangle Town |
| 4. | Squareville | Line Valley |
| 5. | Circle Center | Line Valley |
| 6. | Rectangle Town | Segment City |
| 7. | Squareville | Segment City |
| 8. | Line Valley | Pentagon Park |
| 9. | Segment City | Triangle Town |

Add.

10. 82
+ 43

11. 154
+ 860

12. $15.73
+ 3.56

13. 347
+ 932

14. 234
+ 585

15. $8.25
+ 1.38

16. 3215
+ 4340

17. 392
+ 165

18. $17.86
+ 1.22

19. 2411
328
+ 13

20. 546
30
+ 72

21. $52.32
1.01
+ 7.26

22. 2268 + 1418
23. 268 + 70
24. 823 + 465
25. 465 + 724
26. 67 + 29
27. 5620 + 187
28. 459 + 316
29. 2432 + 6815
30. 425 + 356
31. 5654 + 1165

Find each answer.

32. Jose spent $2.65 for a child's ticket and $3.25 for an adult's ticket. How much did he spend in all?

33. $3.25 was spent for a ticket and $1.25 was spent for food. How much was spent in all?

Is the red path longer, shorter, or the same length as the blue path?

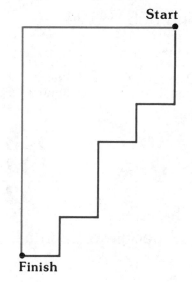

Check your answer by using your centimeter ruler.

# Addition: More than One Renaming

A. 368 people rode the roller coaster.
194 people rode the Ferris wheel.
How many people rode in all?

Find 368 + 194.

Add the ones.
8 + 4 = 12
12 ones =
1 ten 2 ones

Add the tens.
1 + 6 + 9 = 16
16 tens =
1 hundred 6 tens

Add the hundreds.
1 + 3 + 1 = 5

```
    1              1 1            1 1
  368            368            368
+ 194          + 194          + 194
-----          -----          -----
    2             62            562
```

562 people rode in all.

Tell what was done in each example.

B.
$$\begin{array}{r} \overset{1}{}\ \overset{1}{} \\ 4738 \\ +2509 \\ \hline 7247 \end{array}$$

C.
$$\begin{array}{r} \overset{1}{}\ \overset{1}{} \\ \$73.25 \\ +\ \ 7.28 \\ \hline \$80.53 \end{array}$$

D.
$$\begin{array}{r} \overset{1}{}\overset{1}{} \\ 529 \\ 43 \\ +\ \ 82 \\ \hline 654 \end{array}$$

Add.

1.
$$\begin{array}{r} 356 \\ +597 \\ \hline \end{array}$$

2.
$$\begin{array}{r} 2175 \\ +3287 \\ \hline \end{array}$$

3.
$$\begin{array}{r} 2306 \\ +4887 \\ \hline \end{array}$$

4.
$$\begin{array}{r} 258 \\ +175 \\ \hline \end{array}$$

5.
$$\begin{array}{r} \$83.75 \\ +\ 12.98 \\ \hline \end{array}$$

6.
$$\begin{array}{r} 2648 \\ +\ 817 \\ \hline \end{array}$$

7.
$$\begin{array}{r} 6234 \\ +1959 \\ \hline \end{array}$$

8.
$$\begin{array}{r} 167 \\ +\ 65 \\ \hline \end{array}$$

9.
$$\begin{array}{r} 3519 \\ +\ 358 \\ \hline \end{array}$$

10.
$$\begin{array}{r} \$14.59 \\ +\ \ 7.29 \\ \hline \end{array}$$

11.
$$\begin{array}{r} 3281 \\ 123 \\ +\ 935 \\ \hline \end{array}$$

12.
$$\begin{array}{r} 257 \\ 31 \\ +176 \\ \hline \end{array}$$

13.
$$\begin{array}{r} 835 \\ 45 \\ +\ 20 \\ \hline \end{array}$$

14.
$$\begin{array}{r} 3205 \\ 178 \\ +\ 342 \\ \hline \end{array}$$

15.
$$\begin{array}{r} \$18.24 \\ 0.79 \\ +\ \ 0.20 \\ \hline \end{array}$$

16.
$$\begin{array}{r} 4606 \\ +2585 \\ \hline \end{array}$$

17.
$$\begin{array}{r} 597 \\ +316 \\ \hline \end{array}$$

★18.
$$\begin{array}{r} 788 \\ +599 \\ \hline \end{array}$$

★19.
$$\begin{array}{r} 6809 \\ +8391 \\ \hline \end{array}$$

★20.
$$\begin{array}{r} 9999 \\ +1111 \\ \hline \end{array}$$

21. A family spent $29.35 for tickets and $8.59 for food. How much did they spend?

22. 87 people are on the Ferris wheel. 146 people are waiting in line. How many people are there in all?

More practice
Set 23, page 361

# Using Addition

A milk truck made the following deliveries to 10 stores during one month. How many liters of milk were delivered to each store?

| | Store | Liters of whole milk | Liters of skim milk |
|---|---|---|---|
| 1. | A | 3356 | 1925 |
| 2. | B | 2194 | 2047 |
| 3. | C | 4361 | 2783 |
| 4. | D | 1297 | 688 |
| 5. | E | 2834 | 1423 |
| 6. | F | 875 | 516 |
| 7. | G | 1250 | 794 |
| 8. | H | 3086 | 1827 |
| 9. | I | 967 | 641 |
| 10. | J | 5108 | 2748 |

Add across.
Add down.

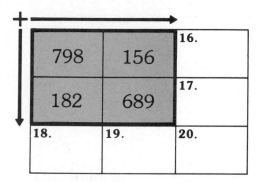

| 215 | 98 | 11. |
| 146 | 74 | 12. |
| 13. | 14. | 15. |

| 798 | 156 | 16. |
| 182 | 689 | 17. |
| 18. | 19. | 20. |

| 3568 | 1927 | 21. |
| 2671 | 1809 | 22. |
| 23. | 24. | 25. |

## Keeping Skillful

1. $\begin{array}{r} 46 \\ -\ 8 \\ \hline \end{array}$  2. $\begin{array}{r} 60 \\ -15 \\ \hline \end{array}$  3. $\begin{array}{r} 82 \\ -36 \\ \hline \end{array}$

4. $\begin{array}{r} 98 \\ -73 \\ \hline \end{array}$  5. $\begin{array}{r} 73 \\ -34 \\ \hline \end{array}$  6. $\begin{array}{r} 67 \\ -29 \\ \hline \end{array}$

7. $\begin{array}{r} 395 \\ -\ 86 \\ \hline \end{array}$  8. $\begin{array}{r} 813 \\ -\ 42 \\ \hline \end{array}$  9. $\begin{array}{r} 560 \\ -\ 17 \\ \hline \end{array}$

10. $\begin{array}{r} 754 \\ -135 \\ \hline \end{array}$  11. $\begin{array}{r} 248 \\ -167 \\ \hline \end{array}$  12. $\begin{array}{r} 843 \\ -126 \\ \hline \end{array}$

13. $\begin{array}{r} 427 \\ -172 \\ \hline \end{array}$  14. $\begin{array}{r} 219 \\ -153 \\ \hline \end{array}$  15. $\begin{array}{r} 971 \\ -252 \\ \hline \end{array}$

16. $\begin{array}{r} 365 \\ -192 \\ \hline \end{array}$  17. $\begin{array}{r} 234 \\ -127 \\ \hline \end{array}$  18. $\begin{array}{r} 908 \\ -156 \\ \hline \end{array}$

19. 93 − 47   20. 87 − 28

21. 478 − 325   22. 148 − 39

23. 615 − 181   24. 280 − 173

25. 319 − 76   26. 784 − 35

27. 918 − 126   28. 304 − 181

29. 483 − 345   30. 916 − 407

# Lab Activity

## Number Game for Two Players

Carla and Joe played this number game with nine cards like these.

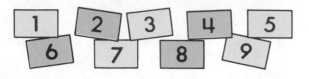

1. They mixed up the cards and put them face down.

2. Carla chose 3 cards. Joe chose 3 cards.

3. Carla used the digits on her cards to write a number. Joe used the digits on his cards to write a number. They kept their numbers a secret.

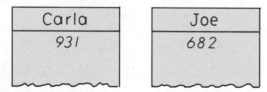

| Carla | Joe |
|-------|-----|
| 931 | 682 |

4. Then they put their cards face down with the others and mixed them up again. Carla and Joe each chose 3 more cards. They wrote another secret number.

| Carla | Joe |
|-------|-----|
| 931 742 | 682 398 |

5. Carla added her two numbers. Joe added his two numbers. They checked each other's addition. Both were correct.

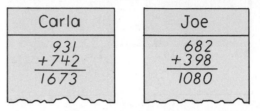

| Carla | Joe |
|-------|-----|
| 931 +742 ‾‾‾‾ 1673 | 682 +398 ‾‾‾‾ 1080 |

6. Carla and Joe compared their sums. Carla had the larger sum so she won one point.

| Round | Carla | Joe |
|-------|-------|-----|
| 1 | 1 | 0 |
| 2 | | |
| 3 | | |

Choose a partner and play this game. Keep score for 10 rounds. At the beginning of each round, start with step 1.

# Chapter 11 Test
## Addition Computation, pages 204–214

Check each answer. If it is correct, write yes. If it is wrong, find the correct answer.

1.
```
   19
   42
 + 36
   97
```

2.
```
   93
   15
 + 25
  123
```

3.
```
  526
  653
+ 409
 1587
```

4.
```
   349
   619
 + 524
  1492
```

5.
```
  $0.75
   0.61
 + 0.43
  $0.79
```

Add.

6.
```
  1624
+ 7247
```

7.
```
  8743
+  193
```

8.
```
  2254
+ 1461
```

9.
```
  4873
+ 3910
```

10.
```
  5382
+  475
```

11.
```
  $29.84
 +  3.14
```

12.
```
  2383
  6122
+  274
```

13.
```
  5420
   234
 +  18
```

14.
```
  3317
+ 2478
```

15.
```
  4956
+ 1732
```

16.
```
  574
+ 338
```

17.
```
  106
+ 798
```

18.
```
  479
+  54
```

19.
```
  2168
+  398
```

20.
```
  7522
+ 1808
```

21.
```
  3375
+ 2819
```

22.
```
  5972
+ 2156
```

23.
```
  2834
+ 6957
```

24.
```
  4516
   239
+  502
```

25.
```
  1495
  1023
+  217
```

# Chapter 12   Subtraction Computation

## Checking Subtraction

**A.** You can check subtraction by using addition.

WHEN I ADD, MY ANSWER IS 894. MY SUBTRACTION IS RIGHT TOO.

WHEN I ADD, MY ANSWER IS 978. I KNOW MY SUBTRACTION IS RIGHT.

Tell how each subtraction problem was checked by addition.

**B.**

$$\begin{array}{r} 279 \\ -\ 42 \\ \hline 237 \end{array} \qquad \begin{array}{r} 42 \\ +237 \\ \hline 279 \end{array}$$

**C.**

$$\begin{array}{r} 96 \\ -37 \\ \hline 59 \end{array} \qquad \begin{array}{r} 37 \\ +59 \\ \hline 96 \end{array}$$

Check each answer. If it is correct, write yes.
If it is wrong, find the correct answer.

| 1. | 2. | 3. | 4. | 5. | 6. |
|---|---|---|---|---|---|
| $\begin{array}{r} 78 \\ -\phantom{0}5 \\ \hline 63 \end{array}$ | $\begin{array}{r} 91 \\ -\phantom{0}7 \\ \hline 84 \end{array}$ | $\begin{array}{r} 63 \\ -54 \\ \hline 19 \end{array}$ | $\begin{array}{r} 45 \\ -12 \\ \hline 23 \end{array}$ | $\begin{array}{r} 632 \\ -\phantom{00}8 \\ \hline 524 \end{array}$ | $\begin{array}{r} \$8.96 \\ -\phantom{0}.39 \\ \hline \$8.67 \end{array}$ |

| 7. | 8. | 9. | 10. | 11. | 12. |
|---|---|---|---|---|---|
| $\begin{array}{r} 283 \\ -191 \\ \hline 192 \end{array}$ | $\begin{array}{r} 192 \\ -153 \\ \hline 42 \end{array}$ | $\begin{array}{r} 876 \\ -\phantom{0}42 \\ \hline 834 \end{array}$ | $\begin{array}{r} 137 \\ -\phantom{0}84 \\ \hline 153 \end{array}$ | $\begin{array}{r} 458 \\ -248 \\ \hline 110 \end{array}$ | $\begin{array}{r} \$7.65 \\ -\phantom{0}3.40 \\ \hline \$4.25 \end{array}$ |

13. $81 - 75 = 8$

14. $56 - 32 = 14$

15. $119 - 83 = 136$

16. $769 - 85 = 784$

17. $345 - 283 = 162$

18. $975 - 467 = 508$

Use the table to find each answer.

19. The greyhound is how much slower than the antelope?

20. The hawk is how much faster than the swift?

21. The cheetah is how much slower than the eagle?

22. The hawk is how much faster than the greyhound?

23. The swift is how much slower than the eagle?

24. The hawk is how much faster than the eagle?

|  | Speed (kilometers per hour) |
|---|---|
| Duck hawk | 291 |
| Golden eagle | 183 |
| Cheetah | 112 |
| Swift | 104 |
| Antelope | 87 |
| Greyhound | 48 |

# Subtraction: Four-Digit Numbers

6539 kg                    2178 kg

A. The elephant weighs how much more?

Find 6539 − 2178.

| Subtract the ones.<br>9 − 8 = 1 | Rename to show 10 more tens.<br>5 hundreds 3 tens =<br>4 hundreds 13 tens<br>Subtract the tens.<br>13 − 7 = 6 | Subtract the hundreds.<br>4 − 1 = 3 | Subtract the thousands.<br>6 − 2 = 4 |
|---|---|---|---|
| $$\begin{array}{r} 6539 \\ -\ 2178 \\ \hline 1 \end{array}$$ | $$\begin{array}{r} {}^{4\ 13} \\ 6\cancel{5}\cancel{3}9 \\ -\ 2178 \\ \hline 61 \end{array}$$ | $$\begin{array}{r} {}^{4\ 13} \\ 6\cancel{5}\cancel{3}9 \\ -\ 2178 \\ \hline 361 \end{array}$$ | $$\begin{array}{r} {}^{4\ 13} \\ 6\cancel{5}\cancel{3}9 \\ -\ 2178 \\ \hline 4361 \end{array}$$ |

The elephant weighs 4361 kilograms more.

Tell what was done in each example.

B.   <sup>4 13</sup>
     5̶3̶84
   − 2471
     2913

C.   <sup>3 15</sup>
     974̶5̶
   −  308
     9437

D.   3867
   − 3214
      653

E.   $26.78
   −  12.53
     $14.25

Subtract.

1.   4587
   − 2165

2.   5963
   − 3612

3.   9781
   −  334

4.   6544
   −  239

5.   $48.35
   −  12.74

6.   7759
   − 5463

7.   2837
   − 1264

8.   4327
   − 2516

9.   7435
   − 4923

10.  $56.92
   −  43.28

11. 6854 − 2541   12. 9756 − 2415   13. 4678 − 3259   14. 7862 − 325

15. 5749 − 3673   16. 3428 − 1276   17. 8695 − 6742   18. 6337 − 254

19. 6347 − 4635   20. 5892 − 3766   21. 3263 − 2451   22. 4835 − 127

Use the table to help you find the answer.

Horse
1378 kg

Ox
1395 kg

Lion
248 kg

Bison
1485 kg

23. The horse weighs how much less than the ox?

24. The ox weighs how much more than the lion?

25. The lion weighs how much less than the bison?

26. The bison weighs how much more than the horse?

More practice
Set 24, page 361

(two hundred nineteen) **219**

# Using Subtraction

Find each difference. Use the code to help you answer the riddle.

What did one clown say to another clown?

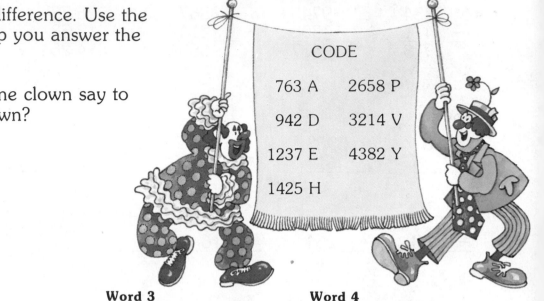

**CODE**

| | |
|---|---|
| 763 A | 2658 P |
| 942 D | 3214 V |
| 1237 E | 4382 Y |
| 1425 H | |

**Word 1**

1. 2782 − 1357

2. 827 − 64

3. 3249 − 35

4. 9563 − 8326

**Word 2**

5. 971 − 208

**Word 3**

6. 6148 − 4723

7. 1486 − 723

8. 4796 − 2138

9. 7839 − 5181

10. 6297 − 1915

**Word 4**

11. 978 − 36

12. 4598 − 3835

13. 9564 − 5182

Subtract.

14. 94
    − 23

15. 53
    − 47

16. $83.45
    − 40.29

17. 149
    − 63

18. 295
    − 87

19. $59.27
    − 37.84

20. 876
    − 459

21. 481
    − 354

22. $74.35
    − 23.61

23. 1682
    − 427

24. 9367
    − 845

25. $37.96
    − 23.88

26. 3158
    − 1915

27. 7845
    − 3662

28. $45.32
    − 21.90

29. 4536
    − 2172

30. 6179
    − 5254

31. $56.94
    − 17.34

32. 32 − 7
33. 75 − 8
34. 58 − 44
35. 67 − 14
36. 982 − 26
37. 436 − 85
38. 748 − 165
39. 518 − 472
40. 2995 − 869
41. 4681 − 302
42. 6789 − 3579
43. 5468 − 2734
44. 9624 − 7281
45. 3764 − 1952

## Time Out

Copy this drawing. Enter the house. Find a path that starts in one room, passes through each door only once, and ends in another room.

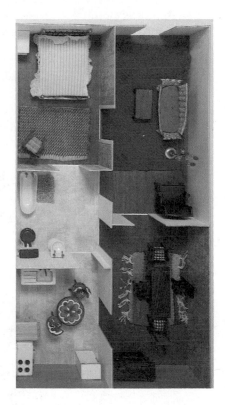

# Subtraction: Two Renamings

**A.** 8642 adults attended a baseball game. 3815 children attended. How many more adults attended?

Find 8642 − 3815.

| Rename to show 10 more ones.<br>4 tens 2 ones =<br>3 tens 12 ones<br>Subtract the ones.<br>12 − 5 = 7 | Subtract the tens.<br>3 − 1 = 2 | Rename to show 10 more hundreds.<br>8 thousands<br>6 hundreds =<br>7 thousands<br>16 hundreds<br>Subtract the hundreds.<br>16 − 8 = 8 | Subtract the thousands.<br>7 − 3 = 4 |
|---|---|---|---|
| 3 12<br>8642<br>− 3815<br>7 | 3 12<br>8642<br>− 3815<br>27 | 7 16 3 12<br>8642<br>− 3815<br>827 | 7 16 3 12<br>8642<br>− 3815<br>4827 |

There were 4827 more adults.

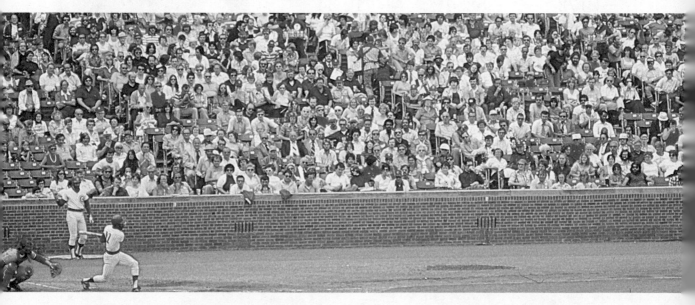

Tell what was done in each example.

B.
$$\overset{6\,13}{\overset{\cancel{3}\,11}{\cancel{7}\cancel{4}\cancel{1}}}$$
$$-\ 389$$
$$\overline{\phantom{0}352}$$

C.
$$\overset{7\,11}{\overset{}{3\cancel{8}\cancel{2}\cancel{5}}}$$
$$\overset{\cancel{1}\,15}{}$$
$$-\ 1746$$
$$\overline{2079}$$

D.
$$\overset{5\,13\,4\,12}{\cancel{6}\cancel{3}\cancel{5}\cancel{2}}$$
$$-\ \phantom{0}728$$
$$\overline{5624}$$

E.
$$\overset{3\,14\ \ 7\ 13}{\$\cancel{4}\cancel{4}.\cancel{8}\cancel{3}}$$
$$-\ 26.56$$
$$\overline{\$18.27}$$

Subtract.

1.
$$343$$
$$-159$$

2.
$$822$$
$$-476$$

3.
$$7652$$
$$-\ 938$$

4.
$$8363$$
$$-\ 715$$

5.
$$\$37.25$$
$$-\ 19.18$$

6.
$$428$$
$$-\ 49$$

7.
$$341$$
$$-\ 87$$

8.
$$7385$$
$$-6576$$

9.
$$6484$$
$$-3728$$

10.
$$\$54.35$$
$$-\ 7.27$$

11.
$$756$$
$$-689$$

12.
$$3725$$
$$-2468$$

13.
$$241$$
$$-\ 79$$

14.
$$8294$$
$$-\ 686$$

15.
$$\$24.53$$
$$-\ 19.25$$

16.
$$4362$$
$$-1724$$

17.
$$2738$$
$$-\ 909$$

★18.
$$5684$$
$$-\ 997$$

★19.
$$6723$$
$$-2928$$

★20.
$$\$86.42$$
$$-\ 47.53$$

21. There were 9461 tickets. 8642 were sold. How many were left?

22. There were 3815 girls and 1908 boys in a group. How many more girls were there?

23. The girls spent $48.34 and the boys spent $23.67. How much less did the boys spend?

★24. 8642 people were at the game. 1375 left before the end. How many stayed?

**More practice**
**Set 25, page 362**

# Subtraction: Two Renamings with Zeros

A. Birds fly south for the winter each year.
The bobolink travels about 6500 kilometers.
The blue goose travels about
2481 kilometers.
About how much farther does the
bobolink travel?

Find 6500 − 2481.

| You need more ones. You need more tens. | Rename to show 10 more tens. 5 hundreds 0 tens = 4 hundreds 10 tens | Rename to show 10 more ones. 10 tens 0 ones = 9 tens 10 ones | Subtract. |
|---|---|---|---|
| $\begin{array}{r} 6500 \\ -\ 2481 \\ \hline \end{array}$ | $\begin{array}{r} {}^{4}6\cancel{5}\overset{10}{0}0 \\ -\ 2481 \\ \hline \end{array}$ | $\begin{array}{r} {}^{9\ 10}6\cancel{5}\cancel{0}0 \\ -\ 2481 \\ \hline \end{array}$ | $\begin{array}{r} {}^{9\ 10}6\cancel{5}\cancel{0}\cancel{0} \\ -\ 2481 \\ \hline 4019 \end{array}$ |

The bobolink travels about 4019 kilometers
farther than the blue goose.

Tell what was done in each example.

$$\begin{array}{c} \overset{9\,10}{\overset{4\,\cancel{10}}{\cancel{5}\cancel{0}\cancel{0}8}} \\ -\ 1643 \\ \hline 3365 \end{array}$$
B.

$$\begin{array}{c} \overset{5\,10\,8\,10}{\cancel{6}\cancel{0}\cancel{9}\cancel{0}} \\ -\ 4258 \\ \hline 1832 \end{array}$$
C.

$$\begin{array}{c} \overset{9\,10}{\overset{6\,\cancel{10}}{7\cancel{0}\cancel{0}}} \\ -\ 86 \\ \hline 614 \end{array}$$
D.

$$\begin{array}{c} \overset{9\,16}{\overset{3\,\cancel{10}}{\$4.\cancel{0}\cancel{6}}} \\ -\ 2.37 \\ \hline \$1.69 \end{array}$$
E.

Subtract.

1.  $\begin{array}{r} 900 \\ -\ 35 \\ \hline \end{array}$
2.  $\begin{array}{r} 520 \\ -\ 34 \\ \hline \end{array}$
3.  $\begin{array}{r} 603 \\ -286 \\ \hline \end{array}$
4.  $\begin{array}{r} 802 \\ -323 \\ \hline \end{array}$
5.  $\begin{array}{r} \$4.00 \\ -\ 2.98 \\ \hline \end{array}$

6.  $\begin{array}{r} 5050 \\ -\ 129 \\ \hline \end{array}$
7.  $\begin{array}{r} 9007 \\ -\ 743 \\ \hline \end{array}$
8.  $\begin{array}{r} 2304 \\ -1257 \\ \hline \end{array}$
9.  $\begin{array}{r} 7065 \\ -4216 \\ \hline \end{array}$
10. $\begin{array}{r} \$67.00 \\ -\ 25.63 \\ \hline \end{array}$

11. $\begin{array}{r} 400 \\ -376 \\ \hline \end{array}$
12. $\begin{array}{r} 605 \\ -\ 86 \\ \hline \end{array}$
13. $\begin{array}{r} 6300 \\ -5248 \\ \hline \end{array}$
14. $\begin{array}{r} 7060 \\ -\ 923 \\ \hline \end{array}$
15. $\begin{array}{r} \$90.80 \\ -\ 7.66 \\ \hline \end{array}$

16. $\begin{array}{r} 5026 \\ -1452 \\ \hline \end{array}$
17. $\begin{array}{r} 7278 \\ -2593 \\ \hline \end{array}$
★18. $\begin{array}{r} 7050 \\ -4276 \\ \hline \end{array}$
★19. $\begin{array}{r} 8064 \\ -\ 578 \\ \hline \end{array}$
★20. $\begin{array}{r} \$40.07 \\ -\ 23.89 \\ \hline \end{array}$

21. Bird watchers counted 2060 doves and 1735 geese. How many more doves were there?

22. A flock of swans had 3007 males and 1642 females. How many more were male?

1060 crows traveled 268 kilometers. 523 swifts traveled 1000 kilometers.

23. There are how many more crows than swifts?

★24. The swifts traveled how much farther than the crows?

**More practice
Set 26, 362**

# Using Subtraction

These mountains are in North America.
The height of each mountain is how many meters
less than Mt. McKinley? than Mt. Logan?
than Mt. Whitney?

| | McKinley 6194 m | Logan 5950 m | Whitney 4418 m |
|---|---|---|---|
| Hood 3424 m | 1. | 2. | 3. |
| Rushmore 1745 m | 4. | 5. | 6. |
| Shasta 4317 m | 7. | 8. | 9. |
| Mitchell 2037 m | 10. | 11. | 12. |
| Washington 1917 m | 13. | 14. | 15. |
| Pikes Peak 4301 m | 16. | 17. | 18. |
| Rainier 4392 m | 19. | 20. | 21. |

Subtract.

22. 
$$\begin{array}{r} 3275 \\ -2468 \end{array}$$

23. 
$$\begin{array}{r} 5831 \\ -3615 \end{array}$$

24. 
$$\begin{array}{r} \$64.92 \\ -\ 18.37 \end{array}$$

25. 
$$\begin{array}{r} 450 \\ -165 \end{array}$$

26. 
$$\begin{array}{r} 704 \\ -386 \end{array}$$

27. 
$$\begin{array}{r} \$8.43 \\ -\ 5.70 \end{array}$$

28. 
$$\begin{array}{r} 1927 \\ -\ 654 \end{array}$$

29. 
$$\begin{array}{r} 1371 \\ -\ 852 \end{array}$$

30. 
$$\begin{array}{r} \$11.55 \\ -\ 6.29 \end{array}$$

31. 
$$\begin{array}{r} 2500 \\ -1472 \end{array}$$

32. 
$$\begin{array}{r} 4700 \\ -1636 \end{array}$$

33. 
$$\begin{array}{r} \$99.80 \\ -\ 53.59 \end{array}$$

34. 
$$\begin{array}{r} 3708 \\ -\ 679 \end{array}$$

35. 
$$\begin{array}{r} 4905 \\ -\ 293 \end{array}$$

36. 
$$\begin{array}{r} \$68.74 \\ -\ 59.09 \end{array}$$

37. 
$$\begin{array}{r} 9005 \\ -3642 \end{array}$$

38. 
$$\begin{array}{r} 7009 \\ -5378 \end{array}$$

39. 
$$\begin{array}{r} \$60.07 \\ -\ 8.25 \end{array}$$

40. 5216 − 87
41. 3421 − 64
42. 400 − 58
43. 600 − 49
44. 2067 − 584
45. 4014 − 731
46. 7493 − 2876
47. 2351 − 1628
48. 806 − 489
49. 902 − 154
50. 8700 − 2351
51. 2300 − 1247

## Keeping Skillful

1. 2168 + 327
2. 335 + 468
3. 1746 + 6538
4. 5347 + 2198
5. 6284 + 245 + 105
6. 17 + 235 + 6334
7. 356 + 84
8. 92 + 478
9. 3274 + 6683
10. 108 + 974
11. 279 + 86 + 127
12. 561 + 98 + 246
13. 852 + 76 + 230
14. 2574 + 3682
15. 330 + 475 + 108
16. 134 + 478 + 247
17. 6423 + 406 + 735
18. 2437 + 5849
19. 510 + 6758
20. 4795 + 2832
21. 627 + 804
22. 5463 + 3728

# Addition and Subtraction Computation

Distance to Yellowstone Park

| | |
|---|---|
| Atlanta | 3014 km |
| Bismarck | 974 km |
| Dallas | 2099 km |
| Helena | 293 km |
| Jackson | 2751 km |
| Los Angeles | 1758 km |
| Tampa | 3690 km |
| New Orleans | 2908 km |
| New York | 3468 km |
| Phoenix | 1552 km |

Use the table to find the answers.

Bismarck is how much closer to Yellowstone than

1. Los Angeles?

2. Tampa?

3. Dallas?

New York is how much farther from Yellowstone than

4. Phoenix?

5. Atlanta?

6. Jackson?

How far is it from

7. Tampa to Yellowstone to Los Angeles?

8. Los Angeles to Yellowstone to Atlanta?

9. Atlanta to Yellowstone to New York?

10. New York to Yellowstone to Dallas?

11. Dallas to Yellowstone to Phoenix?

12. Phoenix to Yellowstone to Bismarck?

13. Bismarck to Yellowstone to Atlanta?

14. Atlanta to Yellowstone to Helena?

15. Helena to Yellowstone to Jackson?

16. Jackson to Yellowstone to New Orleans?

Add across. Add down.

| + | | |
|---|---|---|
| 4234 | 1002 | 17. |
| 1164 | 223 | 18. |
| 19. | 20. | 21. |

| + | | |
|---|---|---|
| 3017 | 2434 | 22. |
| 1128 | 1243 | 23. |
| 24. | 25. | 26. |

Subtract across. Subtract down.

| − | | |
|---|---|---|
| 9006 | 2541 | 27. |
| 874 | 623 | 28. |
| 29. | 30. | 31. |

| − | | |
|---|---|---|
| 6407 | 4025 | 32. |
| 1264 | 907 | 33. |
| 34. | 35. | 36. |

## Keeping Skillful

| | | | | | |
|---|---|---|---|---|---|
| 1. $1 \times 5$ | 2. $4 \times 0$ | 3. $3 \times 3$ | 4. $6 \times 4$ | 5. $5 \times 6$ | 6. $9 \times 2$ |
| 7. $3 \times 6$ | 8. $7 \times 7$ | 9. $2 \times 8$ | 10. $0 \times 9$ | 11. $7 \times 1$ | 12. $4 \times 3$ |
| 13. $8 \times 4$ | 14. $5 \times 3$ | 15. $9 \times 6$ | 16. $7 \times 5$ | 17. $4 \times 9$ | 18. $8 \times 8$ |
| 19. $7 \times 9$ | 20. $6 \times 6$ | 21. $4 \times 5$ | 22. $9 \times 9$ | 23. $3 \times 8$ | 24. $3 \times 7$ |
| 25. $2 \times 8$ | 26. $9 \times 8$ | 27. $6 \times 1$ | 28. $4 \times 7$ | 29. $7 \times 6$ | 30. $5 \times 9$ |
| 31. $9 \times 3$ | 32. $5 \times 5$ | 33. $7 \times 8$ | 34. $8 \times 5$ | 35. $4 \times 4$ | 36. $6 \times 8$ |

# Using Addition and Subtraction

Use the table to find each answer.

1. Tony earned how much in all?

2. Together, how much did Ted and Carlos earn in June?

3. How much money did Lucia earn in all?

4. Carlos earned how much in all?

5. How much more did Mina earn in June than in July?

6. How much less did Ted earn in July than in June?

7. Amy earned how much less than Lucia in June?

**Money Earned in 2 Months**

|        | June    | July    |
|--------|---------|---------|
| Mina   | $14.75  | $13.90  |
| Ted    | $15.26  | $13.15  |
| Carlos | $17.48  | $18.36  |
| Tony   | $20.24  | $24.07  |
| Amy    | $30.58  | $31.82  |
| Lucia  | $34.56  | $35.04  |

Add or subtract. Watch the signs.

8.  $6195 + 283$

9.  $3469 + 827$

10. $4801 + 2359$

11. $2586 + 3351$

12. $1073 + 2456$

13. $5848 - 3167$

14. $3647 - 391$

15. $6150 - 4916$

16. $8049 - 3352$

17. $3182 - 2547$

18. $7187 + 1304$

19. $8963 + 982$

20. $4600 - 4352$

21. $9382 - 258$

22. $9764 - 4485$

**230** (two hundred thirty)

## Adding and Subtracting Large Numbers

Add or subtract.

1. $\begin{array}{r} 68,309 \\ + 18,205 \\ \hline \end{array}$
2. $\begin{array}{r} 93,714 \\ + \quad 658 \\ \hline \end{array}$
3. $\begin{array}{r} 45,362 \\ + \quad 7,472 \\ \hline \end{array}$
4. $\begin{array}{r} 26,573 \\ + 94,184 \\ \hline \end{array}$
5. $\begin{array}{r} 251,048 \\ + 166,243 \\ \hline \end{array}$

6. $\begin{array}{r} 32,696 \\ - \quad 547 \\ \hline \end{array}$
7. $\begin{array}{r} 63,507 \\ - 49,281 \\ \hline \end{array}$
8. $\begin{array}{r} 24,571 \\ - \quad 2,968 \\ \hline \end{array}$
9. $\begin{array}{r} 86,054 \\ - 54,381 \\ \hline \end{array}$
10. $\begin{array}{r} 952,683 \\ - 485,170 \\ \hline \end{array}$

Find each answer.

11. A passenger ship traveled 1145 kilometers on Monday, 1435 kilometers on Tuesday, and 917 kilometers on Wednesday. How far did the ship travel in all?

12. In one hour, the *Queen Elizabeth 2* traveled 52,762 meters and the *United States* traveled 55,580 meters. How much farther did the *United States* travel?

# Problem Solving: Choosing the Operation

**READ**    Ms. Bailey spent $35.68. Mr. Wuttunee
spent $22.83. Ms. Bailey spent how
much more than Mr. Wuttunee?

**DECIDE**    Subtract the amount that Mr. Wuttunee
spent from the amount that Ms. Bailey
spent. Use this number sentence.

$35.68 − $22.83 = ?

**SOLVE**

$$\begin{array}{r} \$35.68 \\ -\ 22.83 \\ \hline \$12.85 \end{array}$$

**ANSWER**    $12.85

For each problem, write a number sentence and give the answer.

1. Mr. Jamison spent $10.99 for lawn tools and $12.58 for a sprinkler. How much did he spend in all?
($10.99 + $12.58 = ?)

2. A small plant stand costs $23.55 and a large plant stand costs $47.00. How much more does the large stand cost?

3. 1128 green plants and 784 cactus plants were watered. How many plants were watered in all?

4. Ms. Janet Palumbo sold 2431 flowers in March and 1570 in April. How many more flowers did she sell in March?

5. $40.46 was spent for flower pots and $20.94 for window boxes. How much was spent in all?

6. Marta bought a terrarium for $23.70 and some plants for $8.24. The terrarium cost how much more than the plants?

7. A lawnmower and a shovel were bought for $89.04. The shovel cost $14.68. How much did the lawnmower cost?

8. Mr. Alber has 3124 plants in his greenhouse and 1056 plants in his store. How many more plants are in his greenhouse?

9. $15.75 was spent for fertilizer. $7.34 was spent for a hose. How much was spent in all?

10. Patricia had 2207 plants. She sold 1852 plants. How many plants were left?

# Problem Solving: Too Much Information

**READ**   1856 people shopped in the morning.
2437 more people shopped in the afternoon.
148 people bought books.
How many people shopped?

**DECIDE**   Add the number of people who shopped in the morning and the number of people who shopped in the afternoon. The number of people who bought books is not needed.

**SOLVE**
```
  1856
+ 2437
  4293
```

**ANSWER**   4293 people

For each problem, tell what information is needed. Do you add or subtract? Give each answer.

**Here's how**

$21.45 was spent for 3 books and $17.29 was spent for 6 records. How much more was spent for books?

*Subtract*
$ 21.45 *books*
−17.29 *records*
$  4.16

1. Mark spent $37.48, Leslie spent $11.95, and Gaynelle spent $28.26. How much did Mark and Gaynelle spend together?

2. Mrs. Hernandez had 1547 stuffed animals and 628 games. She sold 452 stuffed animals. How many stuffed animals were left?

3. Tina spent $18.56 for blouses and $19.73 for shirts. She had $5.00 left. How much did she spend?

4. Cook's Card Shop has 5642 books, 2378 cards, and 1064 magazines. How many more books than cards do they have?

5. Carmen spent $15.24 for tennis shoes and 2 pairs of socks. She spent $26.61 for a tennis racket. How much did she spend in all?

6. Eric spent $32.14 for paint, $15.91 for brushes, and $26.72 for a ladder. The paint cost how much more than the ladder?

7. Connie spent $24.39 on 45 dishes and $13.65 on glasses. How much did she spend in all?

★8. Ms. Swanson spent $40.86 for 4 meters of fabric and $2.75 for 2 meters of ribbon. She gave the clerk 2 twenty-dollar bills and 1 five-dollar bill. How much change did she receive?

## Chapter 12 Test
## Subtraction Computation, pages 216–235

Check each answer. If it is correct, write yes. If it is wrong, find the correct answer.

1.
$$\begin{array}{r} 467 \\ -\ 32 \\ \hline 435 \end{array}$$

2.
$$\begin{array}{r} 853 \\ -117 \\ \hline 744 \end{array}$$

Subtract.

3.
$$\begin{array}{r} 378 \\ -249 \end{array}$$

4.
$$\begin{array}{r} 6725 \\ -4164 \end{array}$$

5.
$$\begin{array}{r} 9142 \\ -\ 730 \end{array}$$

6.
$$\begin{array}{r} 7864 \\ -2427 \end{array}$$

7.
$$\begin{array}{r} 2536 \\ -2391 \end{array}$$

8.
$$\begin{array}{r} 1798 \\ -\ 826 \end{array}$$

9.
$$\begin{array}{r} 547 \\ -398 \end{array}$$

10.
$$\begin{array}{r} 953 \\ -367 \end{array}$$

11.
$$\begin{array}{r} 261 \\ -189 \end{array}$$

12.
$$\begin{array}{r} 3429 \\ -1532 \end{array}$$

13.
$$\begin{array}{r} 5382 \\ -1768 \end{array}$$

14.
$$\begin{array}{r} 8641 \\ -2802 \end{array}$$

15.
$$\begin{array}{r} 4374 \\ -3855 \end{array}$$

16.
$$\begin{array}{r} 400 \\ -317 \end{array}$$

17.
$$\begin{array}{r} 2009 \\ -\ 546 \end{array}$$

18.
$$\begin{array}{r} 8900 \\ -2765 \end{array}$$

19.
$$\begin{array}{r} 5067 \\ -1346 \end{array}$$

20.
$$\begin{array}{r} 3804 \\ -\ 524 \end{array}$$

Add or subtract.

21.
$$\begin{array}{r} 2837 \\ +3548 \end{array}$$

22.
$$\begin{array}{r} 6415 \\ -2709 \end{array}$$

23. Jeff raked 1636 maple leaves and 854 elm leaves. How many leaves did he rake in all?

24. Mrs. Chan had $38.65. She spent $19.29. How much did she have left?

25. Theresa had 1342 flowers. She sold 708 flowers. There were 510 yellow flowers. How many were left?

# Problems Around Us

| Distance from New Orleans | |
|---|---|
| Boston | 3647 km |
| Norfolk | 2819 km |
| Miami | 1373 km |
| Key West | 1058 km |
| Galveston | 752 km |

The distance from New Orleans to Boston is how much more than the distance to

1. Norfolk?    2. Miami?    3. Galveston?    4. Key West?

Find each answer.

5. Jane had 5 bowls with 6 apples in each bowl. How many apples did she have?

6. The Morgan family traveled 246 kilometers on Monday and 376 kilometers on Tuesday. How far did they travel?

7. There were 58 students in the library and 76 students in the gym. How many students were there in all?

8. Ms. Jackson has 8 students in a math group. Each student must do 7 problems. How many problems will the group do in all?

9. At the dog show, there were 7 spaniels, 8 setters, 6 poodles, and 5 bulldogs. How many dogs were there in all?

10. Mona made 6 bead bracelets. She used 9 beads for each bracelet. How many beads did she use?

11. Max had $9.06. He spent $3.79. How much did he have left?

12. Lin had 412 comic books. He sold 295. How many did he have left?

# Individualized Skills Maintenance

## Diagnose

**A** *pages 62–69; 188–193*

Tell what each 4 means.
Use thousands, hundreds, tens, or ones.

6724    4815    2493

**B** *pages 204–213*

347 + 586

7452 + 1394

4058 + 2796

**C** *pages 216–227*

9412 − 7605

8721 − 5643

3006 − 2153

## Practice

**A** Tell what each 7 means.
Use thousands, hundreds, tens, or ones.

1. 7136
2. 2457
3. 5749
4. 2973
5. 2762
6. 2789
7. 5072
8. 1237
9. 7843
10. 6874
11. 7036
12. 8327
13. 9785
14. 2178
15. 7215

**B**

16. 216
   + 592

17. 1395
   + 4263

18. 7819
   + 1364

19. 6274
   + 2196

20. 3842
   + 5629

21. 6543
   + 2954

22. 1389
   + 2177

23. 5837
   + 2916

24. 486
   + 318

25. 2184
   + 3952

**C**

26. 608
   − 396

27. 8165
   − 3952

28. 9273
   − 2765

29. 6500
   − 4293

30. 7085
   − 3457

31. 9215
   − 3702

32. 9635
   − 4268

33. 5070
   − 2946

34. 461
   − 278

35. 7008
   − 3495

# Unit 4 Review

Chapter 10, pages 188–202

Tell what each 6 means. Use thousands, hundreds, tens, or ones.

1. 2618
2. 2165
3. 6537
4. 8716
5. 2176
6. 6508
7. 4061
8. 3672

Give the standard form for each number.

9. two thousand four hundred seventy-three
10. five thousand eighteen
11. six hundred thousand, eight hundred forty-five

Replace the ●. Use < or >.

12. 2178 ● 2163
13. 9865 ● 8956
14. 4739 ● 4860

Give the numbers in order from least to greatest.

15. 2136   8136   9136
16. 7354   7854   7154

Chapter 11, pages 204–214

Add.

17. 3168
    +2917

18. 2165
    +4378

19. 4832
    +1395

20. 916
    +385

Chapter 12, pages 216–235

Subtract.

21. 416
    − 284

22. 6283
    − 4356

23. 8335
    − 3872

24. 5009
    − 2165

Add or subtract.

25. 9853
    − 4576

26. 2138
    + 3067

27. Alice had $34.90. She spent $18.24. How much was left?
28. Jim had $28.47. He earned $15.28. How much did he have in all?

# Unit 4 Test
## Chapters 10–12, pages 188–236

Tell what each 2 means.
Use thousands, hundreds,
tens, or ones.

1. 2168    2. 3245

3. 9012    4. 5206

5. 7524    6. 2537

Give the standard form
for each number.

7. two thousand five hundred
   eighty-six

8. nine hundred fifty-two
   thousand, four hundred
   thirteen

Replace the ●. Use < or >.

9. 8167 ● 6345

10. 5273 ● 5293

11. 6438 ● 6219

Give the numbers in order
from least to greatest.

12. 5872   4872   9872

13. 2148   2948   2748

Add.

| 14. | 518 | 15. | 3854 |
|---|---|---|---|
| | + 279 | | + 4519 |

| 16. | 1894 | 17. | 5138 |
|---|---|---|---|
| | + 2763 | | + 1475 |

Subtract.

| 18. | 735 | 19. | 4138 |
|---|---|---|---|
| | − 284 | | − 1529 |

| 20. | 9427 | 21. | 4090 |
|---|---|---|---|
| | − 3856 | | − 1563 |

Add or subtract.

| 22. | 7512 | 23. | 2158 |
|---|---|---|---|
| | − 3485 | | + 1395 |

24. Melanie drew 168 pictures
    in first grade and
    175 pictures in second
    grade. How many pictures
    did she draw in all?

25. The school library has
    9138 books. 3572 books are
    signed out. How many are
    left in the library?

# Unit 5

# Chapter 13  Division Facts: 2, 3, 4, or 5

## Meaning of Division

**A.** 12 rocks
3 rocks in each group
4 groups of rocks

You can write a **division** sentence for this picture.

$$12 \div 3 = 4$$

Divisor ⤴  ⤴ Quotient

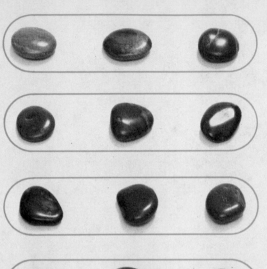

The **divisor** tells how many in each group.

The **quotient** tells how many groups.

**B.** How many in all?   14

How many in each group?   7

How many groups?   2

$14 \div 7 = 2$

Divisor ⤴  ⤴ Quotient

Copy and complete each sentence.

Think:
How many in all?
How many in each group?
How many groups?

1. $10 \div 5 = ?$

2. $8 \div 2 = ?$

3. $15 \div 3 = ?$

4. $18 \div 6 = ?$

5. $28 \div 7 = ?$

6. $20 \div 4 = ?$

7. $12 \div 6 = ?$

8. $21 \div 3 = ?$

*9. How can you use subtraction to find the quotient of $15 \div 3$?

Time Out

Use these cards.

You can use one, two, or three cards. Can you pick up exactly

1 dot? *yes*

2 dots? *no*

3 dots?

4 dots?

5 dots?

6 dots?

7 dots?

8 dots?

9 dots?

Now use these cards. Answer the questions above.

## 2 in Division

You can write a division sentence for each picture.

A. 10 in all
2 in each group
5 groups

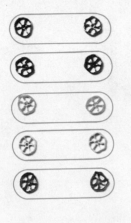

**10 ÷ 2 = 5**

B. 10 in all
5 in each group
2 groups

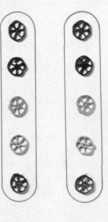

**10 ÷ 5 = 2**

Copy and complete each sentence.

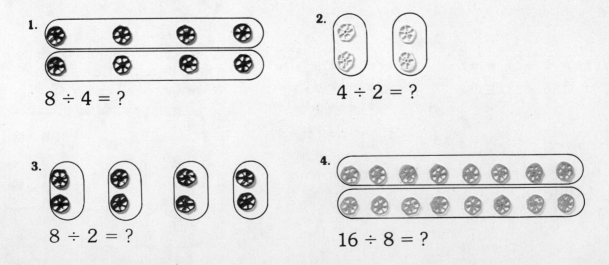

1. 8 ÷ 4 = ?

2. 4 ÷ 2 = ?

3. 8 ÷ 2 = ?

4. 16 ÷ 8 = ?

Copy and complete
each sentence.

5.

$6 \div 3 = ?$

6.

$14 \div 2 = ?$

7.

$18 \div 9 = ?$

Give each answer.

8. $2 \div 2$    9. $4 \div 2$

10. $6 \div 2$    11. $8 \div 2$

12. $10 \div 2$    13. $12 \div 2$

14. $14 \div 2$    15. $16 \div 2$

16. $18 \div 2$    17. $2 \div 1$

18. $8 \div 4$    19. $6 \div 3$

20. $12 \div 6$    21. $10 \div 5$

22. $16 \div 8$    23. $14 \div 7$

24. $8 \div 2$    25. $18 \div 9$

## Keeping Skillful

1. $\begin{array}{r} 4 \\ \times 6 \\ \hline \end{array}$    2. $\begin{array}{r} 1 \\ \times 6 \\ \hline \end{array}$    3. $\begin{array}{r} 9 \\ \times 9 \\ \hline \end{array}$

4. $\begin{array}{r} 8 \\ \times 4 \\ \hline \end{array}$    5. $\begin{array}{r} 6 \\ \times 7 \\ \hline \end{array}$    6. $\begin{array}{r} 9 \\ \times 8 \\ \hline \end{array}$

7. $\begin{array}{r} 8 \\ \times 3 \\ \hline \end{array}$    8. $\begin{array}{r} 3 \\ \times 3 \\ \hline \end{array}$    9. $\begin{array}{r} 7 \\ \times 9 \\ \hline \end{array}$

10. $\begin{array}{r} 4 \\ \times 0 \\ \hline \end{array}$    11. $\begin{array}{r} 7 \\ \times 8 \\ \hline \end{array}$    12. $\begin{array}{r} 4 \\ \times 3 \\ \hline \end{array}$

13. $\begin{array}{r} 7 \\ \times 5 \\ \hline \end{array}$    14. $\begin{array}{r} 5 \\ \times 8 \\ \hline \end{array}$    15. $\begin{array}{r} 6 \\ \times 6 \\ \hline \end{array}$

16. $\begin{array}{r} 5 \\ \times 4 \\ \hline \end{array}$    17. $\begin{array}{r} 7 \\ \times 3 \\ \hline \end{array}$    18. $\begin{array}{r} 9 \\ \times 6 \\ \hline \end{array}$

19. $\begin{array}{r} 4 \\ \times 7 \\ \hline \end{array}$    20. $\begin{array}{r} 6 \\ \times 8 \\ \hline \end{array}$    21. $\begin{array}{r} 6 \\ \times 2 \\ \hline \end{array}$

22. $\begin{array}{r} 8 \\ \times 8 \\ \hline \end{array}$    23. $\begin{array}{r} 2 \\ \times 4 \\ \hline \end{array}$    24. $\begin{array}{r} 3 \\ \times 9 \\ \hline \end{array}$

# 3 in Division

You can write a division sentence for each picture.

A. 15 in all
3 in each group
5 groups

B. 15 in all
5 in each group
3 groups

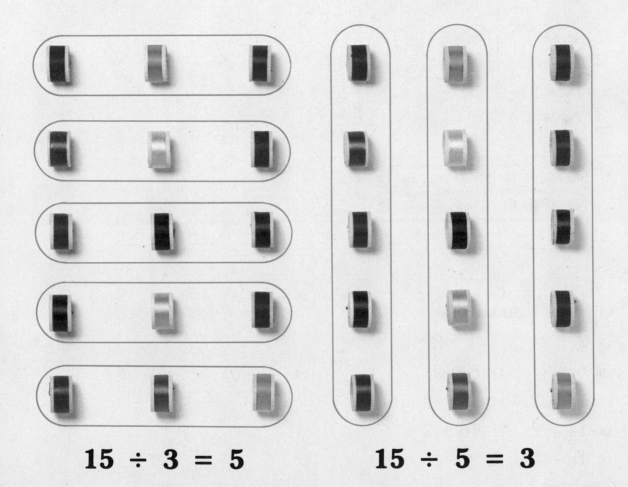

$$15 \div 3 = 5 \qquad 15 \div 5 = 3$$

Copy and complete each sentence.

1.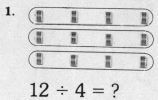

$12 \div 4 = ?$

2.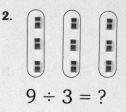

$9 \div 3 = ?$

3. $21 \div 7 = ?$

4. $24 \div 3 = ?$

5. $18 \div 3 = ?$

6. $27 \div 9 = ?$

Give each answer.

7. $3 \div 3$     8. $6 \div 3$     9. $9 \div 3$     10. $12 \div 3$     11. $15 \div 3$

12. $18 \div 3$     13. $21 \div 3$     14. $24 \div 3$     15. $27 \div 3$     16. $3 \div 1$

17. $6 \div 2$     18. $9 \div 3$     19. $12 \div 4$     20. $15 \div 5$     21. $18 \div 6$

22. $21 \div 7$     23. $24 \div 8$     24. $27 \div 9$     25. $10 \div 2$     26. $12 \div 3$

27. $18 \div 6$     28. $6 \div 2$     29. $3 \div 3$     30. $24 \div 8$     31. $18 \div 2$

32. $3 \div 1$     33. $15 \div 5$     34. $14 \div 7$     35. $21 \div 3$     36. $27 \div 3$

More practice
Set 27, page 363

# Using Division Facts

Divide. Use the code to help you answer the riddle below.

What would you do if an elephant sat in front of you at the movies?

**Here's how** $6 \div 3 = 2$  S

| CODE | | | |
|------|---|---|---|
| 1 | V | 6 | I |
| 2 | S | 7 | E |
| 3 | M | 8 | T |
| 4 | H | 9 | O |
| 5 | F | | |

**Word 1**

1. $27 \div 9$
2. $18 \div 3$
3. $14 \div 7$
4. $18 \div 9$

**Word 2**

5. $21 \div 7$
6. $27 \div 3$
7. $16 \div 8$
8. $24 \div 3$

**Word 3**

9. $18 \div 2$
10. $15 \div 3$

**Word 4**

11. $16 \div 2$
12. $8 \div 2$
13. $14 \div 2$

**Word 5**

14. $12 \div 4$
15. $27 \div 3$
16. $3 \div 3$
17. $12 \div 2$
18. $21 \div 3$

Give each answer.

**19.** 6 ÷ 2    **20.** 15 ÷ 3    **21.** 2 ÷ 1    **22.** 14 ÷ 2    **23.** 27 ÷ 3
    6 ÷ 3         15 ÷ 5         2 ÷ 2         14 ÷ 7         27 ÷ 9

**24.** 18 ÷ 3    **25.** 8 ÷ 2    **26.** 24 ÷ 3    **27.** 16 ÷ 2    **28.** 12 ÷ 3
    18 ÷ 6         8 ÷ 4         24 ÷ 8         16 ÷ 8         12 ÷ 4

**29.** 10 ÷ 2    **30.** 3 ÷ 3    **31.** 18 ÷ 2    **32.** 21 ÷ 3    **33.** 12 ÷ 2
    10 ÷ 5         3 ÷ 1         18 ÷ 9         21 ÷ 7         12 ÷ 6

**34.** There are 10 tops. 2 tops are in each box. How many boxes are there?

**35.** There are 14 balls. 7 balls are in each group. How many groups are there?

**36.** There are 21 marbles. 7 marbles are in each bag. How many bags are there?

**37.** There are 12 balloons. 3 balloons are in each group. How many groups are there?

# 4 in Division

A. You can use one picture to show one division fact.

20 in all
5 in each group
4 groups

20 in all
4 in each group
5 groups

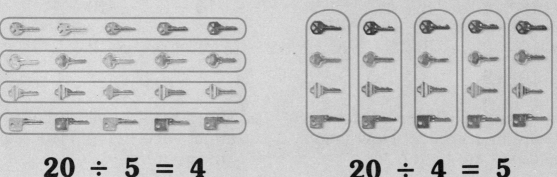

$$20 \div 5 = 4 \qquad 20 \div 4 = 5$$

B. Or you can use one picture to show two division facts.

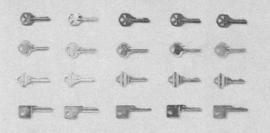

There are 20 in all.

Think of groups of 4.

$20 \div 4 = 5$

Think of groups of 5.

$20 \div 5 = 4$

Copy and complete each sentence.

1.
● ● ● ● ●
● ● ● ● ●
● ● ● ● ●
● ● ● ● ●

$24 \div 4 = ?$

$24 \div 6 = ?$

2.
● ● ● ● ● ● ● ● ●
● ● ● ● ● ● ● ● ●
● ● ● ● ● ● ● ● ●
● ● ● ● ● ● ● ● ●

$36 \div 4 = ?$

$36 \div 9 = ?$

Copy and complete each sentence.

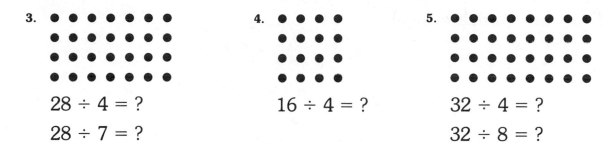

3. 28 ÷ 4 = ?
   28 ÷ 7 = ?

4. 16 ÷ 4 = ?

5. 32 ÷ 4 = ?
   32 ÷ 8 = ?

Give each answer.

| | | | | |
|---|---|---|---|---|
| 6. 4 ÷ 4 | 7. 8 ÷ 4 | 8. 12 ÷ 4 | 9. 16 ÷ 4 | 10. 20 ÷ 4 |
| 11. 24 ÷ 4 | 12. 28 ÷ 4 | 13. 32 ÷ 4 | 14. 36 ÷ 4 | 15. 4 ÷ 1 |
| 16. 8 ÷ 2 | 17. 12 ÷ 3 | 18. 16 ÷ 4 | 19. 20 ÷ 5 | 20. 24 ÷ 6 |
| 21. 28 ÷ 7 | 22. 32 ÷ 8 | 23. 36 ÷ 9 | 24. 27 ÷ 3 | 25. 10 ÷ 2 |
| 26. 36 ÷ 4 | 27. 18 ÷ 2 | 28. 12 ÷ 4 | 29. 21 ÷ 7 | 30. 24 ÷ 6 |
| 31. 4 ÷ 4 | 32. 15 ÷ 3 | 33. 32 ÷ 4 | 34. 20 ÷ 4 | 35. 14 ÷ 7 |

36. There are 20 people. 5 people are at each table. How many tables are there?

37. There are 32 paper plates. 8 paper plates are in each package. How many packages are there?

38. There are 16 sandwiches. 4 sandwiches are in each bag. How many bags are there?

39. There are 28 apples. 4 apples are in each box. How many boxes are there?

# 5 in Division

There are 30 daisies in all.

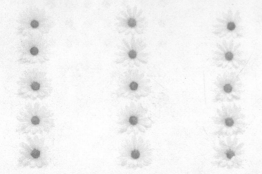

**A.** How many groups of 5?

$$30 \div 5 = 6$$

**B.** How many groups of 6?

$$30 \div 6 = 5$$

**C.** You can write the division in another way.

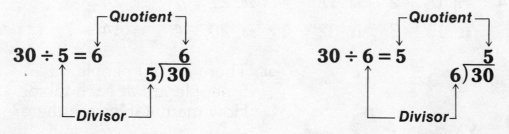

Copy and complete each sentence.

1.
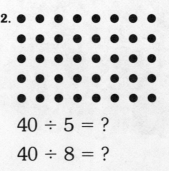

$$35 \div 5 = ?$$

$$35 \div 7 = ?$$

2.

$$40 \div 5 = ?$$

$$40 \div 8 = ?$$

Copy and complete each sentence.

**3.**
● ● ● ● ●
● ● ● ● ●
● ● ● ● ●
● ● ● ● ●
● ● ● ● ●

$25 \div 5 = ?$

**4.**
● ● ● ● ● ● ● ● ●
● ● ● ● ● ● ● ● ●
● ● ● ● ● ● ● ● ●
● ● ● ● ● ● ● ● ●
● ● ● ● ● ● ● ● ●

$45 \div 5 = ?$

$45 \div 9 = ?$

Give each answer.

5. $5 \div 5$  6. $10 \div 5$  7. $15 \div 5$  8. $20 \div 5$  9. $25 \div 5$

10. $30 \div 5$  11. $35 \div 5$  12. $40 \div 5$  13. $45 \div 5$  14. $5 \div 1$

15. $10 \div 2$  16. $15 \div 3$  17. $20 \div 4$  18. $25 \div 5$  19. $30 \div 6$

20. $35 \div 7$  21. $40 \div 8$  22. $45 \div 9$  23. $30 \div 5$  24. $40 \div 5$

25. $15 \div 5$  26. $35 \div 7$  27. $5 \div 1$  28. $45 \div 9$  29. $25 \div 5$

30. $6\overline{)30}$  31. $6\overline{)12}$  32. $4\overline{)24}$  33. $3\overline{)15}$  34. $3\overline{)12}$

35. $8\overline{)16}$  36. $5\overline{)5}$  37. $6\overline{)18}$  38. $7\overline{)28}$  39. $5\overline{)35}$

40. $8\overline{)40}$  41. $9\overline{)27}$  42. $7\overline{)21}$  43. $5\overline{)10}$  44. $1\overline{)1}$

45. $2\overline{)10}$  46. $9\overline{)36}$  47. $5\overline{)45}$  48. $2\overline{)18}$  49. $5\overline{)20}$

**50.** There are 30 orange flowers. 5 are in each row. How many rows are there?

**51.** There are 40 yellow flowers. 5 are in each row. How many rows are there?

**52.** There are 45 red flowers. 9 are in each row. How many rows are there?

**53.** There are 35 blue flowers. 7 are in each row. How many rows are there?

More practice,
Set 28, page 363

(two hundred fifty-three) **253**

# Using Division Facts

How many can you buy if you have

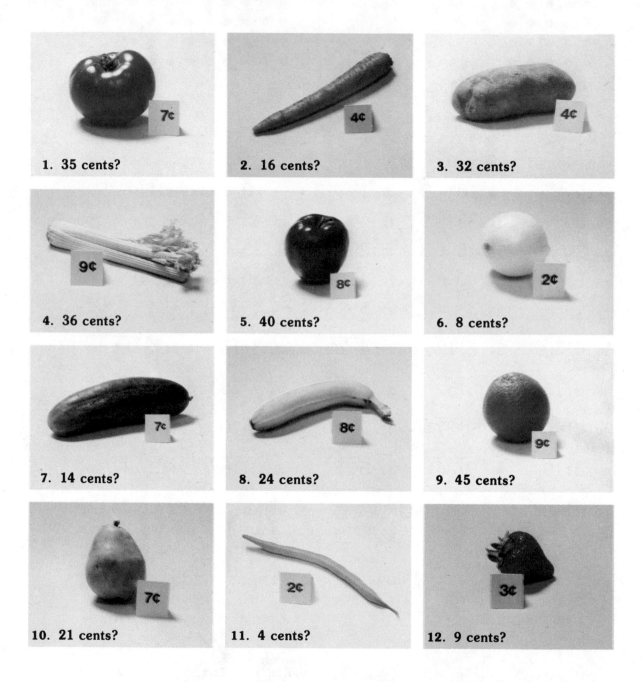

1. 35 cents?

2. 16 cents?

3. 32 cents?

4. 36 cents?

5. 40 cents?

6. 8 cents?

7. 14 cents?

8. 24 cents?

9. 45 cents?

10. 21 cents?

11. 4 cents?

12. 9 cents?

## Use the rule.
## Give each quotient.

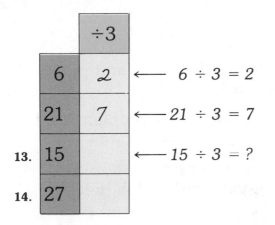

| | ÷3 | |
|---|---|---|
| 6 | 2 | ← 6 ÷ 3 = 2 |
| 21 | 7 | ← 21 ÷ 3 = 7 |
| **13.** 15 | | ← 15 ÷ 3 = ? |
| **14.** 27 | | |

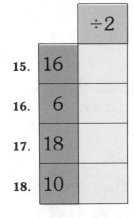

| | ÷2 |
|---|---|
| **15.** 16 | |
| **16.** 6 | |
| **17.** 18 | |
| **18.** 10 | |

| | ÷5 |
|---|---|
| **19.** 15 | |
| **20.** 25 | |
| **21.** 20 | |
| **22.** 40 | |

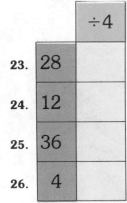

| | ÷4 |
|---|---|
| **23.** 28 | |
| **24.** 12 | |
| **25.** 36 | |
| **26.** 4 | |

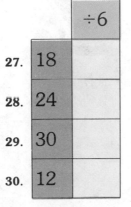

| | ÷6 |
|---|---|
| **27.** 18 | |
| **28.** 24 | |
| **29.** 30 | |
| **30.** 12 | |

**Zero in Division**

## Give each answer.

1. 0 ÷ 2    2. 0 ÷ 4    3. 0 ÷ 1
4. 0 ÷ 7    5. 0 ÷ 8    6. 0 ÷ 3
7. 0 ÷ 6    8. 0 ÷ 9    9. 0 ÷ 25

(two hundred fifty-five) **255**

# Lab Activity

## Division Match
## A Game for 2 Players

Make a set of problem cards and answer cards.

### Problem Cards

Make a card like this for each problem.

$4 \div 2$    $8 \div 2$

$12 \div 2$    $16 \div 2$

$18 \div 9$    $9 \div 3$

$21 \div 3$    $27 \div 9$

$16 \div 4$    $20 \div 4$

$28 \div 4$    $36 \div 4$

$25 \div 5$    $30 \div 5$

$40 \div 5$    $45 \div 5$

### Answer Cards

Use a different color. Make a card like this for each of these numbers.

4

2   4   6   8

2   4   6   8

3   5   7   9

3   5   7   9

### Rules

1. Mix up the cards and put them face down.

2. Turn over one problem card and one answer card.

3. If the problem card and answer card match, keep them.

4. If they do not match, put them face down again.

5. Take turns using steps 2, 3, and 4.

6. Keep playing until all the cards have been matched.

7. The winner is the player with the most cards.

# Chapter 13 Test
## Division Facts, pages 242–256

Copy and complete
each sentence.

1.

$8 \div 2 = ?$

2.

$35 \div 5 = ?$

3.
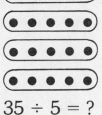

$18 \div 3 = ?$

4.
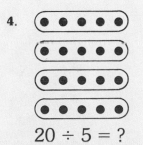

$20 \div 5 = ?$

Give each answer.

5. $10 \div 2$  6. $18 \div 9$

7. $14 \div 7$  8. $16 \div 2$

9. $21 \div 3$  10. $18 \div 6$

11. $27 \div 3$  12. $24 \div 8$

13. $16 \div 4$  14. $28 \div 4$

15. $24 \div 6$  16. $36 \div 9$

17. $45 \div 5$  18. $30 \div 6$

19. $5 \div 1$  20. $40 \div 5$

21. $8 \overline{)32}$  22. $5 \overline{)15}$

23. $3 \overline{)3}$  24. $5 \overline{)25}$

25. $2 \overline{)4}$  26. $3 \overline{)9}$

27. $7 \overline{)35}$  28. $2 \overline{)12}$

29. $3 \overline{)12}$  30. $9 \overline{)45}$

# Chapter 14 Division Facts: 6, 7, 8, or 9

## 6 in Division

There are 42 puppets.

A. How many groups of 6?

$$42 \div 6 = 7 \text{ or } 6\overline{)42}^{\,7}$$

B. How many groups of 7?

$$42 \div 7 = 6 \text{ or } 7\overline{)42}^{\,6}$$

C. Deana drew a picture to help her find the quotient of 54 ÷ 9.

She put 9 marks in a row.

She drew 54 marks in all.

Then she counted the rows of 9 marks.

$$54 \div 9 = 6$$

• **Discuss**  How can you use the picture to find the quotient of 54 ÷ 6?

Copy and complete each sentence.

1. ▲ ▲ ▲ ▲ ▲ ▲ ▲ ▲
   ▲ ▲ ▲ ▲ ▲ ▲ ▲ ▲
   ▲ ▲ ▲ ▲ ▲ ▲ ▲ ▲
   ▲ ▲ ▲ ▲ ▲ ▲ ▲ ▲
   ▲ ▲ ▲ ▲ ▲ ▲ ▲ ▲
   ▲ ▲ ▲ ▲ ▲ ▲ ▲ ▲

   $48 \div 6 = ?$
   $48 \div 8 = ?$

2. ▲ ▲ ▲ ▲ ▲ ▲
   ▲ ▲ ▲ ▲ ▲ ▲
   ▲ ▲ ▲ ▲ ▲ ▲
   ▲ ▲ ▲ ▲ ▲ ▲
   ▲ ▲ ▲ ▲ ▲ ▲
   ▲ ▲ ▲ ▲ ▲ ▲

   $36 \div 6 = ?$

Give each answer.

3. $6 \div 6$  4. $12 \div 6$  5. $18 \div 6$  6. $24 \div 6$  7. $30 \div 6$

8. $36 \div 6$  9. $42 \div 6$  10. $48 \div 6$  11. $54 \div 6$  12. $6 \div 1$

13. $12 \div 2$  14. $18 \div 3$  15. $24 \div 4$  16. $30 \div 5$  17. $36 \div 6$

18. $42 \div 7$  19. $48 \div 8$  20. $54 \div 9$  21. $12 \div 6$  22. $24 \div 4$

23. $54 \div 9$  24. $42 \div 6$  25. $30 \div 5$  26. $48 \div 6$  27. $36 \div 6$

28. $6\overline{)18}$  29. $8\overline{)48}$  30. $6\overline{)54}$  31. $9\overline{)36}$  32. $2\overline{)12}$

33. $6\overline{)24}$  34. $1\overline{)6}$  35. $3\overline{)12}$  36. $7\overline{)42}$  37. $3\overline{)18}$

38. $3\overline{)27}$  39. $8\overline{)32}$  40. $4\overline{)20}$  41. $6\overline{)6}$  42. $6\overline{)30}$

43. There were 48 seats in the puppet theater. 6 seats were in each row. How many rows were there?

44. There were 42 puppets. Each group had 7 puppets. How many groups were there?

More practice
Set 29, page 363

# 7 in Division

There are 56 beads.

**A.** How many groups of 7?

$$56 \div 7 = 8 \text{ or } 7\overline{)56}^{\,8}$$

**B.** How many groups of 8?

$$56 \div 8 = 7 \text{ or } 8\overline{)56}^{\,7}$$

Copy and complete each sentence.

1.

$$63 \div 7 = ?$$
$$63 \div 9 = ?$$

2.

$$49 \div 7 = ?$$

Give each answer.

3. $7 \div 7$     4. $14 \div 7$     5. $21 \div 7$

6. $28 \div 7$     7. $35 \div 7$     8. $42 \div 7$

9. $49 \div 7$     10. $56 \div 7$     11. $63 \div 7$

12. $7 \div 1$     13. $14 \div 2$     14. $21 \div 3$

15. $28 \div 4$     16. $35 \div 5$     17. $42 \div 6$

18. $49 \div 7$     19. $56 \div 8$     20. $63 \div 9$

21. $35 \div 7$     22. $49 \div 7$     23. $14 \div 7$

24. $63 \div 9$     25. $56 \div 7$     26. $21 \div 3$

27. $5\overline{)40}$     28. $6\overline{)48}$     29. $7\overline{)49}$

30. $4\overline{)28}$     31. $3\overline{)9}$     32. $5\overline{)35}$

33. $8\overline{)24}$     34. $7\overline{)63}$     35. $6\overline{)36}$

36. $7\overline{)7}$     37. $6\overline{)18}$     38. $7\overline{)42}$

39. $8\overline{)56}$     40. $5\overline{)10}$     41. $9\overline{)54}$

42. There were 49 beads. 7 beads were on each necklace. How many necklaces were there?

43. There were 35 beads. 7 beads were on each bracelet. How many bracelets were there?

44. There were 42 beads. 6 beads were on each belt. How many belts were there?

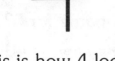

# Using Division Facts

For each exercise, give a number sentence.
Then write yes or no.

Is this a name for 5?

| **Here's how** | $40 \div 8$ | $40 \div 8 = 5$ | *yes* |
|---|---|---|---|
| | $42 \div 7$ | $42 \div 7 = 6$ | *no* |
| | $10 \div 2$ | $10 \div 2 = 5$ | *yes* |
| | $35 \div 7$ | $35 \div 7 = 5$ | *yes* |
| | $28 \div 7$ | $28 \div 7 = 4$ | *no* |

Is this a name for 6?

1. $54 \div 9$
2. $25 \div 5$
3. $49 \div 7$
4. $48 \div 8$
5. $18 \div 3$

Is this a name for 4?

6. $21 \div 7$
7. $30 \div 6$
8. $12 \div 3$
9. $45 \div 9$
10. $32 \div 8$

Is this a name for 8?

11. $16 \div 2$
12. $40 \div 5$
13. $24 \div 8$
14. $8 \div 1$
15. $21 \div 3$

Is this a name for 3?

16. $27 \div 9$
17. $16 \div 4$
18. $4 \div 2$
19. $10 \div 5$
20. $15 \div 5$

Is this a name for 7?

21. $48 \div 6$
22. $63 \div 9$
23. $35 \div 5$
24. $56 \div 8$
25. $36 \div 6$

Is this a name for 9?

26. $32 \div 4$
27. $63 \div 7$
28. $42 \div 6$
29. $54 \div 6$
30. $28 \div 4$

Give each quotient.

| | ÷6 |
|---|---|
| **31.** 12 | |
| **32.** 30 | |
| **33.** 54 | |
| **34.** 42 | |
| **35.** 24 | |
| **36.** 48 | |
| **37.** 36 | |

| | ÷4 |
|---|---|
| **38.** 16 | |
| **39.** 12 | |
| **40.** 24 | |
| **41.** 32 | |
| **42.** 28 | |
| **43.** 36 | |
| **44.** 20 | |

| | ÷5 |
|---|---|
| **45.** 35 | |
| **46.** 10 | |
| **47.** 25 | |
| **48.** 45 | |
| **49.** 30 | |
| **50.** 15 | |
| **51.** 40 | |

| | ÷8 |
|---|---|
| **52.** 48 | |
| **53.** 8 | |
| **54.** 56 | |
| **55.** 24 | |
| **56.** 40 | |
| **57.** 32 | |
| **58.** 16 | |

| | ÷7 |
|---|---|
| **59.** 63 | |
| **60.** 28 | |
| **61.** 49 | |
| **62.** 35 | |
| **63.** 42 | |
| **64.** 7 | |
| **65.** 56 | |

| | ÷9 |
|---|---|
| **66.** 54 | |
| **67.** 45 | |
| **68.** 18 | |
| **69.** 36 | |
| **70.** 9 | |
| **71.** 27 | |
| **72.** 63 | |

# 8 and 9 in Division

There are 72 coins.

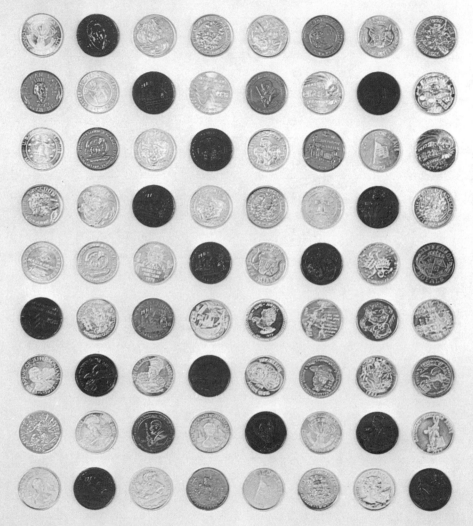

**A.** How many groups of 8?

$$72 \div 8 = 9 \text{ or } 8\overline{)72}^{\,9}$$

**B.** How many groups of 9?

$$72 \div 9 = 8 \text{ or } 9\overline{)72}^{\,8}$$

Copy and complete each sentence.

1.

$64 \div 8 = ?$

2.

$81 \div 9 = ?$

Give each answer.

3. $8 \div 8$    4. $16 \div 8$    5. $24 \div 8$    6. $32 \div 8$    7. $40 \div 8$

8. $48 \div 8$    9. $56 \div 8$    10. $64 \div 8$    11. $72 \div 8$    12. $8 \div 1$

13. $16 \div 2$    14. $24 \div 3$    15. $32 \div 4$    16. $40 \div 5$    17. $48 \div 6$

18. $56 \div 7$    19. $64 \div 8$    20. $72 \div 9$    21. $24 \div 8$    22. $36 \div 6$

23. $9\overline{)9}$    24. $9\overline{)18}$    25. $9\overline{)27}$    26. $9\overline{)36}$    27. $9\overline{)45}$

28. $9\overline{)54}$    29. $9\overline{)63}$    30. $9\overline{)72}$    31. $9\overline{)81}$    32. $1\overline{)9}$

33. $2\overline{)18}$    34. $3\overline{)27}$    35. $4\overline{)36}$    36. $5\overline{)45}$    37. $6\overline{)54}$

38. $7\overline{)63}$    39. $8\overline{)72}$    40. $9\overline{)81}$    41. $3\overline{)27}$    42. $9\overline{)18}$

For each exercise, give how many kinds.

43. 64 buttons
8 of each kind

45. 45 shells
9 of each kind

47. 56 post cards
8 of each kind

44. 63 coins
7 of each kind

46. 72 stamps
8 of each kind

**More practice
Set 30, page 363**

# Using Division Facts

For each exercise, tell how many boxes
Hakim used.

**1.** He had 54. He
put 6 in each box.

**2.** He had 14. He
put 7 in each box.

**3.** He had 72. He
put 8 in each box.

**4.** He had 35. He
put 5 in each box.

**5.** He had 63. He
put 9 in each box.

**6.** He had 40. He
put 5 in each box.

**7.** He had 64. He
put 8 in each box.

**8.** He had 49. He
put 7 in each box.

**9.** He had 20. He
put 5 in each box.

**10.** He had 56. He
put 7 in each box.

**11.** He had 48. He
put 6 in each box.

**12.** He had 42. He
put 6 in each box.

Copy and complete each exercise.
Then write yes or no.

Is this a name for 5?

   **Here's how**   $8\overline{)40}$   $8\overline{)40}^{\,5}$   *yes*

                   $6\overline{)36}$   $6\overline{)36}^{\,6}$   *no*

                   $3\overline{)15}$   $3\overline{)15}^{\,5}$   *yes*

                   $5\overline{)20}$   $5\overline{)20}^{\,4}$   *no*

| Is this a name for 6? | Is this a name for 9? | Is this a name for 3? |
|---|---|---|
| 13. $5\overline{)30}$ | 17. $3\overline{)24}$ | 21. $9\overline{)27}$ |
| 14. $2\overline{)10}$ | 18. $8\overline{)72}$ | 22. $9\overline{)18}$ |
| 15. $9\overline{)54}$ | 19. $7\overline{)63}$ | 23. $8\overline{)24}$ |
| 16. $9\overline{)36}$ | 20. $1\overline{)8}$ | 24. $6\overline{)18}$ |

| Is this a name for 8? | Is this a name for 2? | Is this a name for 7? |
|---|---|---|
| 25. $3\overline{)27}$ | 29. $2\overline{)2}$ | 33. $6\overline{)42}$ |
| 26. $7\overline{)56}$ | 30. $4\overline{)12}$ | 34. $2\overline{)16}$ |
| 27. $9\overline{)81}$ | 31. $6\overline{)12}$ | 35. $4\overline{)24}$ |
| 28. $6\overline{)48}$ | 32. $7\overline{)21}$ | 36. $3\overline{)21}$ |

# Using Division Facts

Divide across. Divide down.

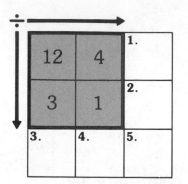

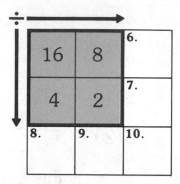

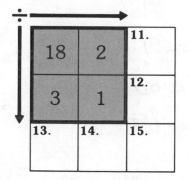

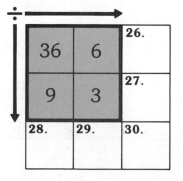

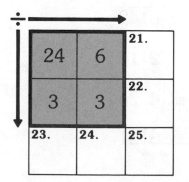

For each exercise, give how many groups.

31. 15 cans
5 cans in each group

32. 18 pins
9 pins in each group

33. 12 balls
3 balls in each group

34. 20 rulers
5 rulers in each group

35. 21 erasers
7 erasers in each group

36. 27 magazines
3 magazines in each group

37. 32 brushes
4 brushes in each group

38. 45 pages
5 pages in each group

39. 72 clips
8 clips in each group

40. 48 pencils
6 pencils in each group

41. 42 workbooks
7 workbooks in each group

42. 54 crayons
6 crayons in each group

43. 56 books
8 books in each group

## Keeping Skillful

1. $\begin{array}{r} 9 \\ \times 4 \\ \hline \end{array}$  2. $\begin{array}{r} 4 \\ \times 4 \\ \hline \end{array}$  3. $\begin{array}{r} 6 \\ \times 7 \\ \hline \end{array}$

4. $\begin{array}{r} 8 \\ \times 8 \\ \hline \end{array}$  5. $\begin{array}{r} 7 \\ \times 5 \\ \hline \end{array}$  6. $\begin{array}{r} 5 \\ \times 8 \\ \hline \end{array}$

7. $\begin{array}{r} 6 \\ \times 2 \\ \hline \end{array}$  8. $\begin{array}{r} 4 \\ \times 1 \\ \hline \end{array}$  9. $\begin{array}{r} 9 \\ \times 8 \\ \hline \end{array}$

10. $\begin{array}{r} 5 \\ \times 4 \\ \hline \end{array}$  11. $\begin{array}{r} 7 \\ \times 7 \\ \hline \end{array}$  12. $\begin{array}{r} 4 \\ \times 6 \\ \hline \end{array}$

13. $\begin{array}{r} 9 \\ \times 9 \\ \hline \end{array}$  14. $\begin{array}{r} 0 \\ \times 9 \\ \hline \end{array}$  15. $\begin{array}{r} 2 \\ \times 8 \\ \hline \end{array}$

16. $\begin{array}{r} 3 \\ \times 4 \\ \hline \end{array}$  17. $\begin{array}{r} 8 \\ \times 3 \\ \hline \end{array}$  18. $\begin{array}{r} 6 \\ \times 5 \\ \hline \end{array}$

19. $\begin{array}{r} 7 \\ \times 8 \\ \hline \end{array}$  20. $\begin{array}{r} 3 \\ \times 7 \\ \hline \end{array}$  21. $\begin{array}{r} 8 \\ \times 6 \\ \hline \end{array}$

22. $\begin{array}{r} 9 \\ \times 7 \\ \hline \end{array}$  23. $\begin{array}{r} 7 \\ \times 6 \\ \hline \end{array}$  24. $\begin{array}{r} 4 \\ \times 8 \\ \hline \end{array}$

# Families of Facts

A. You can use one picture to show four related multiplication and division facts.

Think of 7 groups of 4.

$7 \times 4 = 28$

Separate 28 into groups of 4.

$28 \div 4 = 7$

Think of 4 groups of 7.

$4 \times 7 = 28$

Separate 28 into groups of 7.

$28 \div 7 = 4$

$7 \times 4 = 28$, $28 \div 4 = 7$, $4 \times 7 = 28$, and $28 \div 7 = 4$ are a family of facts.

B. These number sentences also are a family of facts.

$3 \times 3 = 9 \quad 9 \div 3 = 3$

Copy and complete each fact. Circle the
one that does not belong to the family.

**Here's how**

| | |
|---|---|
| $35 \div 5$ | $35 \div 5 = 7$ |
| $5 \times 7$ | $5 \times 7 = 35$ |
| $35 \div 7$ | $35 \div 7 = 5$ |
| $40 \div 8$ | $\boxed{40 \div 8 = 5}$ |
| $7 \times 5$ | $7 \times 5 = 35$ |

| 1. $5 \times 2$ | 2. $72 \div 9$ | 3. $24 \div 8$ | 4. $28 \div 7$ | 5. $6 \times 8$ |
|---|---|---|---|---|
| $5 \times 4$ | $9 \times 8$ | $6 \times 4$ | $9 \times 7$ | $48 \div 8$ |
| $10 \div 2$ | $54 \div 9$ | $24 \div 6$ | $63 \div 7$ | $7 \times 6$ |
| $10 \div 5$ | $72 \div 8$ | $24 \div 4$ | $63 \div 9$ | $48 \div 6$ |
| $2 \times 5$ | $8 \times 9$ | $4 \times 6$ | $7 \times 9$ | $8 \times 6$ |

| 6. $21 \div 7$ | 7. $56 \div 7$ | 8. $8 \times 4$ | 9. $45 \div 9$ | 10. $9 \div 9$ |
|---|---|---|---|---|
| $3 \times 7$ | $56 \div 8$ | $32 \div 4$ | $40 \div 5$ | $9 \div 1$ |
| $21 \div 3$ | $64 \div 8$ | $32 \div 8$ | $9 \times 5$ | $1 \times 9$ |
| $7 \times 3$ | $8 \times 7$ | $8 \times 3$ | $45 \div 5$ | $12 \div 3$ |
| $4 \times 3$ | $7 \times 8$ | $4 \times 8$ | $5 \times 9$ | $9 \times 1$ |

| 11. $9 \times 9$ | 12. $36 \div 6$ | 13. $3 \times 3$ | 14. $49 \div 7$ | 15. $16 \div 2$ |
|---|---|---|---|---|
| $9 \times 2$ | $6 \times 6$ | $9 \div 3$ | $42 \div 7$ | $16 \div 4$ |
| $81 \div 9$ | $36 \div 9$ | $3 \times 2$ | $7 \times 7$ | $4 \times 4$ |

# Using Multiplication and Division Facts

Multiply or divide. Use the code to help you answer the questions.

What kind of animals are hidden in the picture? How many of each kind are hidden?

| CODE | | | |
|---|---|---|---|
| 2 | O | 24 | S |
| 3 | G | 25 | N |
| 4 | W | 28 | T |
| 6 | F | 35 | H |
| 7 | I | 36 | R |
| 9 | D | 40 | E |
| 12 | B | 56 | U |

**Word 1**

1. $18 \div 9$
2. $5 \times 5$
3. $8 \times 5$

**Word 2**

4. $3 \times 4$
5. $63 \div 9$
6. $9 \times 4$
7. $81 \div 9$

**Word 3**

8. $2 \times 3$
9. $6 \div 3$
10. $8 \times 7$
11. $6 \times 6$

**Word 4**

12. $54 \div 6$
13. $10 \div 5$
14. $27 \div 9$
15. $8 \times 3$

**Word 5**

16. $4 \times 7$
17. $32 \div 8$
18. $12 \div 6$

**Word 6**

19. $48 \div 8$
20. $42 \div 6$
21. $6 \times 4$
22. $7 \times 5$

For each exercise, give a number sentence.
Then write yes or no.

Is this a name for 9?

**Here's how**

| | | |
|---|---|---|
| $4 \times 2$ | $4 \times 2 = 8$ | *no* |
| $27 \div 3$ | $27 \div 3 = 9$ | *yes* |
| $56 \div 8$ | $56 \div 8 = 7$ | *no* |
| $3 \times 3$ | $3 \times 3 = 9$ | *yes* |
| $72 \div 8$ | $72 \div 8 = 9$ | *yes* |

Is this a name
for 8?

23. $5 \times 2$

24. $64 \div 8$

25. $14 \div 2$

26. $48 \div 6$

27. $2 \times 4$

Is this a name
for 49?

28. $16 \div 2$

29. $9 \times 5$

30. $7 \times 7$

31. $4 \div 2$

32. $6 \times 7$

Is this a name
for 5?

33. $5 \times 1$

34. $45 \div 9$

35. $3 \times 2$

36. $40 \div 8$

37. $30 \div 6$

Is this a name
for 20?

38. $7 \times 3$

39. $5 \times 4$

40. $5 \div 1$

41. $9 \div 3$

42. $4 \times 5$

Is this a name
for 6?

43. $54 \div 9$

44. $2 \times 2$

45. $36 \div 6$

46. $18 \div 3$

47. $72 \div 9$

Is this a name
for 63?

48. $2 \times 7$

49. $4 \times 4$

50. $24 \div 8$

51. $9 \times 7$

52. $8 \times 9$

# Using Multiplication and Division Facts

Go around each track.
Use the rule in the flag to find each answer.

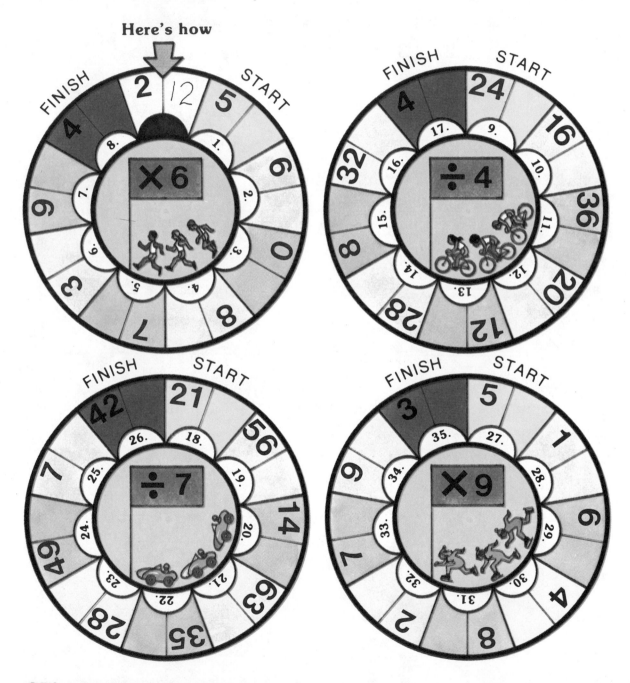

**Here's how**

274 (two hundred seventy-four)

Multiply.

36.  $\begin{array}{r} 3 \\ \times 9 \end{array}$   37.  $\begin{array}{r} 4 \\ \times 7 \end{array}$   38.  $\begin{array}{r} 8 \\ \times 9 \end{array}$

39.  $\begin{array}{r} 2 \\ \times 8 \end{array}$   40.  $\begin{array}{r} 5 \\ \times 6 \end{array}$   41.  $\begin{array}{r} 3 \\ \times 6 \end{array}$

42.  $\begin{array}{r} 5 \\ \times 1 \end{array}$   43.  $\begin{array}{r} 8 \\ \times 8 \end{array}$   44.  $\begin{array}{r} 7 \\ \times 5 \end{array}$

45.  $\begin{array}{r} 8 \\ \times 5 \end{array}$   46.  $\begin{array}{r} 8 \\ \times 4 \end{array}$   47.  $\begin{array}{r} 0 \\ \times 4 \end{array}$

48.  $\begin{array}{r} 8 \\ \times 7 \end{array}$   49.  $\begin{array}{r} 7 \\ \times 3 \end{array}$   50.  $\begin{array}{r} 5 \\ \times 3 \end{array}$

Divide.

51. $9\overline{)36}$   52. $9\overline{)81}$   53. $5\overline{)35}$

54. $8\overline{)72}$   55. $5\overline{)40}$   56. $6\overline{)24}$

57. $5\overline{)45}$   58. $8\overline{)64}$   59. $6\overline{)18}$

60. $6\overline{)48}$   61. $5\overline{)20}$   62. $9\overline{)63}$

63. $3\overline{)21}$   64. $8\overline{)56}$   65. $5\overline{)30}$

## Keeping Skillful

Add.

1. $276 + 417$
2. $4675 + 248$
3. $315 + 352$
4. $34 + 694$
5. $2249 + 6268$

Subtract.

6. $9385 - 4652$
7. $967 - 43$
8. $722 - 354$
9. $6598 - 729$
10. $374 - 289$

Add or subtract.

11. $1763 + 2835$
12. $4880 - 4286$
13. $30 + 87$
14. $829 - 474$
15. $6389 + 2365$
16. $193 - 156$
17. $147 + 137$
18. $7209 - 1726$

# Problem Solving:
# Choosing the Operation

**READ**  A. There are 63 cars. 9 cars are on each train. How many trains are there?

**DECIDE**  Divide the total number of cars by the number of cars on each train. Use this number sentence.

$63 \div 9 = ?$

**SOLVE**

$$9\overline{)63} \quad 7$$

**ANSWER**  7 trains

**READ**  B. There are 8 cars. 9 people are in each car. How many people are there in all?

**DECIDE**  Multiply the number of cars by the number of people in each car. Use this number sentence.

$8 \times 9 = ?$

**SOLVE**

$$\begin{array}{r} 8 \\ \times\ 9 \\ \hline 72 \end{array}$$

**ANSWER**  72 people

For each problem, write a number sentence.
Give the answer.

1. There were 3 adults and
7 children in the group.
How many people were there
in all?
(3 + 7 = ?)

2. There are 8 tickets in a
book. 5 have been used.
How many are left?
(8 − 5 = ?)

3. A train has 5 cars. Each
car has 8 windows. How many
windows are there in all?

4. There are 24 students in a
car. 3 students sit on each
bench. How many benches
are there?

5. The dining car has 7 tables.
2 tables are empty. How
many are not empty?

6. Each trip is 8 kilometers.
The train traveled a distance
of 40 kilometers. How many
trips did the train make?

7. Each car has 4 cabins. How
many cabins are there in
3 cars?

8. Each car has 32 seats.
There are 4 seats in each
row. How many rows are
there?

9. 5 people are in each car.
How many people are in
9 cars?

10. There are 36 cars at the
station. 9 cars are on
each train. How many
trains are there?

11. A train makes 6 stops
during the day and 6 stops
during the night. How many
stops does it make in all?

12. There are 7 tables in the
dining car. Each table has
4 seats. How many seats
are there in all?

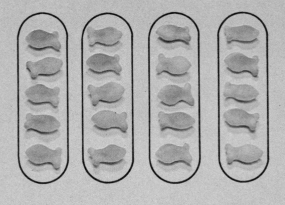

## Side Trip

**Missing Factors**

What number times
5 equals 20?
You need to find the
*missing factor.*

$$? \times 5 = 20$$

Factor  Factor  Product

Think of putting 20 crackers
in groups with 5 in
each group.

$$20 \div 5 = 4$$

There are 4 groups.

4 is the missing factor.

$$4 \times 5 = 20$$

Give each missing factor.

1. $5 \times ? = 15$    2. $? \times 4 = 12$    3. $2 \times ? = 12$    4. $? \times 3 = 21$

5. $? \times 6 = 36$    6. $8 \times ? = 40$    7. $? \times 8 = 48$    8. $8 \times ? = 56$

9. $8 \times ? = 64$    10. $9 \times ? = 81$    11. $? \times 6 = 42$    12. $? \times 9 = 36$

13. $8 \times ? = 8$    14. $? \times 4 = 24$    15. $? \times 6 = 54$    16. $3 \times ? = 9$

17. $? \times 7 = 7$    18. $4 \times ? = 28$    19. $? \times 5 = 35$    20. $? \times 6 = 30$

21. $9 \times ? = 45$    22. $8 \times ? = 16$    23. $? \times 7 = 49$    24. $3 \times ? = 27$

## Chapter 14 Test
## Division Facts, pages 258–278

Divide.

1. $6\overline{)36}$  2. $8\overline{)48}$

3. $6\overline{)54}$  4. $7\overline{)42}$

5. $7\overline{)7}$  6. $7\overline{)49}$

7. $9\overline{)63}$  8. $4\overline{)28}$

9. $5\overline{)40}$  10. $8\overline{)72}$

11. $8\overline{)64}$  12. $4\overline{)32}$

13. $9\overline{)81}$  14. $9\overline{)45}$

15. $2\overline{)18}$  16. $1\overline{)9}$

Multiply or divide.

17. $7 \times 4$    18. $27 \div 9$

19. $35 \div 7$    20. $9 \times 8$

21. $16 \div 4$    22. $25 \div 5$

23. $6 \times 6$    24. $30 \div 6$

25. $3 \times 6$    26. $4 \times 3$

Copy and complete each fact.
Circle the one that does not
belong to the family.

27. $6 \times 7$

    $7 \times 6$

    $42 \div 7$

    $6 \times 8$

    $42 \div 6$

28. $24 \div 8$

    $8 \times 3$

    $24 \div 6$

    $3 \times 8$

    $24 \div 3$

Give each answer.

29. There were 48 tops. 6 tops
were in each box. How many
boxes were there?

30. There were 4 boxes of dolls.
4 dolls were in each box.
How many dolls were there
in all?

# Chapter 15   Fractions and Decimals

## Equal Parts

2 equal parts
Halves

3 equal parts
Thirds

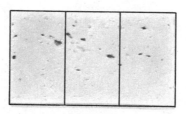

4 equal parts
Fourths

5 equal parts
Fifths

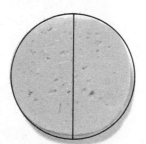

6 equal parts
Sixths

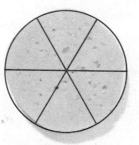

8 equal parts
Eighths

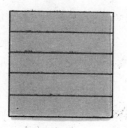

10 equal parts
Tenths

12 equal parts
Twelfths

16 equal parts
Sixteenths

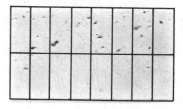

For each picture, tell how many equal parts.
What are the parts called?

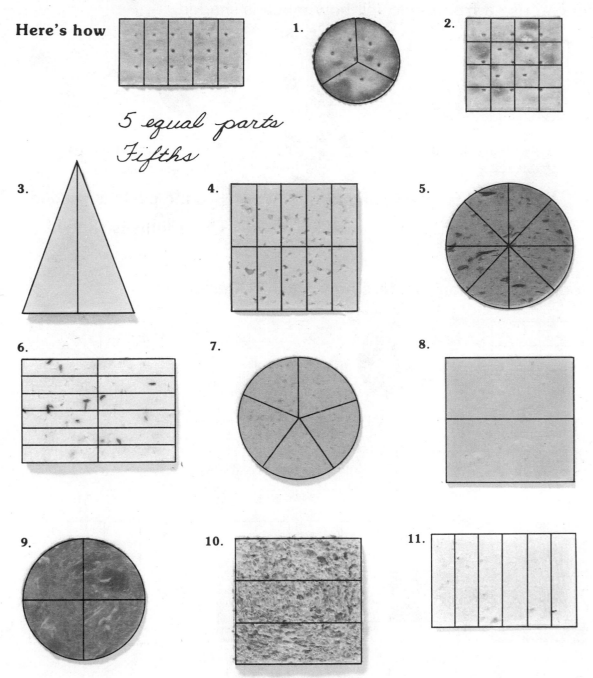

**Here's how**

1.

2.

*5 equal parts
Fifths*

3.

4.

5.

6.

7.

8.

9.

10.

11.

# Part of a Whole

You can use a **fraction** to tell how much is shaded.

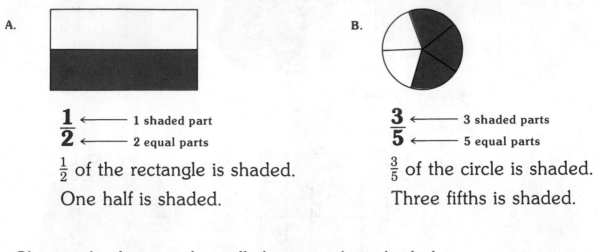

A.

$\dfrac{1}{2}$ ←——— 1 shaded part
←——— 2 equal parts

$\frac{1}{2}$ of the rectangle is shaded.

One half is shaded.

B.

$\dfrac{3}{5}$ ←——— 3 shaded parts
←——— 5 equal parts

$\frac{3}{5}$ of the circle is shaded.

Three fifths is shaded.

Choose the fraction that tells how much is shaded.

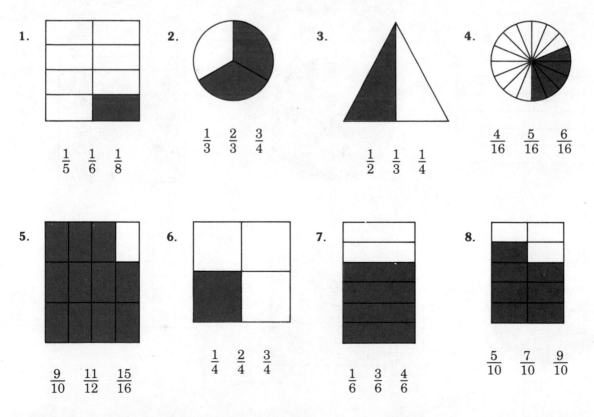

1.  $\frac{1}{5}$  $\frac{1}{6}$  $\frac{1}{8}$

2.  $\frac{1}{3}$  $\frac{2}{3}$  $\frac{3}{4}$

3.  $\frac{1}{2}$  $\frac{1}{3}$  $\frac{1}{4}$

4.  $\frac{4}{16}$  $\frac{5}{16}$  $\frac{6}{16}$

5.  $\frac{9}{10}$  $\frac{11}{12}$  $\frac{15}{16}$

6.  $\frac{1}{4}$  $\frac{2}{4}$  $\frac{3}{4}$

7.  $\frac{1}{6}$  $\frac{3}{6}$  $\frac{4}{6}$

8.  $\frac{5}{10}$  $\frac{7}{10}$  $\frac{9}{10}$

# What fraction tells how much is shaded in each picture?

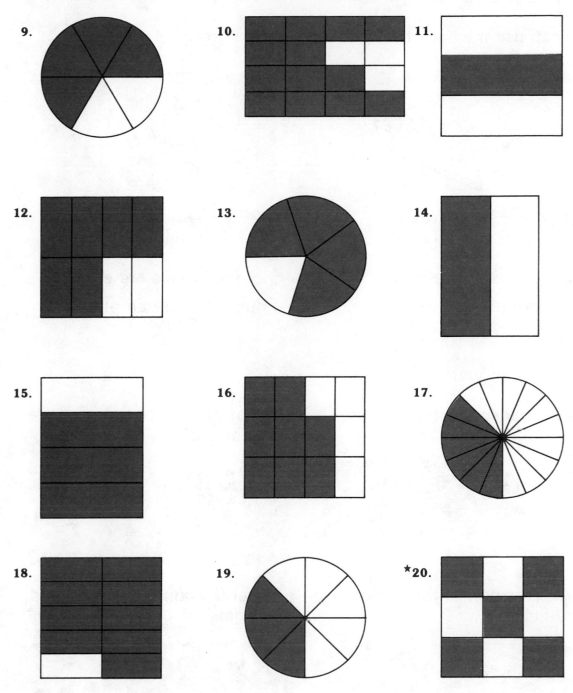

9.

10.

11.

12.

13.

14.

15.

16.

17.

18.

19.

★20.

# Part of a Set

You can use fractions to tell about part of a group.

**A.**

$$\frac{5}{12}$$ ← 5 brown eggs
← 12 eggs in all

$\frac{5}{12}$ of the eggs are brown.

Five twelfths are brown.

**B.**

$$\frac{4}{6}$$ ← 4 empty bottles
← 6 bottles in all

$\frac{4}{6}$ of the bottles are empty.

Four sixths are empty.

Give each answer.

1. What fraction of the pencils are in the box?

2. What fraction of the cups are on the rack?

3. What fraction of the ducks are flying?

4. What fraction of the students are girls?

There are 10 fish.
Give the fraction of fish that look like these.

**5.** **6.** **7.** **8.**

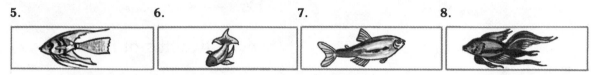

Complete the table.

| | ● ● ● ●<br>● ● ● ●<br>● ● ● ● | ■ ■ ■<br>■ ■ | ▲ ▲ ▲ ▲<br>▲ ▲ ▲<br>▲ ▲ ▲ | ★ ★ ★ ★<br>★ ★ ★ ★<br>★ ★ ★ ★<br>★ ★ ★ ★ |
|---|---|---|---|---|
| How many in all? | 12 | **9.** | **16.** | **23.** |
| How many red? | 4 | **10.** | **17.** | **24.** |
| Fraction<br>(red shapes) | $\frac{4}{12}$ | **11.** | **18.** | **25.** |
| How many blue? | 3 | **12.** | **19.** | **26.** |
| Fraction<br>(blue shapes) | $\frac{3}{12}$ | **13.** | **20.** | **27.** |
| How many green? | 5 | **14.** | **21.** | **28.** |
| Fraction<br>(green shapes) | $\frac{5}{12}$ | **15.** | **22.** | **29.** |

# Writing Fractions

You can use fractions to tell about the red parts.

**A.**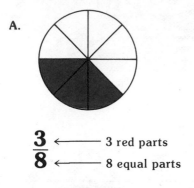

$$\frac{3}{8} \quad \begin{array}{l} \leftarrow \text{ 3 red parts} \\ \leftarrow \text{ 8 equal parts} \end{array}$$

Three eighths of the circle is red.

**B.**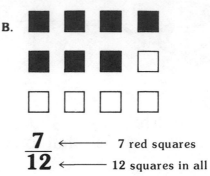

$$\frac{7}{12} \quad \begin{array}{l} \leftarrow \text{ 7 red squares} \\ \leftarrow \text{ 12 squares in all} \end{array}$$

Seven twelfths of the squares are red.

How much is blue? Give a fraction.

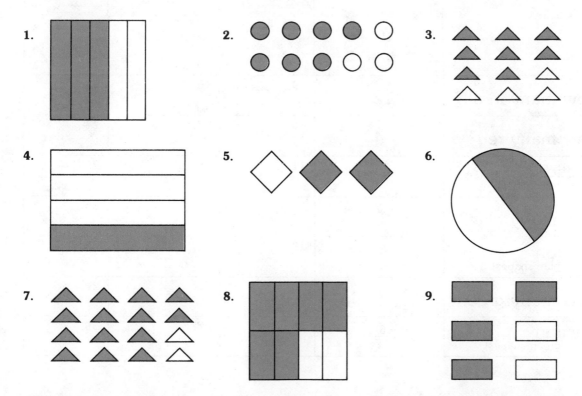

1.

2.

3.

4.

5.

6.

7.

8.

9.

How much is blue? Give a fraction.

10.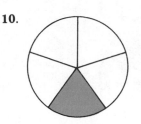

11.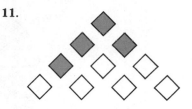

12.

Give each answer.

**Here's how**

three tenths $\frac{3}{10}$

13. one half
14. two thirds
15. four fifths
16. eleven twelfths
17. nine sixteenths
18. seven eighths
19. three fourths
20. one sixth
21. nine tenths
22. two fifths
23. eight tenths
24. six sixteenths
25. three eighths
26. seven twelfths
27. five sixths
28. seven tenths
29. four sixteenths
30. one fourth

Give each word.

**Here's how**

$\frac{13}{16}$ *thirteen sixteenths*

31. $\frac{7}{10}$
32. $\frac{1}{8}$
33. $\frac{3}{12}$
34. $\frac{3}{5}$
35. $\frac{5}{16}$
36. $\frac{4}{6}$
37. $\frac{1}{2}$
38. $\frac{9}{12}$

# Comparing Fractions

**A.**

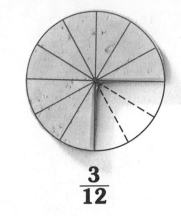

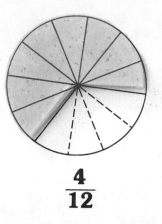

$$\frac{3}{12}$$

$$\frac{4}{12}$$

Paco served $\frac{3}{12}$ of this cheese.     He served $\frac{4}{12}$ of this cheese.

$\frac{3}{12}$ is less than $\frac{4}{12}$.

$$\frac{3}{12} < \frac{4}{12}$$

**B.**

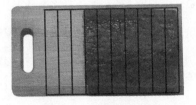

$$\frac{6}{10}$$

$$\frac{3}{10}$$

Paco used $\frac{6}{10}$ of this meat.     He used $\frac{3}{10}$ of this meat.

$\frac{6}{10}$ is greater than $\frac{3}{10}$.

$$\frac{6}{10} > \frac{3}{10}$$

# Which is greater?

**1.**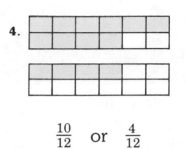

$\frac{1}{4}$ or $\frac{3}{4}$

**2.**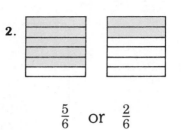

$\frac{5}{6}$ or $\frac{2}{6}$

**3.**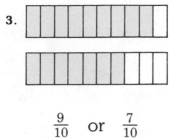

$\frac{9}{10}$ or $\frac{7}{10}$

**4.**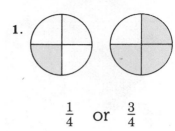

$\frac{10}{12}$ or $\frac{4}{12}$

**5.**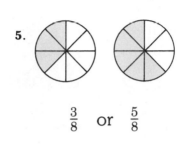

$\frac{3}{8}$ or $\frac{5}{8}$

**6.**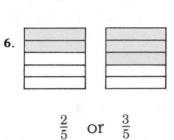

$\frac{2}{5}$ or $\frac{3}{5}$

# Which is less?

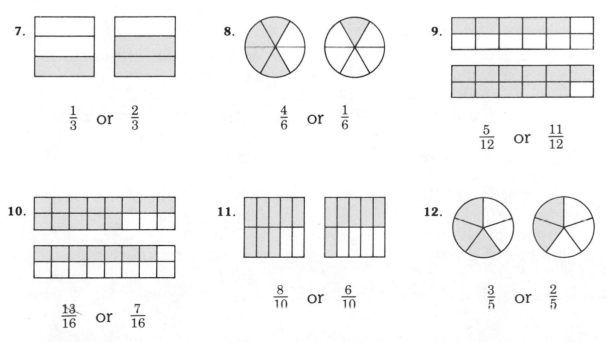

**7.**

$\frac{1}{3}$ or $\frac{2}{3}$

**8.**

$\frac{4}{6}$ or $\frac{1}{6}$

**9.**

$\frac{5}{12}$ or $\frac{11}{12}$

**10.**

$\frac{13}{16}$ or $\frac{7}{16}$

**11.**

$\frac{8}{10}$ or $\frac{6}{10}$

**12.**

$\frac{3}{5}$ or $\frac{2}{5}$

### Fractions in Experiments

Kay put one red card and one blue card into a bag. The two cards were the same size. She shook the bag and drew a card without looking. Kay recorded whether the card was red or blue. She returned the card to the bag. Kay did this experiment 10 times.

This is the table Kay made. Use this table to answer exercises 1-4.

| | Tally | Total |
|------|---------|-------|
| Red | //// | 4 |
| Blue | ////// | 6 |

1. What fraction of the cards were red?
   Number of red cards ⟶ $\frac{░░}{10}$
   Number of draws ⟶

2. Is the fraction close to $\frac{5}{10}$?

3. What fraction of the cards were blue?
   Number of blue cards ⟶ $\frac{░░}{10}$
   Number of draws ⟶

4. Is the fraction close to $\frac{5}{10}$?

Do this experiment and make a table. Use your table to answer exercises 5-8.

5. What fraction of the cards were red?

6. Is the fraction close to $\frac{5}{10}$?

7. What fraction of the cards were blue?

8. Is the fraction close to $\frac{5}{10}$?

9. Repeat the experiment.

10. What fraction of the cards were red? Blue?

11. Are your fractions close to $\frac{5}{10}$?

**290** (two hundred ninety)

# Decimals: Tenths

**A.** This picture represents 1 one.

**B.** Divide 1 one into 10 equal parts. 1 part is 1 tenth.

1 tenth = 0.1

**C.** Divide 1 one into 10 equal parts. 5 parts are 5 tenths.

5 tenths = 0.5

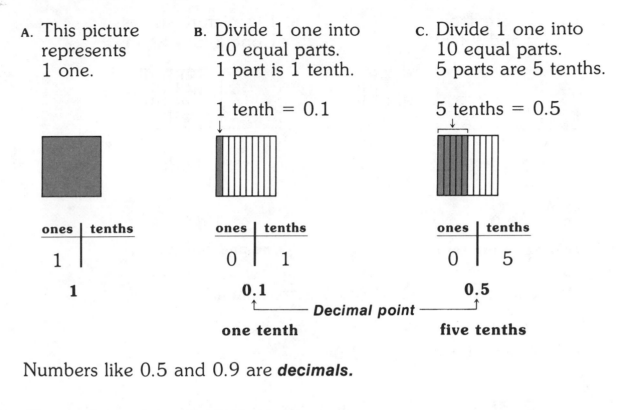

| ones | tenths |
|------|--------|
| 1    |        |

**1**

| ones | tenths |
|------|--------|
| 0    | 1      |

**0.1**

one tenth

| ones | tenths |
|------|--------|
| 0    | 5      |

**0.5**

five tenths

—— *Decimal point* ——

Numbers like 0.5 and 0.9 are **decimals.**

Give a decimal for each shaded part.

**1.**

**2.**

**3.**

**4.**

Give each decimal and its word name.

**5.**

| ones | tenths |
|------|--------|
| 0    | 7      |

**6.**

| ones | tenths |
|------|--------|
| 0    | 3      |

**7.**

| ones | tenths |
|------|--------|
| 0    | 6      |

**8.**

| ones | tenths |
|------|--------|
| 0    | 5      |

**9.**

| ones | tenths |
|------|--------|
| 0    | 4      |

**10.**

| ones | tenths |
|------|--------|
| 0    | 8      |

**11.**

| ones | tenths |
|------|--------|
| 0    | 2      |

**12.**

| ones | tenths |
|------|--------|
| 0    | 9      |

# Decimals: Tenths

A. This picture shows
2 ones and 9 tenths.

B. This picture shows
1 one and 4 tenths.

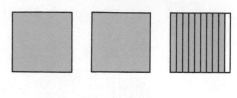

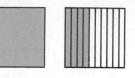

| ones | tenths |
|------|--------|
| 2    | 9      |

2.9

**two and nine tenths**

| ones | tenths |
|------|--------|
| 1    | 4      |

1.4

**one and four tenths**

Numbers like 0.5, 0.7, 1.8, and 4.3 are decimals.

Give a decimal for the shaded part
of each picture.

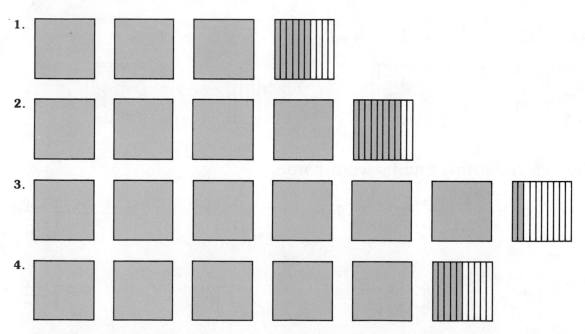

1.

2.

3.

4.

Give a decimal for the shaded part of each picture.

5.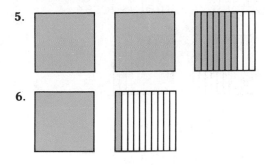

6.

Give each decimal.

7. four tenths

8. two and three tenths

9. seven tenths

10. nine tenths

11. six tenths

12. nine and eight tenths

13. one tenth

14. three and five tenths

15. seven and six tenths

16. four and two tenths

Give each word name.

17. 0.9  18. 3.4  19. 6.2

20. 1.7  21. 0.5  22. 0.3

23. 4.6  24. 0.8  25. 9.1

26. 0.4  27. 5.9  28. 0.7

Remove two of the sticks so that you have 2 squares of different sizes.

Remove two of the sticks so that you have 3 squares of the same size.

Move three of the sticks so that you have 3 squares of the same size.

# Comparing Decimals

**A.** Which decimal is greater?

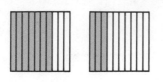

0.7 or 0.3

0.7 is greater than 0.3

0.7 > 0.3

**B.** Which decimal is less?

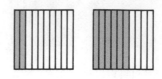

0.2 or 0.6

0.2 is less than 0.6

0.2 < 0.6

Which is greater?

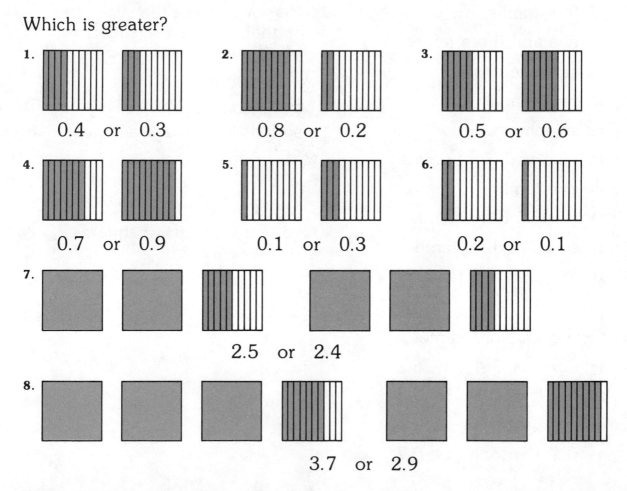

1. 0.4 or 0.3

2. 0.8 or 0.2

3. 0.5 or 0.6

4. 0.7 or 0.9

5. 0.1 or 0.3

6. 0.2 or 0.1

7. 2.5 or 2.4

8. 3.7 or 2.9

Which is less?

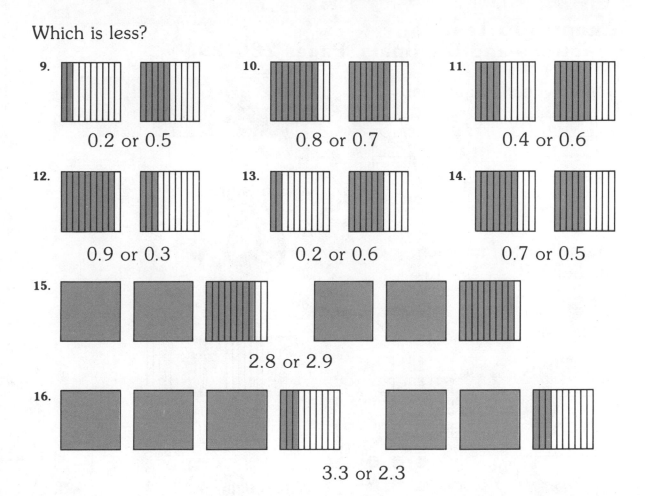

9. 0.2 or 0.5

10. 0.8 or 0.7

11. 0.4 or 0.6

12. 0.9 or 0.3

13. 0.2 or 0.6

14. 0.7 or 0.5

15. 2.8 or 2.9

16. 3.3 or 2.3

## Keeping Skillful

1. $3 \times 2$    2. $5 \times 3$    3. $4 \times 5$    4. $8 \times 3$    5. $5 \times 7$

6. $7 \times 4$    7. $9 \times 7$    8. $2 \times 9$    9. $9 \times 9$    10. $6 \times 8$

11. $8 \times 7$    12. $6 \times 6$    13. $3 \times 7$    14. $6 \times 7$    15. $5 \times 9$

16. $4 \times 2$    17. $2 \times 7$    18. $5 \times 8$    19. $7 \times 0$    20. $8 \times 8$

21. $5 \times 5$    22. $9 \times 4$    23. $0 \times 8$    24. $4 \times 3$    25. $9 \times 6$

26. $7 \times 9$    27. $6 \times 8$    28. $9 \times 8$    29. $7 \times 7$    30. $7 \times 8$

## Chapter 15 Test
## Fractions and Decimals, Pages 280–295

Tell how many equal parts.

1.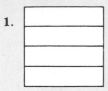

2.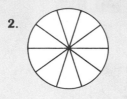

Give a fraction for each shaded part.

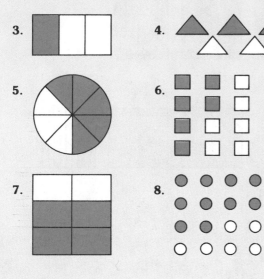

Give a decimal for each shaded part.

9.

10.

11.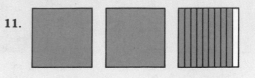

Which is greater?

12.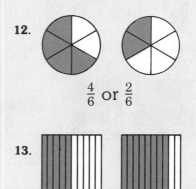

$\frac{4}{6}$ or $\frac{2}{6}$

13.

0.5 or 0.8

Which is less?

14.

$\frac{7}{12}$ or $\frac{5}{12}$

15.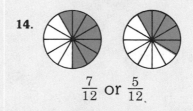

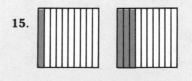

0.1 or 0.3

# Problems Around Us

Tickets: Adult $3 Child $2

**Attendance**

| 248 morning | 368 afternoon |

Find each answer.

1. How many people attended the rodeo?

2. How many more people attended in the afternoon?

3. How much more was the adult's ticket?

How much would it cost for

4. 1 adult and 1 child?

5. 2 adults and 1 child?

6. 2 adults and 3 children?

7. 1 adult and 6 children?

8. 3 adults and 1 child?

9. Tom collected 32 pictures of rodeo stars. He put 8 pictures on each page. How many pages did he fill?

10. Chapa bought 7 sets of pictures. There were 9 in each set. How many pictures did he buy?

11. There were 8 rodeo stars. Each won 4 prizes. They won how many prizes in all?

12. There were 81 people sitting in Section G. There were 9 people in each row. How many rows were in Section G?

# Individualized Skills Maintenance

**Diagnose**

A *pages 150–163; 166–179*

$9 \times 7$

$6 \times 8$

$8 \times 7$

B *pages 242–255; 258–269*

$72 \div 9$

$54 \div 6$

$42 \div 7$

**Practice**

A

1. $\begin{array}{r} 4 \\ \times 9 \\ \hline \end{array}$
2. $\begin{array}{r} 7 \\ \times 6 \\ \hline \end{array}$
3. $\begin{array}{r} 5 \\ \times 8 \\ \hline \end{array}$
4. $\begin{array}{r} 8 \\ \times 7 \\ \hline \end{array}$
5. $\begin{array}{r} 9 \\ \times 6 \\ \hline \end{array}$
6. $\begin{array}{r} 2 \\ \times 7 \\ \hline \end{array}$
7. $\begin{array}{r} 6 \\ \times 4 \\ \hline \end{array}$

8. $\begin{array}{r} 6 \\ \times 3 \\ \hline \end{array}$
9. $\begin{array}{r} 8 \\ \times 2 \\ \hline \end{array}$
10. $\begin{array}{r} 9 \\ \times 8 \\ \hline \end{array}$
11. $\begin{array}{r} 5 \\ \times 5 \\ \hline \end{array}$
12. $\begin{array}{r} 3 \\ \times 8 \\ \hline \end{array}$
13. $\begin{array}{r} 8 \\ \times 8 \\ \hline \end{array}$
14. $\begin{array}{r} 7 \\ \times 9 \\ \hline \end{array}$

15. $\begin{array}{r} 4 \\ \times 7 \\ \hline \end{array}$
16. $\begin{array}{r} 3 \\ \times 9 \\ \hline \end{array}$
17. $\begin{array}{r} 3 \\ \times 5 \\ \hline \end{array}$
18. $\begin{array}{r} 2 \\ \times 9 \\ \hline \end{array}$
19. $\begin{array}{r} 4 \\ \times 8 \\ \hline \end{array}$
20. $\begin{array}{r} 7 \\ \times 7 \\ \hline \end{array}$
21. $\begin{array}{r} 9 \\ \times 9 \\ \hline \end{array}$

B

22. $5\overline{)45}$
23. $3\overline{)15}$
24. $6\overline{)48}$
25. $7\overline{)63}$
26. $6\overline{)18}$

27. $2\overline{)14}$
28. $3\overline{)21}$
29. $2\overline{)18}$
30. $6\overline{)42}$
31. $8\overline{)64}$

32. $9\overline{)81}$
33. $7\overline{)56}$
34. $4\overline{)28}$
35. $8\overline{)72}$
36. $8\overline{)16}$

37. $3\overline{)24}$
38. $4\overline{)36}$
39. $9\overline{)54}$
40. $6\overline{)24}$
41. $5\overline{)25}$

# Unit 5 Review

Chapter 13, pages 242–256
Copy and complete
each sentence.

1.

$12 \div 3 = ?$

$12 \div 4 = ?$

Divide.

2. $21 \div 3$    3. $36 \div 9$

4. $10 \div 2$    5. $35 \div 7$

6. $18 \div 6$    7. $24 \div 4$

Chapter 14, page 258–278
Divide.

8. $9\overline{)81}$    9. $7\overline{)63}$    10. $6\overline{)42}$

11. $9\overline{)72}$    12. $7\overline{)49}$    13. $6\overline{)54}$

Copy and complete each fact.
Circle the one that does not
belong to the family.

14. $8 \times 7$

$56 \div 8$

$56 \div 7$

$7 \times 8$

$54 \div 6$

Find the answer.

15. There are 64 pencils. How
many boxes can be filled
if 8 pencils are put in
each box?

Chapter 15, pages 280–295
Give a fraction for each
shaded part.

16. 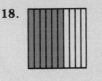    17.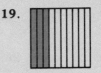

Give a decimal for each
shaded part.

18. 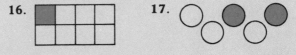    19.

Which is greater?

20.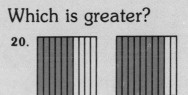

$0.6$   or   $0.8$

21.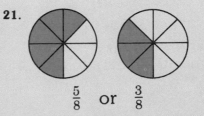

$\frac{5}{8}$   or   $\frac{3}{8}$

## Unit 5 Test
## Chapters 13–15, pages 242–296

Divide.

1. $12 \div 2$     2. $18 \div 3$

3. $21 \div 7$     4. $16 \div 8$

5. $40 \div 8$     6. $12 \div 4$

7. $24 \div 6$     8. $45 \div 5$

9. $7\overline{)42}$     10. $6\overline{)48}$

11. $4\overline{)28}$     12. $6\overline{)36}$

13. $9\overline{)81}$     14. $4\overline{)36}$

15. $8\overline{)32}$     16. $3\overline{)24}$

17. $9\overline{)45}$     18. $9\overline{)72}$

19. $2\overline{)18}$     20. $9\overline{)54}$

21. $3\overline{)27}$     22. $7\overline{)56}$

Find each answer.

23. There are 48 marbles. How many bags can be filled if 8 marbles are put in each bag?

24. There are 9 students. Each student has 4 erasers. How many erasers in all?

Give a fraction for each shaded part.

25.
26.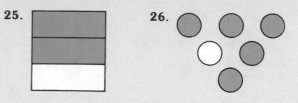

Give a decimal for each shaded part.

27.      28.

29. Which is greater?

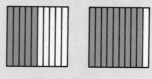

0.5   or   0.9

30. Which is less?

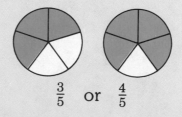

$\frac{3}{5}$   or   $\frac{4}{5}$

# Unit 6

# Chapter 16  Multiplication Computation: One-Digit Multipliers

## Multiplying with 10 or 100

A. There are 5 sheets of stamps.
There are 100 stamps on each sheet.
How many stamps are there in all?

You can add.

```
  100
  100
  100
  100
+ 100
  500
```

Or you can multiply.

$5 \times 100$

**500** ( 5 hundreds )

$5 \times 100 = 500$

B. Tell what was done in this example.

$16 \times 10$

**160** ( 16 tens )

$16 \times 10 = 160$

Multiply.

1. $6 \times 10$   2. $10 \times 59$   3. $43 \times 10$

4. $8 \times 10$   5. $10 \times 7$   6. $5 \times 10$

7. $9 \times 100$   8. $14 \times 100$   9. $100 \times 37$

10. $100 \times 6$   11. $3 \times 100$   12. $8 \times 100$

13. $27 \times 10$   14. $64 \times 100$   15. $82 \times 10$

16. $100 \times 31$   17. $10 \times 35$   18. $24 \times 100$

19. $100 \times 7$   20. $4 \times 10$   21. $91 \times 10$

22. $68 \times 100$   23. $10 \times 78$   24. $100 \times 54$

*25. $63 \times 1000$   *26. $6 \times 10,000$   *27. $94 \times 10,000$

For each exercise, find the number in all.

28. 25 coupon books
    10 coupons in each book

29. 10 rolls of tickets
    85 tickets in each roll

30. 100 boxes of envelopes
    75 envelopes in each box

31. 12 sheets of stamps
    100 stamps on each sheet

**Time Out**

Miguel keeps all of his socks in one drawer.
He has 8 blue socks and 6 brown socks. If
he reaches into the drawer without looking,
what is the least number of socks he can
take out to be sure of getting a pair of
the same color?

# Multiplication: Multiples of 10 and 100

A. There are 3 stacks of pennies.
There are 50 pennies in each stack.
How many pennies are there in all?

You can add.

```
   50
   50
+  50
  150
```

Or you can multiply.

$3 \times 50$

$150$ ( $3 \times 5$ tens = 15 tens )

$3 \times 50 = 150$

Tell what was done in each example.

B. $8 \times 200$

$1600$ ( $8 \times 2$ hundreds = 16 hundreds )

$8 \times 200 = 1600$

C. $400 \times 5$

$2000$ ( 4 hundreds $\times 5$ = 20 hundreds )

$400 \times 5 = 2000$

Multiply.

1. $4 \times 30$    2. $3 \times 30$    3. $30 \times 8$

4. $7 \times 90$    5. $70 \times 4$    6. $6 \times 60$

7. $8 \times 600$    8. $400 \times 4$    9. $9 \times 400$

10. $5 \times 500$    11. $700 \times 6$    12. $5 \times 900$

13. $2 \times 500$    14. $600 \times 5$    15. $4 \times 500$

16. $3 \times 60$    17. $600 \times 9$    18. $40 \times 2$

19. $9 \times 90$    20. $500 \times 8$    21. $90 \times 8$

22. $3 \times 20$    23. $6 \times 200$    24. $50 \times 6$

*25. $7 \times 3000$    *26. $5000 \times 8$    *27. $4 \times 7000$

*28. $8000 \times 8$    *29. $60{,}000 \times 7$    *30. $3 \times 40{,}000$

For each exercise, find the total number in all.

31. 2 bags of silver dollars
30 dollars in each bag

32. 5 rolls of nickels
20 nickels in each roll

33. 9 rolls of dimes
50 dimes in each roll

34. 3 bags of quarters
300 quarters in each bag

35. 7 bundles of dollar bills
500 bills in each bundle

36. 8 bags of pennies
700 pennies in each bag

37. 6 rolls of quarters
40 quarters in each roll

38. 4 rolls of pennies
50 pennies in each roll

39. 7 bags of dimes
800 dimes in each bag

More practice
Set 31, page 364

# Multiplication: No Renaming

A. A pancake griddle holds 12 pancakes. How many pancakes will 4 griddles hold?

Think of 12 as 10 and 2.

Find 4 × 12.

$$\begin{array}{r} 12 \\ \times\ 4 \\ \hline 8 \end{array}$$

Multiply the ones.
4 × 2 = 8

Show 8 ones.

$$\begin{array}{r} 12 \\ \times\ 4 \\ \hline 48 \end{array}$$

Multiply the tens.
4 × 1 ten = 4 tens

Show 4 tens.

Four griddles will hold 48 pancakes.

B. Tell how to
find 3 × 231.

$$
\begin{array}{r}
231 \\
\times\ \ 3 \\
\hline
3
\end{array}
$$

$$
\begin{array}{r}
231 \\
\times\ \ 3 \\
\hline
93
\end{array}
$$

$$
\begin{array}{r}
231 \\
\times\ \ 3 \\
\hline
693
\end{array}
$$

C. Tell how to
find 4 × 52.

$$
\begin{array}{r}
52 \\
\times\ \ 4 \\
\hline
8
\end{array}
$$

$$
\begin{array}{r}
52 \\
\times\ \ 4 \\
\hline
208
\end{array}
$$

Multiply.

1.  $\begin{array}{r} 11 \\ \times\ 4 \\ \hline \end{array}$   2.  $\begin{array}{r} 14 \\ \times\ 2 \\ \hline \end{array}$   3.  $\begin{array}{r} 43 \\ \times\ 2 \\ \hline \end{array}$   4.  $\begin{array}{r} 22 \\ \times\ 3 \\ \hline \end{array}$

5.  $\begin{array}{r} 41 \\ \times\ 6 \\ \hline \end{array}$   6.  $\begin{array}{r} 74 \\ \times\ 2 \\ \hline \end{array}$   7.  $\begin{array}{r} 32 \\ \times\ 4 \\ \hline \end{array}$   8.  $\begin{array}{r} 31 \\ \times\ 5 \\ \hline \end{array}$

9.  $\begin{array}{r} 423 \\ \times\ 2 \\ \hline \end{array}$   10.  $\begin{array}{r} 133 \\ \times\ 3 \\ \hline \end{array}$   11.  $\begin{array}{r} 200 \\ \times\ 4 \\ \hline \end{array}$   12.  $\begin{array}{r} 332 \\ \times\ 3 \\ \hline \end{array}$

13.  $\begin{array}{r} 50 \\ \times\ 6 \\ \hline \end{array}$   14.  $\begin{array}{r} 122 \\ \times\ 4 \\ \hline \end{array}$   15.  $\begin{array}{r} 71 \\ \times\ 7 \\ \hline \end{array}$   16.  $\begin{array}{r} 74 \\ \times\ 2 \\ \hline \end{array}$

17.  $\begin{array}{r} 52 \\ \times\ 3 \\ \hline \end{array}$   18.  $\begin{array}{r} 312 \\ \times\ 3 \\ \hline \end{array}$   19.  $\begin{array}{r} 90 \\ \times\ 8 \\ \hline \end{array}$   20.  $\begin{array}{r} 300 \\ \times\ 2 \\ \hline \end{array}$

21.  $\begin{array}{r} 83 \\ \times\ 3 \\ \hline \end{array}$   22.  $\begin{array}{r} 211 \\ \times\ 4 \\ \hline \end{array}$   ★23.  $\begin{array}{r} 1332 \\ \times\ 3 \\ \hline \end{array}$   ★24.  $\begin{array}{r} 14{,}231 \\ \times\ 2 \\ \hline \end{array}$

25. A milk container holds 32 cups of milk.
Mr. Standing Hawk filled 4 containers.
How many cups of milk were there in all?

26. Mr. Kingman served bacon to 132 people.
He gave each person 3 bacon strips.
How many bacon strips did he serve?

27. Mrs. Garza put 2 orange slices on each
plate. She put orange slices on
421 plates. How many orange slices
did she use?

# Multiplication: One Renaming

A. Lela bought 4 packs of balloons. She paid 23 cents for each pack. How much did she spend in all?

Find $4 \times 23$.

$$
\begin{array}{r}
1 \\
23 \\
\times\ 4 \\
\hline
2
\end{array}
$$

Multiply the ones.
$4 \times 3 = 12$

Show 12 as 1 ten 2 ones.

$$
\begin{array}{r}
1 \\
23 \\
\times\ 4 \\
\hline
92
\end{array}
$$

Multiply the tens.
$4 \times 2$ tens = 8 tens
Add the 1 ten.

Show 9 tens.

Lela paid 92 cents for the balloons.

B. Tell how to
find 5 × 19.

$$\begin{array}{r} {}^{4}\phantom{0} \\ 19 \\ \times\ 5 \\ \hline 5 \end{array}$$

$$\begin{array}{r} {}^{4}\phantom{0} \\ 19 \\ \times\ 5 \\ \hline 95 \end{array}$$

Multiply.

1. $\begin{array}{r} 16 \\ \times\ 4 \\ \hline \end{array}$   2. $\begin{array}{r} 25 \\ \times\ 3 \\ \hline \end{array}$   3. $\begin{array}{r} 38 \\ \times\ 2 \\ \hline \end{array}$   4. $\begin{array}{r} 14 \\ \times\ 7 \\ \hline \end{array}$

5. $\begin{array}{r} 19 \\ \times\ 2 \\ \hline \end{array}$   6. $\begin{array}{r} 12 \\ \times\ 8 \\ \hline \end{array}$   7. $\begin{array}{r} 13 \\ \times\ 7 \\ \hline \end{array}$   8. $\begin{array}{r} 18 \\ \times\ 4 \\ \hline \end{array}$

9. $\begin{array}{r} 14 \\ \times\ 5 \\ \hline \end{array}$   10. $\begin{array}{r} 15 \\ \times\ 4 \\ \hline \end{array}$   11. $\begin{array}{r} 37 \\ \times\ 2 \\ \hline \end{array}$   12. $\begin{array}{r} 26 \\ \times\ 3 \\ \hline \end{array}$

C. Tell how to
find 2 × 35.

$$\begin{array}{r} {}^{1}\phantom{0} \\ 35 \\ \times\ 2 \\ \hline 0 \end{array}$$

$$\begin{array}{r} {}^{1}\phantom{0} \\ 35 \\ \times\ 2 \\ \hline 70 \end{array}$$

13. $\begin{array}{r} 27 \\ \times\ 3 \\ \hline \end{array}$   14. $\begin{array}{r} 45 \\ \times\ 2 \\ \hline \end{array}$   15. $\begin{array}{r} 14 \\ \times\ 6 \\ \hline \end{array}$   16. $\begin{array}{r} 27 \\ \times\ 2 \\ \hline \end{array}$

17. $\begin{array}{r} 24 \\ \times\ 4 \\ \hline \end{array}$   18. $\begin{array}{r} 29 \\ \times\ 3 \\ \hline \end{array}$   19. $\begin{array}{r} 16 \\ \times\ 5 \\ \hline \end{array}$   20. $\begin{array}{r} 17 \\ \times\ 4 \\ \hline \end{array}$

21. $\begin{array}{r} 13 \\ \times\ 6 \\ \hline \end{array}$   22. $\begin{array}{r} 17 \\ \times\ 5 \\ \hline \end{array}$   23. $\begin{array}{r} 47 \\ \times\ 2 \\ \hline \end{array}$   24. $\begin{array}{r} 23 \\ \times\ 4 \\ \hline \end{array}$

25. Clarence bought 5 party hats.
He spent 15 cents for each hat.
How much did he spend for the 5 hats?

26. Ingrid bought 3 prizes.
She spent 24 cents for each prize.
How much did she spend in all?

★27. Three balloons cost 29 cents.
How much do 6 of these balloons cost?

★28. Two tickets cost 19 cents.
How much do 8 of these tickets cost?

# Multiplication: One-Digit and Two-Digit Numbers

**A.** Leroy Lion's heart beats 45 times a minute. How many times does Leroy's heart beat in 3 minutes?

Find 3 × 45.

$$\begin{array}{r} 1 \\ \mathbf{45} \\ \times\ \mathbf{3} \\ \hline \mathbf{5} \end{array}$$

Multiply the ones.
3 × 5 = 15

Show 1 ten 5 ones.

$$\begin{array}{r} 1 \\ \mathbf{45} \\ \times\ \mathbf{3} \\ \hline \mathbf{135} \end{array}$$

Multiply the tens.
3 × 4 tens = 12 tens
Add the 1 ten.

Show 13 tens.

Leroy's heart beats 135 times in 3 minutes.

**B.** Tell how to find 5 × 86.

$$\begin{array}{r} 3 \\ \mathbf{86} \\ \times\ \mathbf{5} \\ \hline \mathbf{0} \end{array}$$

$$\begin{array}{r} 3 \\ \mathbf{86} \\ \times\ \mathbf{5} \\ \hline \mathbf{430} \end{array}$$

Multiply.

| 1. | 68 × 2 | 2. | 79 × 3 | 3. | 34 × 5 | 4. | 95 × 2 | 5. | 58 × 4 | 6. | 89 × 5 |

| 7. | 35 × 8 | 8. | 46 × 6 | 9. | 67 × 2 | 10. | 93 × 6 | 11. | 19 × 8 | 12. | 62 × 8 |

| 13. | 55 × 9 | 14. | 17 × 9 | 15. | 43 × 9 | 16. | 97 × 5 | 17. | 89 × 4 | 18. | 57 × 7 |

| 19. | 92 × 7 | 20. | 73 × 8 | 21. | 84 × 6 | 22. | 59 × 7 | 23. | 69 × 8 | 24. | 88 × 6 |

Herbert Horse's heart beats 42 times a minute. How many times does it beat in

25. 6 minutes?

26. 9 minutes?

27. 5 minutes?

Ella Elephant's heart beats 36 times a minute. How many times does it beat in

31. 4 minutes?

32. 7 minutes?

33. 100 minutes?

Heather Hummingbird's heart beats 15 times a second. How many times does it beat in

28. 7 seconds?

29. 8 seconds?

30. 10 seconds?

Polly Person's heart beats 4800 times an hour. How many times does it beat in

★34. 2 hours?

★35. 5 hours?

★36. 10 hours?

**More practice
Set 32, page 364**

(three hundred eleven) **311**

# Multiplication: One-Digit and Three-Digit Numbers

**A.** Ms. Jordan buys food for the school cafeteria. She bought 6 boxes of hamburgers. There were 216 hamburgers in each box. How many hamburgers did she buy?

**B.** Tell how to find $2 \times 454$.

$$\begin{array}{r} 454 \\ \times\ \ 2 \\ \hline 8 \end{array}$$

Find $6 \times 216$.

$$\begin{array}{r} ^3 \\ 216 \\ \times\ \ \ 6 \\ \hline 6 \end{array}$$

$6 \times 6 = 36$

Show 3 tens 6 ones.

$$\begin{array}{r} ^1 \\ 454 \\ \times\ \ 2 \\ \hline 08 \end{array}$$

$$\begin{array}{r} ^3 \\ 216 \\ \times\ \ \ 6 \\ \hline 96 \end{array}$$

$6 \times 1$ ten $= 6$ tens
Add the 3 tens.

Show 9 tens.

$$\begin{array}{r} ^1 \\ 454 \\ \times\ \ 2 \\ \hline 908 \end{array}$$

$$\begin{array}{r} ^3 \\ 216 \\ \times\ \ \ 6 \\ \hline 1296 \end{array}$$

$6 \times 2$ hundreds $= 12$ hundreds

Show 12 hundreds.

Ms. Jordan bought 1296 hamburgers.

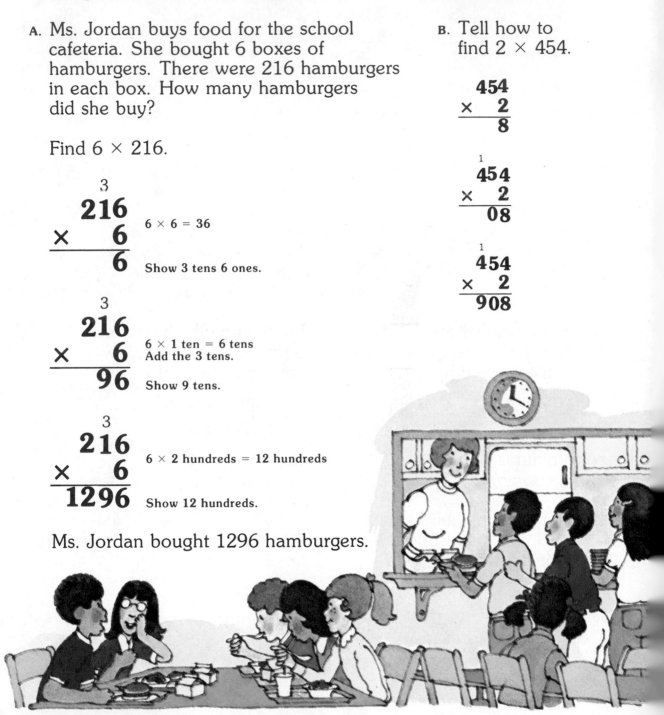

Multiply.

1. 116
   × 4

2. 613
   × 7

3. 113
   × 7

4. 419
   × 3

5. 243
   × 3

6. 471
   × 8

7. 842
   × 4

8. 283
   × 3

9. 112
   × 5

10. 364
    × 2

11. 914
    × 6

12. 521
    × 6

13. 723
    × 4

14. 851
    × 9

15. 253
    × 2

16. 327
    × 2

17. 152
    × 4

18. 126
    × 3

★19. 3142
    × 4

★20. 5813
    × 3

21. There are 8 milk cartons in each crate. How many cartons are in 112 crates?

22. Each can of juice will make 192 glasses of juice. How many glasses of juice can be made from 3 cans?

23. There are 315 packs of catsup in a box. How many packs of catsup are in 5 boxes?

24. There are 225 apples in a box. How many apples are in 3 boxes?

**More practice**
Set 33, page 364

## Using Multiplication

**TICKETS**

| TICKETS | |
| --- | --- |
| **New York to Chicago** | |
| Coach | $ 58 |
| First Class | $ 114 |
| **New York to Omaha** | |
| Coach | $ 118 |
| First Class | $ 191 |
| **Chicago to San Francisco** | |
| Coach | $ 123 |
| First Class | $ 215 |

For each exercise, find how much the tickets will cost.

1. 5 coach tickets from New York to Chicago
   (Find 5 × $58.)

2. 5 first-class tickets from New York to Chicago
   (Find 5 × $114.)

3. 2 coach tickets from New York to Omaha

4. 3 first-class tickets from New York to Omaha

5. 4 coach tickets from Chicago to San Francisco

6. 6 first-class tickets from Chicago to San Francisco

★7. 3 first-class tickets from New York to Chicago
   and then from Chicago to San Francisco

Multiply.

8. $\begin{array}{r} 118 \\ \times\ 5 \\ \hline \end{array}$
9. $\begin{array}{r} 182 \\ \times\ 3 \\ \hline \end{array}$
10. $\begin{array}{r} 17 \\ \times\ 5 \\ \hline \end{array}$

11. $\begin{array}{r} 124 \\ \times\ 2 \\ \hline \end{array}$
12. $\begin{array}{r} 23 \\ \times\ 4 \\ \hline \end{array}$
13. $\begin{array}{r} 624 \\ \times\ 4 \\ \hline \end{array}$

14. $\begin{array}{r} 63 \\ \times\ 2 \\ \hline \end{array}$
15. $\begin{array}{r} 82 \\ \times\ 4 \\ \hline \end{array}$
16. $\begin{array}{r} 251 \\ \times\ 3 \\ \hline \end{array}$

17. $\begin{array}{r} 41 \\ \times\ 6 \\ \hline \end{array}$
18. $\begin{array}{r} 49 \\ \times\ 8 \\ \hline \end{array}$
19. $\begin{array}{r} 315 \\ \times\ 2 \\ \hline \end{array}$

20. $\begin{array}{r} 131 \\ \times\ 7 \\ \hline \end{array}$
21. $\begin{array}{r} 312 \\ \times\ 3 \\ \hline \end{array}$
22. $\begin{array}{r} 231 \\ \times\ 5 \\ \hline \end{array}$

23. $\begin{array}{r} 714 \\ \times\ 3 \\ \hline \end{array}$
24. $\begin{array}{r} 78 \\ \times\ 6 \\ \hline \end{array}$
25. $\begin{array}{r} 232 \\ \times\ 4 \\ \hline \end{array}$

26. $83 \times 7$
27. $8 \times 400$
28. $9 \times 65$
29. $5 \times 381$
30. $283 \times 3$
31. $500 \times 7$
32. $5 \times 851$
33. $97 \times 8$
34. $6 \times 900$
35. $9 \times 88$
36. $349 \times 2$
37. $500 \times 5$

## Keeping Skillful

Add.

1. $\begin{array}{r} 57 \\ +\ 89 \\ \hline \end{array}$
2. $\begin{array}{r} 385 \\ +\ 124 \\ \hline \end{array}$
3. $\begin{array}{r} 592 \\ +\ 650 \\ \hline \end{array}$

4. $\begin{array}{r} 275 \\ +\ 738 \\ \hline \end{array}$
5. $\begin{array}{r} 3817 \\ +\ 2427 \\ \hline \end{array}$
6. $\begin{array}{r} 5483 \\ +\ 7088 \\ \hline \end{array}$

Subtract.

7. $\begin{array}{r} 94 \\ -\ 69 \\ \hline \end{array}$
8. $\begin{array}{r} 215 \\ -\ 183 \\ \hline \end{array}$
9. $\begin{array}{r} 520 \\ -\ 117 \\ \hline \end{array}$

10. $\begin{array}{r} 427 \\ -\ 338 \\ \hline \end{array}$
11. $\begin{array}{r} 4407 \\ -\ 1271 \\ \hline \end{array}$
12. $\begin{array}{r} 8316 \\ -\ 5821 \\ \hline \end{array}$

Add or subtract.

13. $\begin{array}{r} 703 \\ -\ 528 \\ \hline \end{array}$
14. $\begin{array}{r} 815 \\ +\ 109 \\ \hline \end{array}$
15. $\begin{array}{r} 346 \\ +\ 782 \\ \hline \end{array}$

16. $\begin{array}{r} 371 \\ -\ 359 \\ \hline \end{array}$
17. $\begin{array}{r} 2844 \\ +\ 5056 \\ \hline \end{array}$
18. $\begin{array}{r} 8900 \\ -\ 2715 \\ \hline \end{array}$

19. $\begin{array}{r} 4206 \\ -\ 1342 \\ \hline \end{array}$
20. $\begin{array}{r} 3978 \\ +\ 6204 \\ \hline \end{array}$
21. $\begin{array}{r} 6075 \\ -\ 3749 \\ \hline \end{array}$

### Multiplication Trail

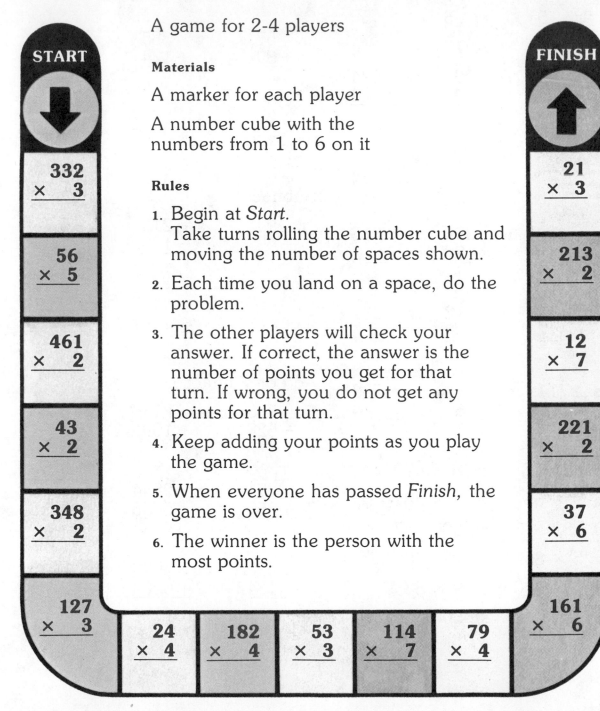

A game for 2-4 players

**Materials**

A marker for each player

A number cube with the numbers from 1 to 6 on it

**Rules**

1. Begin at *Start.*
   Take turns rolling the number cube and moving the number of spaces shown.

2. Each time you land on a space, do the problem.

3. The other players will check your answer. If correct, the answer is the number of points you get for that turn. If wrong, you do not get any points for that turn.

4. Keep adding your points as you play the game.

5. When everyone has passed *Finish,* the game is over.

6. The winner is the person with the most points.

START

$332 \times 3$

$56 \times 5$

$461 \times 2$

$43 \times 2$

$348 \times 2$

$127 \times 3$

$24 \times 4$

$182 \times 4$

$53 \times 3$

$114 \times 7$

$79 \times 4$

$161 \times 6$

FINISH

$21 \times 3$

$213 \times 2$

$12 \times 7$

$221 \times 2$

$37 \times 6$

# Chapter 16 Test
## Multiplication Computation:
## One-Digit Multipliers, pages 302–316

Multiply.

1. $7 \times 10$

2. $10 \times 36$

3. $50 \times 10$

4. $100 \times 8$

5. $52 \times 100$

6. $4 \times 40$

7. $2 \times 30$

8. $40 \times 6$

9. $500 \times 6$

10. $7 \times 300$

11. $\begin{array}{r} 42 \\ \times\ 2 \\ \hline \end{array}$  12. $\begin{array}{r} 31 \\ \times\ 5 \\ \hline \end{array}$

13. $\begin{array}{r} 21 \\ \times\ 3 \\ \hline \end{array}$  14. $\begin{array}{r} 324 \\ \times\ \ 2 \\ \hline \end{array}$

15. $\begin{array}{r} 15 \\ \times\ 4 \\ \hline \end{array}$  16. $\begin{array}{r} 46 \\ \times\ 2 \\ \hline \end{array}$

17. $\begin{array}{r} 35 \\ \times\ 7 \\ \hline \end{array}$  18. $\begin{array}{r} 84 \\ \times\ 4 \\ \hline \end{array}$

19. $\begin{array}{r} 68 \\ \times\ 6 \\ \hline \end{array}$  20. $\begin{array}{r} 519 \\ \times\ \ 5 \\ \hline \end{array}$

21. $\begin{array}{r} 541 \\ \times\ \ 8 \\ \hline \end{array}$  22. $\begin{array}{r} 917 \\ \times\ \ 4 \\ \hline \end{array}$

23. $\begin{array}{r} 193 \\ \times\ \ 2 \\ \hline \end{array}$  24. $\begin{array}{r} 38 \\ \times\ 9 \\ \hline \end{array}$

25. $\begin{array}{r} 68 \\ \times\ 8 \\ \hline \end{array}$  26. $\begin{array}{r} 861 \\ \times\ \ 7 \\ \hline \end{array}$

27. $\begin{array}{r} 28 \\ \times\ 2 \\ \hline \end{array}$  28. $\begin{array}{r} 417 \\ \times\ \ 5 \\ \hline \end{array}$

29. $\begin{array}{r} 35 \\ \times\ 2 \\ \hline \end{array}$  30. $\begin{array}{r} 941 \\ \times\ \ 9 \\ \hline \end{array}$

# Chapter 17 Area and Volume

## Angles

These pictures show **angles.**

Angles that form square corners are called **right angles.**
You can use the square corner of a card to test for
right angles. These pictures show right angles.

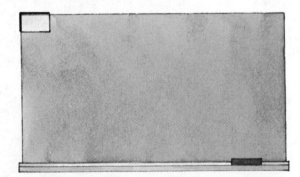

Does the picture show an angle? Write yes or no.

1.

2.

3.

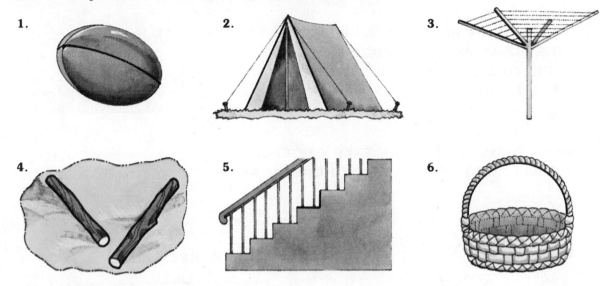

4.

5.

6.

Is the angle a right angle? You may use a card to
help you. Write yes or no.

7.

8.

9.

10.

11.

12.

13.

14.

15.

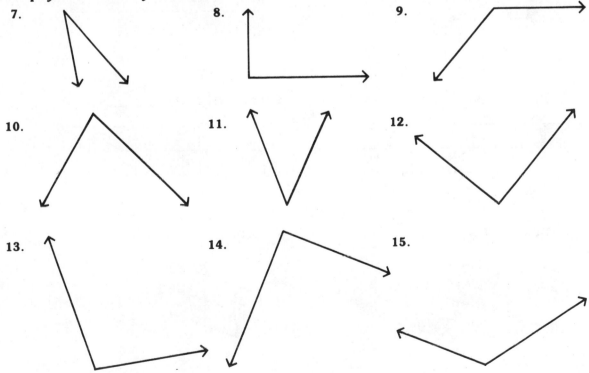

# Area

Nick found the **area** of a table top. He used a tile shaped like a triangle as the unit of area. The area of the table top is 20 units.

Unit of area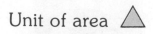

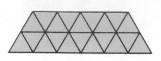

A unit of area is given for each exercise. Use this unit to find the area of the shape.

1. Unit of area

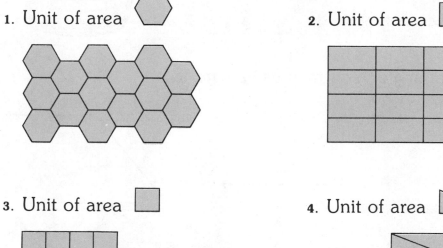

2. Unit of area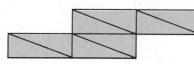

3. Unit of area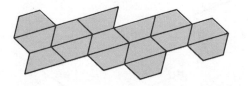

4. Unit of area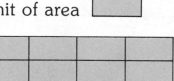

5. Unit of area

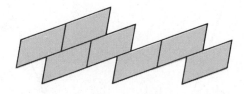

6. Unit of area

For each exercise, tell about how many of the given units
of area cover each shape. The same shape is shown
in each exercise.

7. Unit of area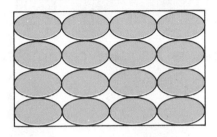

8. Unit of area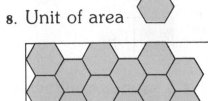

9. Unit of area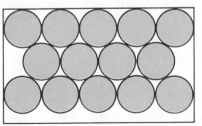

10. Unit of area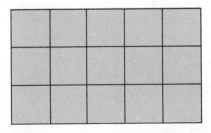

11. Unit of area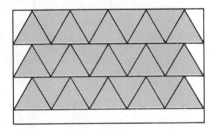

12. Unit of area

° **Discuss** Which unit of area do you think
gives the most accurate measure?

# Square Centimeter

The **square centimeter** is a standard unit of area.

1 cm
1 cm

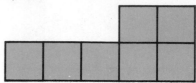

The area is 1 square centimeter.     The area is 7 square centimeters.

The square centimeter is the unit of area.
For each exercise, give the area in square centimeters.

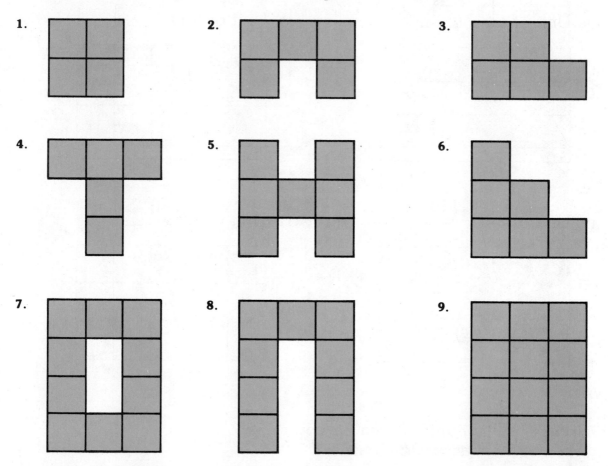

1.

2.

3.

4.

5.

6.

7.

8.

9.

For each exercise, give the area in square centimeters.

**10.**

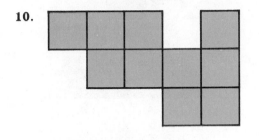

**11.**

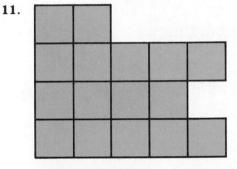

**12.**

Use centimeter grid paper.
Draw a shape for each area.

**13.** 5 square centimeters

**14.** 8 square centimeters

**15.** 10 square centimeters

**16.** 13 square centimeters

How many triangles?

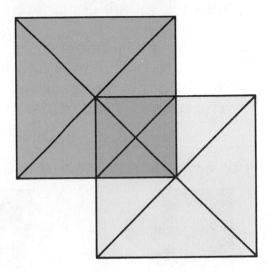

How many rectangles?

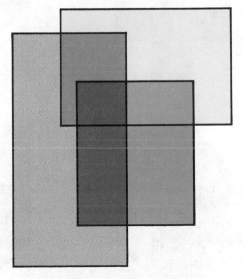

# Area: Half Units

A. Two halves of a square centimeter make 1 square centimeter.

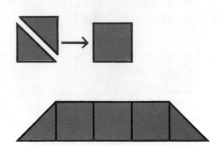

B. This shape is made up of 3 square centimeters and two halves of a square centimeter. The area is 4 square centimeters.

For each exercise, give the area in square centimeters.

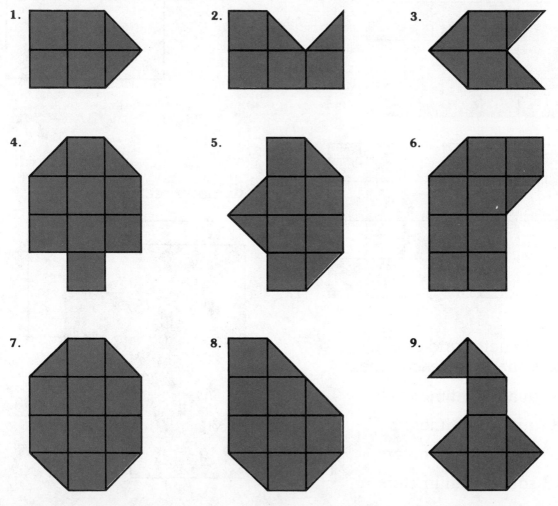

1.

2.

3.

4.

5.

6.

7.

8.

9.

For each exercise, give the area
in square centimeters.

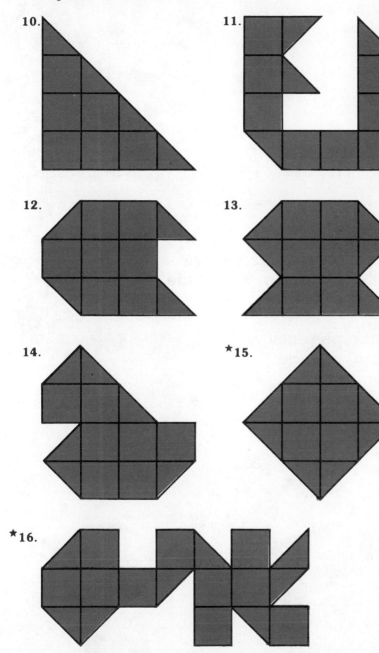

10.

11.

12.

13.

14.

*15.

*16.

## Keeping Skillful

1. 48 ÷ 8
2. 21 ÷ 7
3. 40 ÷ 5
4. 32 ÷ 4
5. 64 ÷ 8
6. 30 ÷ 6
7. 24 ÷ 3
8. 42 ÷ 7
9. 36 ÷ 4
10. 45 ÷ 5
11. 81 ÷ 9
12. 56 ÷ 8
13. 72 ÷ 9
14. 49 ÷ 7
15. 63 ÷ 9
16. 56 ÷ 7
17. 24 ÷ 6
18. 63 ÷ 7
19. 28 ÷ 4
20. 72 ÷ 8
21. 35 ÷ 7
22. 27 ÷ 3
23. 54 ÷ 6

# Three-Dimensional Shapes

These pictures show a **sphere,**
a **rectangular prism,** and a **cube.**

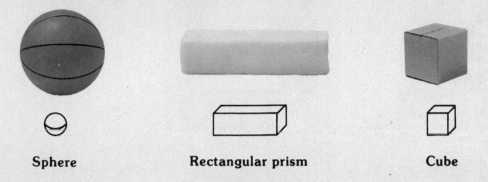

| Sphere | Rectangular prism | Cube |

•**Discuss**  Name objects in your classroom that are
shaped like a sphere, a rectangular prism, or a cube.

Name the shape each object represents.
Use sphere, rectangular prism, or cube.

1.  2.  3.

4.  5.  6.

7.  8.  9.

Give the name for each shape. Use sphere, rectangular prism, cube, or none of these.

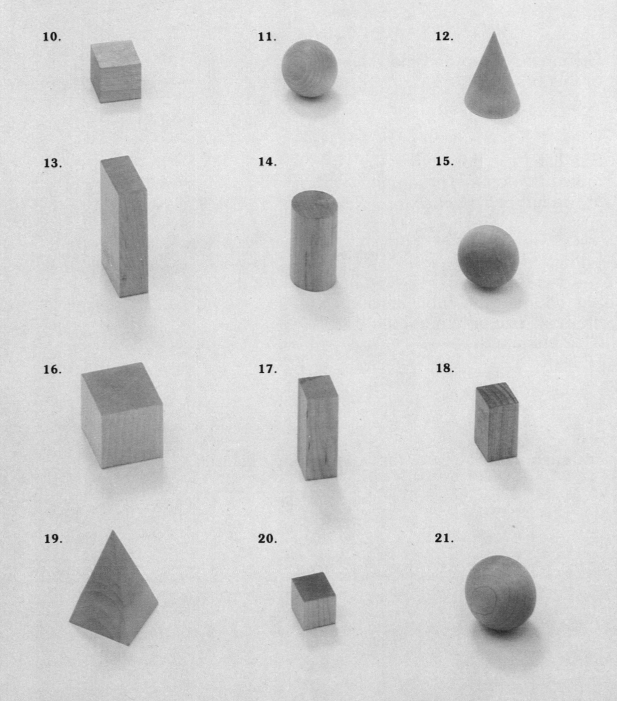

10.

11.

12.

13.

14.

15.

16.

17.

18.

19.

20.

21.

# Volume

Gwen wanted to find the **volume** of this box.

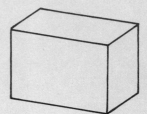

She filled the box with units of volume. These units are called **cubic units.**

 1 cubic unit

She counted the cubic units in the box. The volume of the box is 12 cubic units.

For each exercise, give the volume in cubic units.

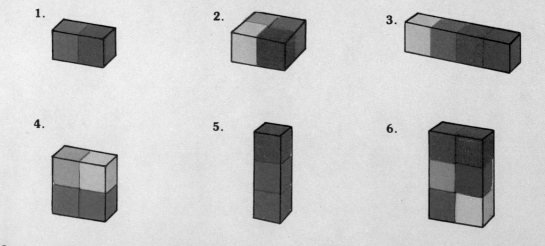

1.

2.

3.

4.

5.

6.

For each exercise, give the volume in cubic units. Remember to count the cubes that you cannot see.

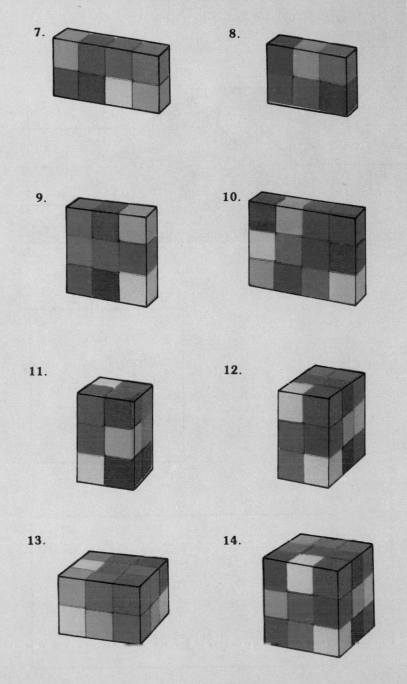

7.

8.

9.

10.

11.

12.

13.

14.

## Keeping Skillful

1. $4 \times 8$
2. $9 + 3$
3. $21 \div 7$
4. $12 - 5$
5. $48 \div 8$
6. $3 \times 9$
7. $11 - 3$
8. $5 + 8$
9. $42 \div 6$
10. $7 - 4$
11. $7 \times 4$
12. $6 \times 9$
13. $7 + 9$
14. $45 \div 5$
15. $15 - 9$
16. $9 + 8$
17. $9 \times 8$
18. $63 \div 9$
19. $8 + 7$
20. $13 - 8$
21. $56 \div 7$
22. $72 \div 8$
23. $7 \times 9$

### Triangular Puzzle Pieces

You can make different shapes by using only triangles. You need centimeter grid paper, a ruler, a pencil, and scissors. Use your ruler and pencil. Copy these triangles on the grid paper. Cut them out.

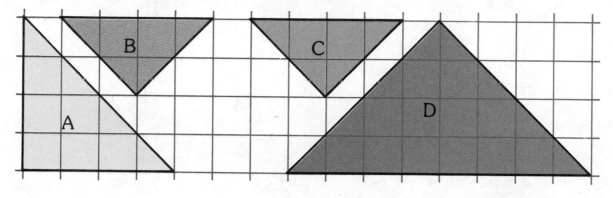

Use the triangles to make each shape. Do not overlap the triangles, and do not leave space between the triangles.

Use triangles A, B, and C.

Use triangles A, B, C, and D.

Use triangles A, B, C, and D.

# Chapter 17 Test
## Area and Volume, pages 318–330

Is the angle a right angle?
Write yes or no.

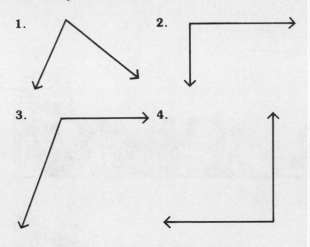

1.

2.

3.

4.

For each exercise, give the
area in square centimeters.

5.

6.

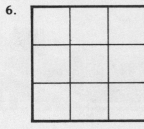

7.

8.

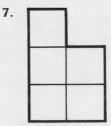

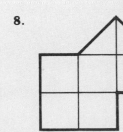

Give the name for each shape.
Use rectangular prism ( ▱ ),
sphere ( ⊖ ), or cube ( ▱ ).

9.

10.

11.

For each exercise, give the
volume in cubic units.

1 cubic unit

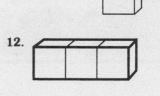

12.

13.

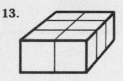

14.

15.

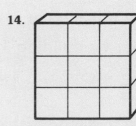

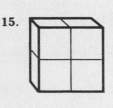

# Chapter 18 Division Computation: One-Digit Divisors

## Meaning of Division:
## The Number in Each Group

There are 15 people and 5 roller coaster cars.
The same number of people are in each car.
How many people are in each car?

**One person sat in each car.**

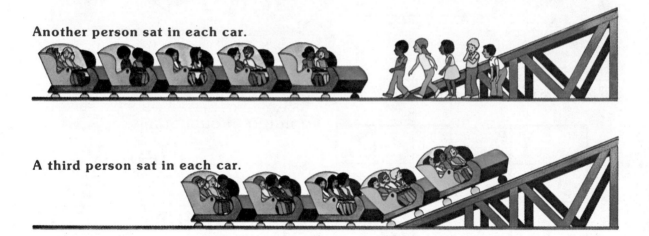

**Another person sat in each car.**

**A third person sat in each car.**

All of the people are seated.
There are 3 people in each car.

You find the answer by dividing 15 by 5.

$$5\overline{)15}^{\,3}$$

There are 3 people in each car.

Give each answer.

1. 40 race cars are on 8 tracks. Each track has the same number of cars. How many cars are on each track?

2. 30 people sat at 5 tables. The same number were at each table. How many people sat at each table?

3. There were 36 people in 9 cars. The same number were in each car. How many people were in each car?

4. There were 18 cars on 2 roads. The same number were on each road. How many cars were on each road?

5. It takes 42 minutes to go on 6 rides. Each ride takes the same amount of time. How long does each ride take?

6. There were 72 people on 9 boats. The same number were on each boat. How many people were on each boat?

7. There were 63 seats on 7 planes. The same number were on each plane. How many seats were on each plane?

8. 20 horses pulled 5 carts. Each cart was pulled by the same number of horses. How many horses pulled each cart?

9. There were 49 people on 7 rides. The same number were on each ride. How many people were on each ride?

10. There were 24 horns on 8 cars. The same number were on each car. How many horns were on each car?

## Keeping Skillful

1. $12 \div 3$
2. $24 \div 6$
3. $30 \div 6$
4. $27 \div 9$
5. $49 \div 7$
6. $8 \div 1$
7. $48 \div 8$
8. $54 \div 6$
9. $18 \div 6$
10. $25 \div 5$
11. $28 \div 7$
12. $45 \div 5$
13. $32 \div 4$
14. $81 \div 9$
15. $56 \div 7$
16. $36 \div 6$
17. $35 \div 7$
18. $16 \div 8$
19. $21 \div 7$
20. $72 \div 8$
21. $10 \div 5$
22. $64 \div 8$
23. $42 \div 6$

## Meaning of Division: The Number of Groups

Lamar has 25 peaches. How many bags of 7 peaches can he fill? How many peaches will be left over?

Separate 25 into groups of 7.

Draw 25 marks. Circle groups of 7.

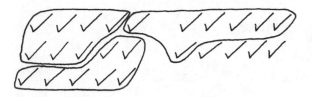

There are 3 bags of peaches. There are 4 peaches left over.

For each exercise, give the number of groups and the number left over. You can draw pictures to help you.

1. Clifton has 18 oranges. How many bags of 4 oranges can he fill? How many oranges will be left over?

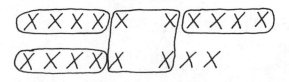

▦ bags, ▦ oranges left over

2. Carolina has 20 apples. How many trays of 8 apples can she make? How many apples will be left over?

▦ trays, ▦ apples left over

For each exercise, give the number of groups and the number left over. You can draw pictures to help you.

3. Javier has 23 pears. How many trays of 6 pears can he make? How many pears will be left over?

4. Inez has 10 cucumbers. How many trays of 8 cucumbers can she make? How many cucumbers will be left over?

5. Kathy has 35 ears of corn. How many bags of 4 ears can she fill? How many ears will be left over?

6. Lamont has 27 plums. How many bags of 3 plums can he fill? How many plums will be left over?

7. Susan has 42 onions. How many bags of 9 onions can she fill? How many onions will be left over?

8. David has 18 beets. How many bunches of 6 beets can he make? How many beets will be left over?

9. Pedro has 39 carrots. How many bunches of 8 carrots can he make? How many carrots will be left over?

10. Kazuko has 45 limes. How many bags of 7 limes can she fill? How many limes will be left over?

11. Rene has 32 lemons. How many trays of 6 lemons can she make? How many lemons will be left over?

12. Karen has 42 potatoes. How many bags of 5 potatoes can she fill? How many potatoes will be left over?

★13. Leon has 25 tomatoes. How many bags of one dozen tomatoes can he fill? How many tomatoes will be left over?

## Time Out

I'm a four-digit number.
All my digits are the same.
If you multiply me by 3,
9999 is my name.

What number am I?

# One-Digit Quotients: Remainders

A. Gloria has 50 feathers.
She uses 8 feathers to make a puppet.
How many puppets can she make?
How many feathers will be left over?

Find 50 ÷ 8.

$$8\overline{)50}$$

Divide. How many 8s in 50?   6

$$\begin{array}{r} 6 \\ 8\overline{)50} \\ -48 \\ \hline 2 \end{array}$$

Write 6 above the 0.

Multiply. 6 × 8 = 48
Subtract. The remainder is 2.

$$\begin{array}{r} 6 \text{ R2} \\ 8\overline{)50} \\ -48 \\ \hline 2 \end{array}$$

Write R2 in the answer.

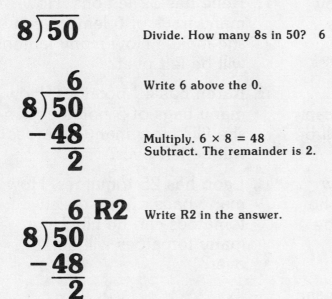

When you divide 50 by 8, the answer
is 6 remainder 2.

Quotient
6 R2  ← Remainder
Divisor ⟶ 8)50

She can make 6 puppets.
There will be 2 feathers left over.

Tell what was done in each step.

B. Find 67 ÷ 7.    C. Find 45 ÷ 9.

$$7\overline{)67} \quad \begin{array}{r} 9\ R4 \\ -63 \\ \hline 4 \end{array}$$

$$9\overline{)45} \quad \begin{array}{r} 5 \\ -45 \\ \hline 0 \end{array}$$

Divide.

1. $4\overline{)14}$    2. $2\overline{)13}$    3. $5\overline{)15}$    4. $3\overline{)16}$    5. $7\overline{)31}$    6. $9\overline{)24}$

7. $3\overline{)22}$    8. $2\overline{)11}$    9. $5\overline{)8}$    10. $4\overline{)8}$    11. $3\overline{)14}$    12. $2\overline{)19}$

13. $9\overline{)54}$    14. $6\overline{)27}$    15. $5\overline{)44}$    16. $4\overline{)39}$    17. $8\overline{)47}$    18. $6\overline{)57}$

19. $9\overline{)77}$    20. $7\overline{)55}$    21. $5\overline{)28}$    22. $6\overline{)49}$    23. $7\overline{)63}$    24. $8\overline{)59}$

25. $7\overline{)64}$    26. $8\overline{)64}$    27. $4\overline{)33}$    28. $6\overline{)52}$    29. $8\overline{)75}$    30. $9\overline{)68}$

31. Jason uses 5 pipe cleaners to make a doll. How many dolls can he make with 36 pipe cleaners? How many pipe cleaners will be left over?

32. Sally uses 8 felt squares to make a clown. How many clowns can she make with 54 felt squares? How many felt squares will be left over?

33. Regina uses 6 craft sticks to make a puppet. How many puppets can she make with 25 craft sticks? How many craft sticks will be left over?

34. Roberto uses 7 eyes to make each sea monster. How many sea monsters can he make with 60 eyes? How many eyes will be left over?

More practice
Set 34, page 365

# Two-Digit Quotients: No Remainders

A. Martin had 4 dimes and 2 pennies. He divided the 42¢ among 3 people. Each person received the same amount. How much did each person receive?

Find 42 ÷ 3.

Divide the 4 dimes among the 3 people. Each will get 1 dime. You used 3 of the dimes

$$
\begin{array}{r}
1\phantom{2} \\
3\overline{)42} \\
-3\phantom{2} \\
\hline
1\phantom{2}
\end{array}
$$

Divide 4 tens by 3.
Think: How many 3s in 4? **1**
Write 1 above the 4 tens.
Multiply. 1 × 3 = 3
Subtract. 4 − 3 = 1

$$
\begin{array}{r}
1\phantom{2} \\
3\overline{)42} \\
-3\downarrow \\
\hline
12
\end{array}
$$

Bring down the 2 ones.
There are 12 ones.

There is one dime left. Change the dime into 10 pennies. Now you have 12 pennies.

$$
\begin{array}{r}
14 \\
3\overline{)42} \\
-3\phantom{2} \\
\hline
12 \\
-12 \\
\hline
0
\end{array}
$$

Divide 12 by 3.
Think: How many 3s in 12? **4**
Write 4 above the 2.
Multiply. 4 × 3 = 12
Subtract. 12 − 12 = 0
The remainder is 0.

Divide the 12 pennies among the 3 people. Give each 4 pennies. You used all 12 of the pennies.

Each person will get 14¢.

Tell what was done in each step.

**B.** Find 96 ÷ 3.      **c.** Find 90 ÷ 2.

$$\begin{array}{r} 3 \\ 3\overline{)96} \\ -9 \\ \hline 0 \end{array}$$
$$\begin{array}{r} 4 \\ 2\overline{)90} \\ -8 \\ \hline 1 \end{array}$$

$$\begin{array}{r} 32 \\ 3\overline{)96} \\ -9\downarrow \\ \hline 06 \\ -6 \\ \hline 0 \end{array}$$
$$\begin{array}{r} 45 \\ 2\overline{)90} \\ -8\downarrow \\ \hline 10 \\ -10 \\ \hline 0 \end{array}$$

Divide.

1. $2\overline{)42}$    2. $3\overline{)39}$    3. $4\overline{)48}$    4. $3\overline{)93}$    5. $4\overline{)88}$    6. $9\overline{)99}$

7. $2\overline{)34}$    8. $4\overline{)56}$    9. $4\overline{)76}$    10. $5\overline{)65}$    11. $3\overline{)72}$    12. $5\overline{)85}$

13. $8\overline{)88}$    14. $6\overline{)78}$    15. $7\overline{)91}$    16. $6\overline{)96}$    17. $2\overline{)98}$    18. $3\overline{)81}$

19. $2\overline{)68}$    20. $6\overline{)84}$    21. $5\overline{)90}$    22. $4\overline{)60}$    23. $3\overline{)69}$    ★24. $2\overline{)80}$

25. 2 pens cost 54¢. Each pen costs the same amount. How much does each pen cost?

26. 3 tickets cost 48¢. Each ticket costs the same amount. How much does each ticket cost?

27. A pencil cost 5¢. Yoko has 75¢. How many pencils can she buy?

28. A balloon costs 4¢. Saul has 92¢. How many balloons can he buy?

More practice
Set 35, page 365

# Two-Digit Quotients: Remainders

**A.** Laveeta's mechanic shop has 98 tires. How many sets of 4 tires can she sell? How many tires will be left over?

Find 98 ÷ 4.

$$\begin{array}{r} 2 \\ 4{\overline{\smash{)}98}} \\ -8 \\ \hline 1 \end{array}$$

Divide 9 tens by 4.
Think: How many 4s in 9? *2*
Write 2 above the 9 tens.

Multiply. 2 × 4 = 8

Subtract. 9 − 8 = 1

$$\begin{array}{r} 24 \\ 4{\overline{\smash{)}98}} \\ -8\downarrow \\ \hline 18 \\ -16 \\ \hline 2 \end{array}$$

Bring down the 8.
Divide 18 by 4.
Think: How many 4s in 18? *4*
Write 4 above the 8.
Multiply. 4 × 4 = 16

Subtract. 18 − 16 = 2

$$\begin{array}{r} 24 \;\; R2 \\ 4{\overline{\smash{)}98}} \\ -8\downarrow \\ \hline 18 \\ -16 \\ \hline 2 \end{array}$$

The quotient is 24.
The remainder is 2.

She can sell 24 sets of tires.
There will be 2 tires left over.

**B.** Tell what was done in each step.

$$\begin{array}{r} 2 \\ 3{\overline{\smash{)}80}} \\ -6 \\ \hline 2 \end{array}$$

$$\begin{array}{r} 26 \\ 3{\overline{\smash{)}80}} \\ -6\downarrow \\ \hline 20 \\ -18 \\ \hline 2 \end{array}$$

$$\begin{array}{r} 26 \;\; R2 \\ 3{\overline{\smash{)}80}} \\ -6\downarrow \\ \hline 20 \\ -18 \\ \hline 2 \end{array}$$

Divide.

1. $3\overline{)37}$    2. $2\overline{)53}$    3. $6\overline{)89}$

4. $7\overline{)89}$    5. $6\overline{)82}$    6. $4\overline{)63}$

7. $8\overline{)91}$    8. $7\overline{)92}$    9. $4\overline{)90}$

10. $2\overline{)77}$    11. $8\overline{)98}$    12. $6\overline{)88}$

13. $4\overline{)79}$    14. $2\overline{)67}$    15. $4\overline{)99}$

★16. $2\overline{)61}$    ★17. $9\overline{)92}$    ★18. $8\overline{)84}$

19. There are 95 mufflers in the shop. How many cases of 4 can be filled? How many will be left over?

20. There are 76 spark plugs. How many sets of 6 can be sold? How many will be left over?

21. 7 wrenches will fit in a tool box. There are 80 wrenches. How many tool boxes can be filled? How many wrenches will be left over?

22. 8 cans of motor oil will fit on each shelf. There are 93 cans of oil. How many shelves can be filled? How many cans will be left over?

More practice
Set 36, page 365

## Using Division Computation

For each exercise, tell the number of stacks.
Then tell how many pennies are left over.

Sheila has 96 pennies.
She puts them in stacks with

1. 2 in each stack.
   Think: 2)96
2. 3 in each stack.
   Think: 3)96
3. 4 in each stack.
4. 5 in each stack.
5. 6 in each stack.
6. 7 in each stack.
7. 8 in each stack.
*8. 9 in each stack.

Larry has 97 pennies.
He puts them in stacks with

9. 2 in each stack.
10. 3 in each stack.
11. 4 in each stack.
12. 5 in each stack.
13. 6 in each stack.
14. 7 in each stack.
15. 8 in each stack.
*16. 9 in each stack.

*17. Look at exercises 1–8. How many ways can Sheila stack the 96 pennies so that there are no pennies left over?

*18. Look at exercises 9–16. How many ways can Larry stack the 97 pennies so that there are no pennies left over?

Divide.

19. $55 \div 2$
20. $27 \div 4$
21. $88 \div 8$
22. $28 \div 2$
23. $47 \div 7$
24. $26 \div 3$
25. $92 \div 8$
26. $65 \div 4$
27. $87 \div 3$
28. $51 \div 3$
29. $55 \div 4$
30. $62 \div 2$
31. $36 \div 7$
32. $38 \div 4$
33. $84 \div 3$
34. $88 \div 4$
35. $82 \div 5$
36. $29 \div 5$
37. $87 \div 7$
38. $64 \div 3$
39. $84 \div 4$
40. $98 \div 7$

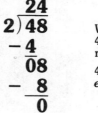

## Even and Odd Numbers

**A.** Find $73 \div 2$.

$$\begin{array}{r} 36 \text{ R1} \\ 2\overline{)73} \\ -6 \phantom{0} \\ \hline 13 \\ -12 \\ \hline 1 \end{array}$$

When you divide 73 by 2, the remainder is 1.

73 is an *odd number*.

**B.** Find $48 \div 2$.

$$\begin{array}{r} 24 \\ 2\overline{)48} \\ -4 \phantom{0} \\ \hline 08 \\ -8 \\ \hline 0 \end{array}$$

When you divide 48 by 2, the remainder is 0.

48 is an *even number*.

• **Discuss** What is the remainder when you divide an even number by 2?

• **Discuss** What is the remainder when you divide an odd number by 2?

Tell if the number is even or odd.

1. 2    2. 8    3. 7    4. 6

5. 3    6. 9    7. 5    8. 4

9. 10    10. 33    11. 19    12. 23

13. 27    14. 18    15. 12    16. 26

17. 54    18. 65    19. 56    20. 49

21. 98    22. 45    23. 72    24. 30

25. 74    26. 53    27. 77    28. 85

Choose the correct answer.

29. The digits 0, 2, 4, 6, and 8 are in the ones place of an (even, odd) number.

30. The digits 1, 3, 5, 7, and 9 are in the ones place of an (even, odd) number.

Tell if the number is even or odd. Do not divide.

31. 457    32. 676    33. 321

34. 1274    35. 9000    36. 5288

37. 32,403    38. 151,295

39. 831,242    40. 1,238,459

# Problem Solving: Choosing the Operation

READ    Roger pasted 72 pictures on 4 pages
        He put the same number on
        each page. How many pictures did
        Roger put on each page?

DECIDE    Divide the total number of pictures
          by the number of pages. Use this
          number sentence.

          $72 \div 4 = ?$

SOLVE
$$\begin{array}{r} 18 \\ 4\overline{)72} \\ -4\phantom{0} \\ \hline 32 \\ -32 \\ \hline 0 \end{array}$$

ANSWER    18 pictures

Write a number sentence. Give each answer.

1. Nancy had $4.50. She paid $3.29 for film.
   How much money did she have left?
   ($4.50 − $3.29 = ?)

2. Mr. Blake used 175 feet of movie film.
   Later he used 150 feet more. How many
   feet of film did he use in all?
   (175 + 150 = ?)

3. Ricardo has 6 rolls of film. There are 24
   pictures on each roll. How many pictures
   are there in all?
   (6 × 24 = ?)

4. Mahalia has 90¢. How many 5¢ pictures can she buy?

5. Toni took 252 pictures. 29 pictures were not good. How many of them were good?

6. Al bought 5 rolls of film. There were 36 pictures on each roll. How many pictures were there in all?

7. Mark had 8 pictures made. He paid 12¢ for each picture. How much did he pay in all?

8. Arnetta paid $1.19 for film. She paid $1.75 for flash cubes. How much did she pay in all?

9. Dave put 84 pictures in a book. He used 6 pages. He put the same number of pictures on each page. How many pictures did he put on each page?

10. Color film costs $1.89. Black and white film costs $1.09. How much more does color film cost?

11. 75 students had their pictures taken in 3 groups. There were the same number in each group. How many students were in each group?

*12. 3 rolls of movie film costs $6.78. How much does one roll cost?

## Keeping Skillful

1. $142 - 38$
2. $58 \div 2$
3. $245 + 127$
4. $32 \times 3$
5. $2 \times 49$
6. $380 - 212$
7. $74 \div 5$
8. $305 + 817$
9. $4 \times 56$
10. $864 + 437$
11. $98 \div 7$
12. $907 - 169$
13. $2175 - 1128$
14. $712 \times 8$
15. $1273 + 2149$
16. $3192 + 2678$
17. $98 \div 6$
18. $5600 - 3473$
19. $91 \div 4$
20. $68 \times 5$
21. $97 \div 3$
22. $527 \times 2$

## Chapter 18 Test
## Division Computation, pages 332–345

Divide.

1. $5\overline{)32}$    2. $6\overline{)19}$

3. $7\overline{)42}$    4. $8\overline{)70}$

5. $4\overline{)11}$    6. $9\overline{)41}$

7. $6\overline{)54}$    8. $4\overline{)18}$

9. $9\overline{)35}$    10. $3\overline{)36}$

11. $3\overline{)75}$    12. $5\overline{)70}$

13. $2\overline{)92}$    14. $2\overline{)84}$

15. $8\overline{)96}$    16. $2\overline{)69}$

17. $3\overline{)95}$    18. $5\overline{)94}$

19. $6\overline{)89}$    20. $4\overline{)87}$

21. $7\overline{)97}$    22. $4\overline{)95}$

23. $4\overline{)64}$    24. $6\overline{)68}$

25. $3\overline{)96}$    26. $4\overline{)92}$

27. $3\overline{)59}$    28. $3\overline{)81}$

29. $2\overline{)27}$    30. $7\overline{)84}$

Give each answer.

31. There are 15 puppet shows each week. How many shows are there in 9 weeks?

32. John has 54 beads. He needs 3 beads to make one puppet. How many puppets can he make?

33. Kazumi sold 115 tickets. Carole sold 246 tickets. How many tickets did they sell in all?

34. There are 96 seats in the puppet theater. There are 8 rows. Each row has the same number of seats. How many seats are in each row?

35. Demond had $1.73. He bought a ticket for $1.25. How much money did he have left?

## Problems Around Us

Pinocchio's Nose
Grows 8 centimeters for each lie
Now 64 centimeters long

Use the picture to help you find each answer.

1. How much more must Pinocchio's nose grow to be 200 centimeters long?

2. How much longer is his nose now than when it measured 48 centimeters?

3. How many lies has Pinocchio told so far?

4. If he told 25 lies, how long would Pinocchio's nose be?

Find each answer.

5. There are 39 ladybugs. Each has 8 spots. How many spots are there in all?

6. There are 99 seeds in 3 pumpkins. Each pumpkin has the same number of seeds. How many seeds are in each pumpkin?

7. A librarian has 4 shelves and 96 books. She will put the same number on each shelf. How many books will she put on each shelf?

8. Jenny has 3 packages of baseball cards. Each package has 50 cards. Jenny has how many baseball cards?

9. There were 24 students using 2 slides. Each slide had 8 steps. How many steps were there in all?

10. Bryan has 48 eggs in 6 baskets. Each basket holds the same number of eggs. How many eggs are in each basket?

# Individualized Skills Maintenance

**Diagnose**

**A** *pages 306–315*

8 × 72

5 × 271

4 × 319

**B** *pages 336–342*

73 ÷ 9

95 ÷ 5

86 ÷ 7

**Practice**

**A**

1. $\begin{array}{r} 12 \\ \times\ 3 \\ \hline \end{array}$
2. $\begin{array}{r} 13 \\ \times\ 2 \\ \hline \end{array}$
3. $\begin{array}{r} 21 \\ \times\ 3 \\ \hline \end{array}$
4. $\begin{array}{r} 16 \\ \times\ 2 \\ \hline \end{array}$
5. $\begin{array}{r} 12 \\ \times\ 7 \\ \hline \end{array}$
6. $\begin{array}{r} 25 \\ \times\ 3 \\ \hline \end{array}$

7. $\begin{array}{r} 46 \\ \times\ 4 \\ \hline \end{array}$
8. $\begin{array}{r} 29 \\ \times\ 8 \\ \hline \end{array}$
9. $\begin{array}{r} 48 \\ \times\ 7 \\ \hline \end{array}$
10. $\begin{array}{r} 217 \\ \times\ 3 \\ \hline \end{array}$
11. $\begin{array}{r} 417 \\ \times\ 2 \\ \hline \end{array}$
12. $\begin{array}{r} 132 \\ \times\ 4 \\ \hline \end{array}$

13. $\begin{array}{r} 413 \\ \times\ 5 \\ \hline \end{array}$
14. $\begin{array}{r} 621 \\ \times\ 9 \\ \hline \end{array}$
15. $\begin{array}{r} 715 \\ \times\ 6 \\ \hline \end{array}$
16. $\begin{array}{r} 183 \\ \times\ 2 \\ \hline \end{array}$
17. $\begin{array}{r} 251 \\ \times\ 4 \\ \hline \end{array}$
18. $\begin{array}{r} 591 \\ \times\ 8 \\ \hline \end{array}$

19. $\begin{array}{r} 712 \\ \times\ 7 \\ \hline \end{array}$
20. $\begin{array}{r} 38 \\ \times\ 5 \\ \hline \end{array}$
21. $\begin{array}{r} 924 \\ \times\ 3 \\ \hline \end{array}$
22. $\begin{array}{r} 47 \\ \times\ 8 \\ \hline \end{array}$
23. $\begin{array}{r} 139 \\ \times\ 2 \\ \hline \end{array}$
24. $\begin{array}{r} 472 \\ \times\ 4 \\ \hline \end{array}$

**B**

25. $9\overline{)86}$
26. $8\overline{)35}$
27. $3\overline{)25}$
28. $4\overline{)37}$
29. $7\overline{)50}$

30. $8\overline{)89}$
31. $4\overline{)92}$
32. $2\overline{)47}$
33. $6\overline{)95}$
34. $9\overline{)99}$

35. $5\overline{)75}$
36. $8\overline{)95}$
37. $3\overline{)79}$
38. $4\overline{)48}$
39. $5\overline{)64}$

40. $6\overline{)82}$
41. $3\overline{)98}$
42. $7\overline{)81}$
43. $6\overline{)81}$
44. $2\overline{)98}$

# Unit 6 Review

Chapter 16, pages 302–316
Multiply.

1. $10 \times 9$

2. $16 \times 100$

3. $13 \times 10$

4. $40 \times 7$

5. $4 \times 300$

6. $\begin{array}{r} 34 \\ \times\ 2 \\ \hline \end{array}$
7. $\begin{array}{r} 51 \\ \times\ 6 \\ \hline \end{array}$
8. $\begin{array}{r} 72 \\ \times\ 7 \\ \hline \end{array}$

9. $\begin{array}{r} 96 \\ \times\ 3 \\ \hline \end{array}$
10. $\begin{array}{r} 617 \\ \times\ 4 \\ \hline \end{array}$
11. $\begin{array}{r} 812 \\ \times\ 8 \\ \hline \end{array}$

Chapter 17, pages 318–330
Is the angle a right angle?
Write yes or no.

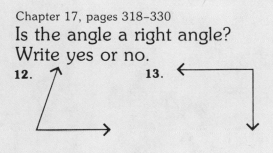

12.          13.

Name each shape. Use sphere, rectangular prism, or cube.

14.          15.          16.

For each exercise, give the area in square centimeters.

17.
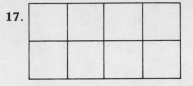

For each exercise, give the volume in cubic units.

18.

Chapter 18, pages 332–345
Divide.

19. $7\overline{)57}$     20. $9\overline{)84}$     21. $3\overline{)23}$

22. $6\overline{)77}$     23. $2\overline{)59}$     24. $4\overline{)87}$

25. $5\overline{)61}$     26. $8\overline{)89}$     27. $6\overline{)94}$

28. There are 6 pads of paper. Each pad has 116 sheets. How many sheets of paper are there in all?

29. There were 72 monkeys in 9 trees. The same number were in each tree. How many monkeys were in each tree?

# Unit 6 Test
## Chapters 16–18, pages 302–346

Multiply.

1. $8 \times 10$    2. $100 \times 6$

3. $16 \times 10$   4. $50 \times 9$

5. $600 \times 6$   6. $400 \times 8$

7. $\begin{array}{r} 31 \\ \times\ 5 \\ \hline \end{array}$    8. $\begin{array}{r} 24 \\ \times\ 2 \\ \hline \end{array}$    9. $\begin{array}{r} 51 \\ \times\ 4 \\ \hline \end{array}$

10. $\begin{array}{r} 93 \\ \times\ 3 \\ \hline \end{array}$   11. $\begin{array}{r} 25 \\ \times\ 7 \\ \hline \end{array}$   12. $\begin{array}{r} 67 \\ \times\ 8 \\ \hline \end{array}$

13. $\begin{array}{r} 328 \\ \times\ 3 \\ \hline \end{array}$   14. $\begin{array}{r} 425 \\ \times\ 2 \\ \hline \end{array}$   15. $\begin{array}{r} 916 \\ \times\ 5 \\ \hline \end{array}$

Is the angle a right angle?
Write yes or no.

16.
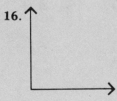

17.

For each exercise, give the area in square centimeters.

18.
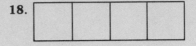

For each exercise, give the volume in cubic units.

19.
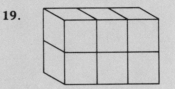

Divide.

20. $2\overline{)17}$    21. $6\overline{)15}$

22. $8\overline{)79}$    23. $9\overline{)65}$

24. $3\overline{)34}$    25. $7\overline{)82}$

26. $5\overline{)73}$    27. $8\overline{)94}$

28. $4\overline{)65}$    29. $6\overline{)83}$

30. Ms. Whitewing has 52 tubes of paint. She uses 2 tubes for each painting. How many paintings can she make?

# End-of-Book Test

Add.

1. 5
   +8

2. 7
   +9

3. 6
   +7

4. 2
   +4

5. 32
   +47

6. 38
   +14

7. 528
   +317

8. 385
   +297

9. $16 + 9 + 34$

Subtract.

10. 16
    − 7

11. 18
    − 9

12. 12
    − 6

13. 15
    − 8

14. 63
    −52

15. 73
    −25

16. 308
    −187

17. 342
    −154

Multiply.

18. 2
    ×9

19. 3
    ×4

20. 5
    ×3

21. 8
    ×6

22. 7
    ×6

23. 9
    ×8

24. 62
    × 4

25. 38
    × 2

Divide.

26. $2\overline{)14}$

27. $3\overline{)18}$

28. $4\overline{)20}$

29. $7\overline{)56}$

30. $8\overline{)64}$

31. $9\overline{)63}$

32. $3\overline{)29}$

33. $7\overline{)86}$

34. Which is greater?

$\frac{2}{3}$ or $\frac{1}{3}$

**Continued on next page**

35. Use $ and . to show the amount for *6 dollars*, *4 dimes*, and *7 pennies*.

36. Which is less?

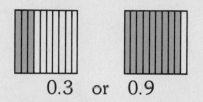

0.3   or   0.9

Replace the ●. Use < or >.

37. 58 ● 76   38. 872 ● 842

Give the numbers in order. Begin with the least number.

39. 24   26   25

40. 367   387   327

Tell what each 8 means. Use thousands, hundreds, tens, or ones.

41. 698   42. 8267

Give the standard form for each number.

43. sixty-five

44. one thousand seven hundred ninety-eight

45. Would you use meters or kilometers to measure the length of a room?

46. Give the area in square centimeters.

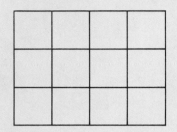

Find each answer.

47. Paul had 15 shells. He gave away 8 of them. He had how many left?

48. Megan had 5 stacks of coins. She had 7 coins in each stack. How many coins did she have in all?

49. Max found 8 yellow rocks and 5 white rocks. He found how many rocks in all?

50. Arlene has 18 spools. She uses 3 of them to make each toy. How many toys can she make?

# More Practice

## Set 1   *pages 8–9*

Give the numbers in order.
Start with the least number.

1. 4   6   3   5   **2.** 11   9   12   10   **3.** 15   17   16   14

**4.** 26   24   23   25   **5.** 33   31   34   32   **6.** 46   44   47   45

**7.** 59   57   60   58   **8.** 66   64   67   65   **9.** 73   72   74   71

## Set 2   *pages 22–23*

| **1.** 5 | **2.** 2 | **3.** 4 | **4.** 0 | **5.** 6 | **6.** 3 | **7.** 6 | **8.** 1 |
|---|---|---|---|---|---|---|---|
| +3 | +4 | +6 | +1 | +3 | +4 | +2 | +6 |

| **9.** 3 | **10.** 5 | **11.** 8 | **12.** 4 | **13.** 3 | **14.** 0 | **15.** 7 | **16.** 5 |
|---|---|---|---|---|---|---|---|
| +3 | +2 | +2 | +4 | +5 | +9 | +2 | +1 |

**17.** 3 + 0   **18.** 1 + 4   **19.** 5 + 5   **20.** 2 + 2   **21.** 7 + 3   **22.** 2 + 8

**23.** 7 + 1   **24.** 6 + 4   **25.** 3 + 7   **26.** 2 + 0   **27.** 5 + 4   **28.** 3 + 2

## Set 3   *pages 24–25*

| **1.** 7 | **2.** 4 | **3.** 5 | **4.** 9 | **5.** 3 | **6.** 7 | **7.** 7 | **8.** 7 |
|---|---|---|---|---|---|---|---|
| +4 | +9 | +7 | +2 | +8 | +5 | +7 | +9 |

| **9.** 6 | **10.** 9 | **11.** 8 | **12.** 4 | **13.** 6 | **14.** 6 | **15.** 8 | **16.** 8 |
|---|---|---|---|---|---|---|---|
| +9 | +4 | +8 | +8 | +6 | +7 | +3 | +9 |

**17.** 6 + 5   **18.** 4 + 7   **19.** 9 + 3   **20.** 5 + 8   **21.** 9 + 7   **22.** 8 + 4

**23.** 5 + 9   **24.** 8 + 6   **25.** 9 + 9   **26.** 7 + 5   **27.** 9 + 4   **28.** 7 + 6

**Set 4**  *pages 28–29*

1. $\begin{array}{r} 7 \\ -4 \\ \hline \end{array}$
2. $\begin{array}{r} 5 \\ -2 \\ \hline \end{array}$
3. $\begin{array}{r} 10 \\ -4 \\ \hline \end{array}$
4. $\begin{array}{r} 8 \\ -1 \\ \hline \end{array}$
5. $\begin{array}{r} 3 \\ -0 \\ \hline \end{array}$
6. $\begin{array}{r} 10 \\ -6 \\ \hline \end{array}$
7. $\begin{array}{r} 4 \\ -1 \\ \hline \end{array}$

8. $\begin{array}{r} 8 \\ -7 \\ \hline \end{array}$
9. $\begin{array}{r} 10 \\ -7 \\ \hline \end{array}$
10. $\begin{array}{r} 7 \\ -5 \\ \hline \end{array}$
11. $\begin{array}{r} 7 \\ -7 \\ \hline \end{array}$
12. $\begin{array}{r} 9 \\ -6 \\ \hline \end{array}$
13. $\begin{array}{r} 4 \\ -2 \\ \hline \end{array}$
14. $\begin{array}{r} 6 \\ -3 \\ \hline \end{array}$

15. $8 - 5$   16. $5 - 4$   17. $10 - 9$   18. $3 - 2$   19. $9 - 7$
20. $5 - 1$   21. $8 - 2$   22. $6 - 2$   23. $7 - 0$   24. $10 - 5$

**Set 5**  *pages 30–31*

1. $\begin{array}{r} 13 \\ -5 \\ \hline \end{array}$
2. $\begin{array}{r} 11 \\ -4 \\ \hline \end{array}$
3. $\begin{array}{r} 17 \\ -8 \\ \hline \end{array}$
4. $\begin{array}{r} 15 \\ -6 \\ \hline \end{array}$
5. $\begin{array}{r} 12 \\ -5 \\ \hline \end{array}$
6. $\begin{array}{r} 13 \\ -9 \\ \hline \end{array}$
7. $\begin{array}{r} 11 \\ -9 \\ \hline \end{array}$

8. $\begin{array}{r} 14 \\ -6 \\ \hline \end{array}$
9. $\begin{array}{r} 14 \\ -5 \\ \hline \end{array}$
10. $\begin{array}{r} 12 \\ -8 \\ \hline \end{array}$
11. $\begin{array}{r} 16 \\ -9 \\ \hline \end{array}$
12. $\begin{array}{r} 11 \\ -2 \\ \hline \end{array}$
13. $\begin{array}{r} 14 \\ -8 \\ \hline \end{array}$
14. $\begin{array}{r} 12 \\ -3 \\ \hline \end{array}$

15. $16 - 8$   16. $13 - 4$   17. $11 - 6$   18. $13 - 7$   19. $12 - 6$   20. $13 - 3$
21. $15 - 7$   22. $11 - 7$   23. $18 - 9$   24. $11 - 3$   25. $14 - 7$   26. $16 - 5$

**Set 6**  *pages 66–67*

Is 5 in the tens place? Write yes or no.

1. 524   2. 156   3. 356   4. 505   5. 571   6. 253   7. 597

Is 8 in the ones place? Write yes or no.

8. 328   9. 814   10. 268   11. 889   12. 387   13. 938   14. 879

Give the standard form for each number.

15. two hundred one   16. fifty-six   17. four hundred nineteen

(three hundred fifty-five) **355**

## More Practice

### Set 7   *pages 68–69*

What digit is in the tens place?

**1.** 347   **2.** 291   **3.** 658   **4.** 170   **5.** 249   **6.** 352   **7.** 988

What digit is in the hundreds place?

**8.** 632   **9.** 471   **10.** 395   **11.** 721   **12.** 467   **13.** 143   **14.** 992

### Set 8   *pages 74–75*

Count by twos.

**1.** Begin at 14. Stop at 24.   **2.** Begin at 242. Stop at 252.

**3.** Begin at 134. Stop at 146.   **4.** Begin at 458. Stop at 466.

Count by fives.

**5.** Begin at 35. Stop at 65.   **6.** Begin at 115. Stop at 140.

**7.** Begin at 665. Stop at 690.   **8.** Begin at 920. Stop at 945.

### Set 9   *pages 88–89*

| | | | | | | |
|---|---|---|---|---|---|---|
| **1.** 58 <br> + 5 | **2.** 37 <br> + 7 | **3.** 76 <br> + 4 | **4.** 29 <br> + 3 | **5.** 45 <br> + 9 | **6.** 17 <br> + 9 | **7.** 68 <br> + 7 |
| **8.** 32 <br> + 9 | **9.** 26 <br> + 69 | **10.** 37 <br> + 45 | **11.** 58 <br> + 26 | **12.** 14 <br> + 36 | **13.** 49 <br> + 28 | **14.** 64 <br> + 19 |
| **15.** 13 <br> + 57 | **16.** 29 <br> + 47 | **17.** 76 <br> + 9 | **18.** 33 <br> + 8 | **19.** 57 <br> + 6 | **20.** 28 <br> + 3 | **21.** 45 <br> + 37 |

**Set 10** *pages 90–91*

1. 435
+ 25

2. 259
+ 34

3. 637
+ 35

4. 306
+ 25

5. 924
+ 16

6. 149
+ 38

7. 376
+ 107

8. 625
+ 348

9. 167
+ 226

10. 437
+ 123

11. 419
+ 532

12. 258
+ 206

13. 424
+ 458

14. 538
+ 23

15. 529
+ 125

16. 718
+ 18

17. 419
+ 256

18. 376
+ 14

**Set 11** *pages 92–93*

1. 137
+ 92

2. 747
+ 70

3. 591
+ 95

4. 385
+ 21

5. 494
+ 64

6. 152
+ 72

7. 287
+ 91

8. 252
+ 183

9. 560
+ 346

10. 353
+ 561

11. 392
+ 147

12. 282
+ 691

13. 194
+ 583

14. 166
+ 281

15. 474
+ 164

16. 183
+ 244

17. 854
+ 92

18. 563
+ 66

**Set 12** *pages 98–99*

1. 53
29
+ 8

2. 57
23
+ 4

3. 24
36
+ 31

4. 28
32
+ 3

5. 27
45
+ 17

6. 18
46
+ 26

7. 262
30
+ 12

8. 223
184
+ 62

9. 536
92
+ 180

10. 254
362
+ 143

11. 541
170
+ 197

12. 39
153
+ 204

# More Practice

## Set 13 *pages 108–109*

| | | | | | | |
|---|---|---|---|---|---|---|
| 1. 40<br>− 5 | 2. 73<br>− 7 | 3. 52<br>− 3 | 4. 36<br>− 7 | 5. 81<br>− 8 | 6. 44<br>− 8 | 7. 62<br>− 4 |

| | | | | | | |
|---|---|---|---|---|---|---|
| 8. 67<br>−39 | 9. 36<br>−28 | 10. 45<br>−27 | 11. 60<br>−21 | 12. 35<br>−26 | 13. 92<br>−36 | 14. 83<br>−74 |

## Set 14 *pages 110–111*

| | | | | | |
|---|---|---|---|---|---|
| 1. 980<br>− 4 | 2. 171<br>− 4 | 3. 254<br>− 7 | 4. 320<br>− 8 | 5. 185<br>− 36 | 6. 171<br>− 49 |

| | | | | | |
|---|---|---|---|---|---|
| 7. 482<br>− 48 | 8. 571<br>− 27 | 9. 752<br>− 37 | 10. 766<br>−318 | 11. 692<br>−646 | 12. 365<br>−218 |

| | | | | | |
|---|---|---|---|---|---|
| 13. 580<br>−536 | 14. 676<br>−357 | 15. 971<br>−568 | 16. 243<br>−229 | 17. 583<br>−418 | 18. 361<br>−316 |

## Set 15 *pages 112–113*

| | | | | | |
|---|---|---|---|---|---|
| 1. 438<br>− 85 | 2. 556<br>− 83 | 3. 206<br>− 12 | 4. 716<br>− 61 | 5. 767<br>− 74 | 6. 969<br>− 84 |

| | | | | | |
|---|---|---|---|---|---|
| 7. 325<br>− 64 | 8. 214<br>− 32 | 9. 424<br>− 73 | 10. 509<br>− 53 | 11. 815<br>−453 | 12. 359<br>−167 |

| | | | | | |
|---|---|---|---|---|---|
| 13. 429<br>−190 | 14. 802<br>−721 | 15. 746<br>−574 | 16. 867<br>−391 | 17. 537<br>−243 | 18. 639<br>−376 |

**Set 16** *pages 118–119*

| 1. $3.25<br>− 1.16 | 2. $7.20<br>+ 1.45 | 3. $1.40<br>+ 0.25 | 4. $2.93<br>− 1.80 | 5. $4.65<br>+ 1.25 |
|---|---|---|---|---|
| 6. $9.60<br>− 0.80 | 7. $1.75<br>+ 1.42 | 8. $2.29<br>− 1.45 | 9. $3.50<br>+ 1.50 | 10. $0.80<br>+ 0.04 |
| 11. $1.94<br>+ 0.52 | 12. $4.73<br>+ 1.07 | 13. $0.85<br>− 0.48 | 14. $3.48<br>− 0.19 | 15. $9.35<br>− 3.50 |

**Set 17** *pages 154–155*

1. $2 \times 5$  2. $4 \times 2$  3. $3 \times 6$  4. $9 \times 3$  5. $8 \times 2$  6. $3 \times 4$
7. $2 \times 3$  8. $3 \times 3$  9. $2 \times 6$  10. $2 \times 4$  11. $5 \times 3$  12. $7 \times 3$
13. $9 \times 2$  14. $3 \times 9$  15. $2 \times 8$  16. $8 \times 3$  17. $6 \times 2$  18. $6 \times 3$
19. $3 \times 7$  20. $4 \times 3$  21. $2 \times 2$  22. $7 \times 2$  23. $2 \times 9$  24. $5 \times 2$

**Set 18** *pages 160–161*

| 1. 7<br>× 5 | 2. 2<br>× 7 | 3. 4<br>× 4 | 4. 5<br>× 6 | 5. 2<br>× 5 | 6. 3<br>× 3 | 7. 3<br>× 9 | 8. 4<br>× 6 |
|---|---|---|---|---|---|---|---|
| 9. 9<br>× 4 | 10. 3<br>× 6 | 11. 9<br>× 5 | 12. 2<br>× 9 | 13. 4<br>× 5 | 14. 4<br>× 2 | 15. 5<br>× 8 | 16. 5<br>× 7 |
| 17. 3<br>× 4 | 18. 8<br>× 2 | 19. 6<br>× 4 | 20. 5<br>× 3 | 21. 5<br>× 5 | 22. 5<br>× 9 | 23. 2<br>× 3 | 24. 4<br>× 9 |
| 25. 4<br>× 8 | 26. 6<br>× 5 | 27. 2<br>× 2 | 28. 3<br>× 8 | 29. 7<br>× 4 | 30. 6<br>× 2 | 31. 7<br>× 3 | 32. 5<br>× 4 |

# More Practice

**Set 19**  *pages 168–169*

| | | | | | | | |
|---|---|---|---|---|---|---|---|
| 1. 5 ×2 | 2. 1 ×1 | 3. 2 ×6 | 4. 7 ×0 | 5. 3 ×3 | 6. 6 ×6 | 7. 4 ×5 | 8. 3 ×5 |
| 9. 9 ×4 | 10. 6 ×8 | 11. 2 ×4 | 12. 8 ×4 | 13. 6 ×1 | 14. 4 ×7 | 15. 0 ×3 | 16. 6 ×3 |
| 17. 5 ×9 | 18. 9 ×1 | 19. 4 ×0 | 20. 2 ×8 | 21. 9 ×6 | 22. 5 ×5 | 23. 1 ×5 | 24. 7 ×6 |

**Set 20**  *pages 174–175*

| | | | | | | | |
|---|---|---|---|---|---|---|---|
| 1. 8 ×7 | 2. 2 ×5 | 3. 6 ×4 | 4. 7 ×7 | 5. 6 ×8 | 6. 0 ×4 | 7. 5 ×3 | 8. 4 ×7 |
| 9. 5 ×7 | 10. 4 ×5 | 11. 2 ×8 | 12. 3 ×6 | 13. 8 ×8 | 14. 9 ×2 | 15. 7 ×6 | 16. 5 ×8 |
| 17. 7 ×9 | 18. 6 ×5 | 19. 8 ×1 | 20. 9 ×4 | 21. 3 ×9 | 22. 9 ×8 | 23. 6 ×6 | 24. 9 ×9 |

**Set 21**  *pages 192–193*

Is 6 in the thousands place? Write yes or no.

1. 6037   2. 2664   3. 4368   4. 6897   5. 6430   6. 629

Is 3 in the hundreds place? Write yes or no.

7. 3952   8. 6235   9. 9308   10. 341   11. 3431   12. 5372

**Set 22**   *pages 206–207*

| 1. 2417 +4561 | 2. 4318 +1462 | 3. 1536 +2390 | 4. 2745 +1823 | 5. 1426 +7556 | 6. 7247 +1942 |
|---|---|---|---|---|---|
| 7. 7600 + 534 | 8. 8145 + 607 | 9. 2304 + 489 | 10. 1476 + 271 | 11. 3467 + 192 | 12. 5728 + 871 |

**Set 23**   *pages 210–211*

| 1. 784 +159 | 2. 493 +277 | 3. 366 +534 | 4. 379 + 33 | 5. 478 + 27 | 6. 603 + 98 |
|---|---|---|---|---|---|
| 7. 4677 + 126 | 8. 3519 + 958 | 9. 5142 +1885 | 10. 3420 +1786 | 11. 6156 +2385 | 12. 2718 +3843 |
| 13. 7026 +1897 | 14. 4573 +1675 | 15. 5916 +2437 | 16. 6213 +1959 | 17. 2964 +4572 | 18. 1395 +7297 |

**Set 24**   *pages 218–219*

| 1. 571 − 62 | 2. 782 −354 | 3. 473 −259 | 4. 828 −594 | 5. 719 −655 | 6. 638 −195 |
|---|---|---|---|---|---|
| 7. 4595 −2136 | 8. 2478 −1763 | 9. 9578 −7654 | 10. 6397 −1228 | 11. 5376 −4523 | 12. 3886 − 549 |

13. $293 - 46$     14. $359 - 178$     15. $578 - 293$     16. $828 - 347$

17. $384 - 168$     18. $393 - 289$     19. $2839 - 659$     20. $4565 - 1842$

21. $7529 - 2819$     22. $8498 - 3756$     23. $6853 - 761$     24. $5247 - 4702$

## More Practice

**Set 25**  *pages 222-223*

| | | | | | |
|---|---|---|---|---|---|
| 1. 561<br>− 72 | 2. 752<br>−384 | 3. 453<br>−279 | 4. 824<br>−598 | 5. 719<br>−655 | 6. 635<br>−198 |
| 7. 4195<br>−2536 | 8. 2473<br>−1768 | 9. 9548<br>−6674 | 10. 6327<br>−1298 | 11. 5372<br>−4526 | 12. 3846<br>− 589 |
| 13. 243<br>− 96 | 14. 358<br>−179 | 15. 573<br>−298 | 16. 827<br>−348 | 17. 364<br>−186 | 18. 383<br>−299 |

**Set 26**  *pages 224-225*

| | | | | | |
|---|---|---|---|---|---|
| 1. 800<br>− 76 | 2. 500<br>− 38 | 3. 700<br>−241 | 4. 206<br>− 98 | 5. 608<br>−219 | 6. 805<br>−357 |
| 7. 2800<br>−1543 | 8. 4900<br>−3683 | 9. 8070<br>−4526 | 10. 5090<br>−4158 | 11. 3008<br>−1726 | 12. 6004<br>−3981 |
| 13. 7502<br>−4036 | 14. 4830<br>− 925 | 15. 9670<br>−1854 | 16. 8063<br>−5247 | 17. 680<br>−395 | 18. 340<br>−145 |

**Set 27**  *pages 246-247*

| | | | | | |
|---|---|---|---|---|---|
| 1. $4 \div 2$ | 2. $6 \div 2$ | 3. $24 \div 3$ | 4. $6 \div 3$ | 5. $10 \div 5$ | 6. $21 \div 3$ |
| 7. $27 \div 3$ | 8. $3 \div 3$ | 9. $14 \div 7$ | 10. $18 \div 2$ | 11. $8 \div 4$ | 12. $8 \div 2$ |
| 13. $12 \div 4$ | 14. $24 \div 8$ | 15. $12 \div 2$ | 16. $15 \div 3$ | 17. $18 \div 6$ | 18. $18 \div 9$ |
| 19. $10 \div 2$ | 20. $14 \div 2$ | 21. $21 \div 7$ | 22. $9 \div 3$ | 23. $18 \div 9$ | 24. $16 \div 8$ |
| 25. $16 \div 2$ | 26. $12 \div 6$ | 27. $18 \div 3$ | 28. $12 \div 3$ | 29. $2 \div 1$ | 30. $9 \div 3$ |
| 31. $27 \div 9$ | 32. $15 \div 5$ | 33. $16 \div 8$ | 34. $21 \div 3$ | 35. $8 \div 2$ | 36. $15 \div 3$ |

**Set 28**  *pages 252–253*

1. $4\overline{)8}$  2. $8\overline{)32}$  3. $5\overline{)5}$  4. $3\overline{)9}$  5. $9\overline{)36}$  6. $7\overline{)35}$  7. $4\overline{)24}$

8. $5\overline{)30}$  9. $4\overline{)16}$  10. $2\overline{)14}$  11. $8\overline{)24}$  12. $3\overline{)15}$  13. $9\overline{)18}$  14. $4\overline{)28}$

15. $5\overline{)20}$  16. $6\overline{)24}$  17. $9\overline{)45}$  18. $5\overline{)40}$  19. $7\overline{)21}$  20. $4\overline{)12}$  21. $2\overline{)4}$

22. $27 \div 3$  23. $32 \div 4$  24. $15 \div 5$  25. $6 \div 3$  26. $45 \div 9$  27. $30 \div 6$

28. $10 \div 5$  29. $12 \div 6$  30. $36 \div 4$  31. $40 \div 8$  32. $16 \div 8$  33. $12 \div 3$

34. $4 \div 1$  35. $28 \div 7$  36. $20 \div 4$  37. $25 \div 5$  38. $35 \div 5$  39. $18 \div 6$


**Set 29**  *pages 258–259*

1. $7\overline{)42}$  2. $5\overline{)30}$  3. $2\overline{)18}$  4. $4\overline{)32}$  5. $5\overline{)25}$  6. $3\overline{)12}$  7. $2\overline{)12}$

8. $4\overline{)8}$  9. $7\overline{)35}$  10. $1\overline{)3}$  11. $7\overline{)28}$  12. $6\overline{)54}$  13. $5\overline{)40}$  14. $7\overline{)21}$

15. $8\overline{)48}$  16. $4\overline{)36}$  17. $6\overline{)24}$  18. $6\overline{)6}$  19. $3\overline{)15}$  20. $5\overline{)20}$  21. $9\overline{)45}$

22. $27 \div 9$  23. $1 \div 1$  24. $18 \div 6$  25. $6 \div 3$  26. $9 \div 3$  27. $20 \div 4$

28. $36 \div 9$  29. $24 \div 3$  30. $14 \div 7$  31. $42 \div 6$  32. $4 \div 2$  33. $10 \div 5$

34. $24 \div 4$  35. $16 \div 4$  36. $54 \div 9$  37. $40 \div 8$  38. $48 \div 6$  39. $36 \div 6$


**Set 30**  *pages 264–265*

1. $7\overline{)49}$  2. $9\overline{)36}$  3. $3\overline{)18}$  4. $9\overline{)81}$  5. $3\overline{)24}$  6. $6\overline{)42}$  7. $1\overline{)5}$

8. $5\overline{)30}$  9. $3\overline{)12}$  10. $7\overline{)56}$  11. $4\overline{)16}$  12. $8\overline{)32}$  13. $3\overline{)15}$  14. $8\overline{)48}$

15. $2\overline{)10}$  16. $2\overline{)4}$  17. $8\overline{)40}$  18. $4\overline{)8}$  19. $8\overline{)72}$  20. $3\overline{)27}$  21. $5\overline{)25}$

22. $3 \div 3$  23. $6 \div 2$  24. $24 \div 6$  25. $9 \div 3$  26. $12 \div 6$  27. $35 \div 5$

28. $63 \div 9$  29. $18 \div 9$  30. $16 \div 8$  31. $36 \div 6$  32. $20 \div 4$  33. $64 \div 8$

34. $21 \div 7$  35. $72 \div 9$  36. $14 \div 7$  37. $45 \div 9$  38. $28 \div 7$  39. $54 \div 6$

# More Practice

**Set 31**  *pages 304–305*

1. $2 \times 20$  2. $30 \times 5$  3. $70 \times 9$  4. $8 \times 40$  5. $6 \times 700$

6. $9 \times 400$  7. $4 \times 600$  8. $3 \times 900$  9. $60 \times 3$  10. $50 \times 4$

11. $600 \times 2$  12. $200 \times 7$  13. $80 \times 5$  14. $6 \times 800$  15. $3 \times 700$

16. $9 \times 20$  17. $80 \times 8$  18. $5 \times 90$  19. $300 \times 8$  20. $5 \times 500$

21. $4 \times 700$  22. $700 \times 7$  23. $9 \times 90$  24. $20 \times 8$  25. $800 \times 9$

**Set 32**  *pages 310–311*

1. $76 \times 2$  2. $32 \times 7$  3. $47 \times 5$  4. $82 \times 6$  5. $56 \times 3$  6. $39 \times 8$  7. $24 \times 9$

8. $77 \times 4$  9. $56 \times 5$  10. $19 \times 6$  11. $75 \times 3$  12. $63 \times 4$  13. $98 \times 6$  14. $25 \times 8$

15. $89 \times 3$  16. $27 \times 9$  17. $65 \times 5$  18. $28 \times 7$  19. $87 \times 2$  20. $44 \times 8$  21. $53 \times 6$

**Set 33**  *pages 312–313*

1. $148 \times 2$  2. $117 \times 5$  3. $342 \times 4$  4. $412 \times 8$  5. $329 \times 3$  6. $215 \times 6$  7. $663 \times 3$

8. $515 \times 5$  9. $746 \times 2$  10. $219 \times 4$  11. $331 \times 8$  12. $516 \times 6$  13. $972 \times 3$  14. $721 \times 7$

15. $832 \times 4$  16. $441 \times 5$  17. $643 \times 2$  18. $191 \times 9$  19. $513 \times 7$  20. $882 \times 3$  21. $954 \times 2$

**Set 34**  *pages 336–337*

1. $3\overline{)20}$   2. $5\overline{)48}$   3. $2\overline{)7}$   4. $6\overline{)42}$   5. $8\overline{)43}$   6. $8\overline{)76}$   7. $5\overline{)9}$

8. $4\overline{)37}$   9. $9\overline{)45}$   10. $3\overline{)28}$   11. $8\overline{)35}$   12. $7\overline{)58}$   13. $6\overline{)40}$   14. $5\overline{)32}$

15. $9\overline{)66}$   16. $7\overline{)51}$   17. $2\overline{)17}$   18. $6\overline{)34}$   19. $9\overline{)80}$   20. $7\overline{)46}$   21. $4\overline{)30}$

22. $3\overline{)19}$   23. $8\overline{)15}$   24. $6\overline{)25}$   25. $2\overline{)16}$   26. $7\overline{)38}$   27. $3\overline{)26}$   28. $9\overline{)72}$

29. $8\overline{)57}$   30. $4\overline{)18}$   31. $2\overline{)14}$   32. $9\overline{)42}$   33. $4\overline{)26}$   34. $6\overline{)51}$   35. $5\overline{)49}$


**Set 35**  *pages 338–339*

1. $2\overline{)36}$   2. $4\overline{)68}$   3. $3\overline{)78}$   4. $2\overline{)64}$   5. $3\overline{)54}$   6. $4\overline{)44}$   7. $6\overline{)72}$

8. $7\overline{)84}$   9. $2\overline{)46}$   10. $4\overline{)52}$   11. $3\overline{)57}$   12. $7\overline{)98}$   13. $4\overline{)84}$   14. $6\overline{)66}$

15. $2\overline{)58}$   16. $3\overline{)51}$   17. $5\overline{)95}$   18. $2\overline{)74}$   19. $6\overline{)90}$   20. $5\overline{)55}$   21. $8\overline{)96}$

22. $3\overline{)45}$   23. $7\overline{)77}$   24. $5\overline{)70}$   25. $3\overline{)39}$   26. $5\overline{)60}$   27. $4\overline{)96}$   28. $4\overline{)72}$

29. $2\overline{)86}$   30. $4\overline{)64}$   31. $2\overline{)94}$   32. $3\overline{)75}$   33. $5\overline{)80}$   34. $3\overline{)63}$   35. $2\overline{)52}$


**Set 36**  *pages 340–341*

1. $4\overline{)73}$   2. $3\overline{)65}$   3. $7\overline{)88}$   4. $2\overline{)67}$   5. $5\overline{)76}$   6. $6\overline{)87}$   7. $3\overline{)74}$

8. $8\overline{)95}$   9. $5\overline{)71}$   10. $3\overline{)56}$   11. $5\overline{)89}$   12. $6\overline{)93}$   13. $2\overline{)97}$   14. $7\overline{)79}$

15. $4\overline{)55}$   16. $3\overline{)85}$   17. $2\overline{)49}$   18. $8\overline{)99}$   19. $5\overline{)81}$   20. $4\overline{)66}$   21. $2\overline{)63}$

22. $6\overline{)88}$   23. $2\overline{)95}$   24. $4\overline{)69}$   25. $7\overline{)85}$   26. $2\overline{)89}$   27. $5\overline{)98}$   28. $4\overline{)67}$

29. $6\overline{)79}$   30. $8\overline{)89}$   31. $5\overline{)93}$   32. $7\overline{)96}$   33. $6\overline{)75}$   34. $4\overline{)86}$   35. $7\overline{)99}$

36. $7\overline{)34}$   37. $4\overline{)59}$   38. $2\overline{)27}$   39. $5\overline{)51}$   40. $3\overline{)52}$   41. $9\overline{)97}$   42. $5\overline{)68}$

# Metric System

### Length

The basic unit of length is the meter*. The distance from a door knob to the floor is about 1 meter.

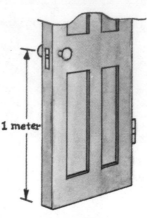

Millimeter, centimeter, and kilometer are other commonly used units of length.

The thickness of a dime is about 1 millimeter.

The distance across a fingernail is about 1 centimeter.

The length of ten football fields placed end to end is about 1 kilometer.

### Mass (weight)**

The basic unit of mass is the kilogram. The mass of this football is about 1 kilogram.

Gram is another commonly used unit of mass. The mass of a dollar bill is about 1 gram.

The mass of a grain of sand is about 1 milligram.

### Capacity

The basic unit of capacity is the liter*. This milk carton holds about 1 liter.

Milliliter is another commonly used unit of capacity. An eyedropper holds about 1 milliliter of liquid.

*The word *meter* may also be spelled *metre*, and the word *liter* may be spelled *litre*. The -er spelling is in common usage in the United States and appears in this program.

**The units of mass are often referred to as units of weight. In common usage and in this program, the term *weight* is generally used to mean *mass* and the term *weigh* to mean *determine the mass of* or *have a mass of*.

## Area

Square centimeter and square meter are commonly used units of area in the metric system.

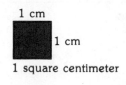

1 square centimeter

## Volume

The cubic centimeter is a commonly used unit of volume. If the cube shown here were filled with water, the amount of water would be 1 milliliter. The mass of the water would be 1 gram.

A cube with a volume of 1 cubic decimeter measures 1 decimeter, or 10 centimeters, on each edge. If a cubic decimeter were filled with water, the amount of water would be 1 liter. The mass of the water would be 1 kilogram.

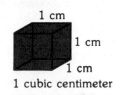

1 cubic centimeter

## Temperature

The Celsius scale is commonly used in countries employing the metric system.

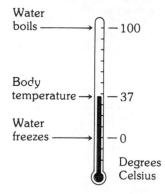

Water boils — 100
Body temperature — 37
Water freezes — 0
Degrees Celsius

## Prefixes and Symbols

This table shows the most common prefixes in the metric system, as well as their symbols and meanings.

| Prefix | Symbol | Meaning |
| --- | --- | --- |
| mega- | M | million |
| kilo- | k | thousand |
| hecto- | h | hundred |
| deka- | da | ten |
| deci- | d | tenth |
| centi- | c | hundredth |
| milli- | m | thousandth |
| micro- | $\mu$ | millionth |

This display relates some of the prefixes in the metric system to the base-ten numeration system.

| kilo- thousands | hecto- hundreds | deka- tens | ones | deci- tenths | centi- hundredths | milli- thousandths |
| --- | --- | --- | --- | --- | --- | --- |

Here are official symbols for some common metric measures. They do not need periods. You need not add an -s for the plural form.

| | |
| --- | --- |
| meter | m |
| kilometer | km |
| centimeter | cm |
| millimeter | mm |
| liter | L |
| milliliter | mL |
| kilogram | kg |
| gram | g |
| square meter | $m^2$ |
| square centimeter | $cm^2$ |
| cubic meter | $m^3$ |
| cubic centimeter | $cm^3$ |

# Tables

## Metric System

**Length**

$$10 \text{ millimeters (mm)} = 1 \text{ centimeter (cm)}$$
$$\left.\begin{array}{l} 10 \text{ centimeters} \\ 100 \text{ millimeters} \end{array}\right\} = 1 \text{ decimeter (dm)}$$
$$\left.\begin{array}{l} 10 \text{ decimeters} \\ 100 \text{ centimeters} \end{array}\right\} = 1 \text{ meter (m)}$$
$$1000 \text{ meters} = 1 \text{ kilometer (km)}$$

**Area**

$$100 \text{ square millimeters (mm}^2) = 1 \text{ square centimeter (cm}^2)$$
$$10,000 \text{ square centimeters} = 1 \text{ square meter (m}^2)$$
$$100 \text{ square meters} = 1 \text{ are (a)}$$
$$10,000 \text{ square meters} = 1 \text{ hectare (ha)}$$

**Volume**

$$1000 \text{ cubic millimeters (mm}^3) = 1 \text{ cubic centimeter (cm}^3)$$
$$1000 \text{ cubic centimeters} = 1 \text{ cubic decimeter (dm}^3)$$
$$1,000,000 \text{ cubic centimeters} = 1 \text{ cubic meter (m}^3)$$

**Mass (weight)**

$$1000 \text{ milligrams (mg)} = 1 \text{ gram (g)}$$
$$1000 \text{ grams} = 1 \text{ kilogram (kg)}$$
$$1000 \text{ kilograms} = 1 \text{ metric ton (t)}$$

**Capacity**

$$1000 \text{ milliliters (mL)} = 1 \text{ liter (L)}$$

## Customary System

**Length**

$$12 \text{ inches (in.)} = 1 \text{ foot (ft.)}$$
$$\left.\begin{array}{l} 3 \text{ feet} \\ 36 \text{ inches} \end{array}\right\} = 1 \text{ yard (yd.)}$$
$$\left.\begin{array}{l} 1760 \text{ yards} \\ 5280 \text{ feet} \end{array}\right\} = 1 \text{ mile (mi.)}$$
$$6076 \text{ feet} = 1 \text{ nautical mile}$$

**Area**

$$144 \text{ square inches (sq. in.)} = 1 \text{ square foot (sq. ft.)}$$
$$9 \text{ square feet} = 1 \text{ square yard (sq. yd.)}$$
$$4840 \text{ square yards} = 1 \text{ acre (A.)}$$

**Volume**

$$1728 \text{ cubic inches (cu. in.)} = 1 \text{ cubic foot (cu. ft.)}$$
$$27 \text{ cubic feet} = 1 \text{ cubic yard (cu. yd.)}$$

**Weight**

$$16 \text{ ounces (oz.)} = 1 \text{ pound (lb.)}$$
$$2000 \text{ pounds} = 1 \text{ ton (T.)}$$

**Capacity**

$$8 \text{ fluid ounces (fl. oz.)} = 1 \text{ cup (c.)}$$
$$2 \text{ cups} = 1 \text{ pint (pt.)}$$
$$2 \text{ pints} = 1 \text{ quart (qt.)}$$
$$4 \text{ quarts} = 1 \text{ gallon (gal.)}$$

## Time

$$60 \text{ seconds} = 1 \text{ minute}$$
$$60 \text{ minutes} = 1 \text{ hour}$$
$$24 \text{ hours} = 1 \text{ day}$$
$$7 \text{ days} = 1 \text{ week}$$
$$\left.\begin{array}{l} 365 \text{ days} \\ 52 \text{ weeks} \\ 12 \text{ months} \end{array}\right\} = 1 \text{ year}$$
$$366 \text{ days} = 1 \text{ leap year}$$

## Addition-Subtraction Table

| + | 0 | 1 | 2 | 3 | 4 | 5 | 6 | 7 | 8 | 9 |
|---|---|---|---|---|---|---|---|---|---|---|
| 0 | 0 | 1 | 2 | 3 | 4 | 5 | 6 | 7 | 8 | 9 |
| 1 | 1 | 2 | 3 | 4 | 5 | 6 | 7 | 8 | 9 | 10 |
| 2 | 2 | 3 | 4 | 5 | 6 | 7 | 8 | 9 | 10 | 11 |
| 3 | 3 | 4 | 5 | 6 | 7 | 8 | 9 | 10 | 11 | 12 |
| 4 | 4 | 5 | 6 | 7 | 8 | 9 | 10 | 11 | 12 | 13 |
| 5 | 5 | 6 | 7 | 8 | 9 | 10 | 11 | 12 | 13 | 14 |
| 6 | 6 | 7 | 8 | 9 | 10 | 11 | 12 | 13 | 14 | 15 |
| 7 | 7 | 8 | 9 | 10 | 11 | 12 | 13 | 14 | 15 | 16 |
| 8 | 8 | 9 | 10 | 11 | 12 | 13 | 14 | 15 | 16 | 17 |
| 9 | 9 | 10 | 11 | 12 | 13 | 14 | 15 | 16 | 17 | 18 |

## Multiplication-Division Table

| × | 1 | 2 | 3 | 4 | 5 | 6 | 7 | 8 | 9 |
|---|---|---|---|---|---|---|---|---|---|
| 1 | 1 | 2 | 3 | 4 | 5 | 6 | 7 | 8 | 9 |
| 2 | 2 | 4 | 6 | 8 | 10 | 12 | 14 | 16 | 18 |
| 3 | 3 | 6 | 9 | 12 | 15 | 18 | 21 | 24 | 27 |
| 4 | 4 | 8 | 12 | 16 | 20 | 24 | 28 | 32 | 36 |
| 5 | 5 | 10 | 15 | 20 | 25 | 30 | 35 | 40 | 45 |
| 6 | 6 | 12 | 18 | 24 | 30 | 36 | 42 | 48 | 54 |
| 7 | 7 | 14 | 21 | 28 | 35 | 42 | 49 | 56 | 63 |
| 8 | 8 | 16 | 24 | 32 | 40 | 48 | 56 | 64 | 72 |
| 9 | 9 | 18 | 27 | 36 | 45 | 54 | 63 | 72 | 81 |

# Glossary

**Acute angle**  An angle that has a measure less than 90°

**Addend**  A number that is added. In 8 + 4 – 12, the addends are 8 and 4.

**Angle** (∠)  Two rays with the same endpoint.

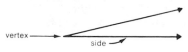

**Area**  A number indicating the size of the inside of a plane figure. The area of this figure is 8 square units.

**Associative property of addition**  The way in which addends are grouped does not affect the sum. Also called the grouping property of addition.
(7 + 2) + 5 = 7 + (2 + 5)

**Associative property of multiplication**  The way in which factors are grouped does not affect the product. Also called the grouping property of multiplication.
(7 × 2) × 5 = 7 × (2 × 5)

**Average**  A number obtained by dividing the sum of two or more addends by the number of addends.

**Basic fact**  A number sentence that has at least two one-digit numbers. The sentences below are examples of basic facts.
7 + 2 = 9    16 – 7 = 9
5 × 3 = 15    8 ÷ 4 = 2

**Cardinal number**  A number used to count or to tell how many, such as *three*.

**Central angle**  An angle with its vertex at the center of a circle.

**Circle**  A plane figure with all of its points the same distance from a given point called the *center*.

**Circumference**  The distance around a circle.

**Common denominator**  A common multiple of two or more denominators. A common denominator for $\frac{1}{6}$ and $\frac{3}{8}$ is 48.

**Common factor**  A number that is a factor of two or more numbers. A common factor of 6 and 12 is 3.

**Common multiple**  A number that is a multiple of two or more numbers. A common multiple of 4 and 6 is 12.

**Commutative property of addition**  The order in which numbers are added does not affect the sum. Also called the order property of addition.
4 + 6 = 6 + 4

**Commutative property of multiplication**  The order in which numbers are multiplied does not affect the product. Also called the order property of multiplication.
4 × 6 – 6 × 4

**Composite number**  A whole number, greater than 0, that has more than two factors. 12 is a composite number because it has more than two factors: 1, 2, 3, 4, 6, and 12.

**Cone**  A space figure shaped like this.

**Congruent**  Having the same size and the same shape.

**Cross-products**  For the ratios $\frac{3}{4}$ and $\frac{9}{12}$, the cross-products are 3 × 12 and 4 × 9.

**Cube**  A prism with all square faces.

**Cylinder**  A space figure shaped like this.

**Decimal**  A number that is written using place value and a decimal point.
3.84    0.076
decimal point

**Degree** (of an angle)  A unit for measuring angles.

90 degrees

**Denominator**  *See* Fraction.

**Diagonal**  In a polygon, a segment that connects one vertex to another vertex but is not a side of the polygon.

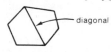
diagonal

**Diameter**   In a circle, a segment that passes through the center and has its endpoints on the circle.

diameter

**Difference**   The answer to a subtraction problem. In $95 - 68 = 27$, the difference is 27.

**Digit**   Any of the single symbols used to write numbers. In the base-ten system, the digits are 0, 1, 2, 3, 4, 5, 6, 7, 8, and 9.

**Distributive property**   A distributive property that relates multiplication and addition is used in this number sentence.
$$4 \times (7 + 3) =$$
$$(4 \times 7) + (4 \times 3)$$

**Dividend**   A number that is divided by another number. In $48 \div 6 = 8$, the dividend is 48.

**Divisor**   A number that divides another number. In $48 \div 6 = 8$, the divisor is 6.

**Edge**   In a space figure, a segment where two faces meet.

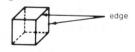

edge

**Endpoint**   The point at the end of a segment or ray.

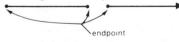

endpoint

**Equal fractions**   Fractions that name the same number. $\frac{2}{3}$ and $\frac{8}{12}$ are equal fractions.

**Equal ratios**   Ratios indicating the same rate or comparison, such as $\frac{3}{4}$ and $\frac{9}{12}$. Cross-products of equal ratios are equal. $3 \times 12 = 4 \times 9$.

**Equation**   A mathematical sentence that uses the $=$ symbol.
$$14 - 7 = 7$$

**Equilateral triangle**   A triangle with all three sides congruent.

**Even number**   A whole number with a factor of 2.

**Expanded form**   The expanded form for 5176 is $5000 + 100 + 70 + 6$.

**Exponent**   In $4^3$, the exponent is 3. It tells that 4 is to be used as a factor three times.
$$4^3 = 4 \times 4 \times 4$$

**Face**   A flat surface that is part of a polyhedron.

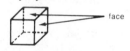

face

**Factor**   A number to be multiplied. In $3 \times 7 = 21$, the factors are 3 and 7.

**Family of facts**   The related number sentences for addition and subtraction (or multiplication and division) that contain all the same numbers.
$$5 + 3 = 8 \qquad 8 - 3 = 5$$
$$3 + 5 = 8 \qquad 8 - 5 = 3$$

**Fraction**   A number such as $\frac{2}{3}$. In $\frac{2}{3}$, the numerator 2 tells how many equal parts or items are being considered. The denominator 3 gives the total number of equal parts or items.

**Graph**   (1)A picture used to show data. The data may be shown by a bar graph, a circle graph, a line graph, or a pictograph. (2)Points on a grid matched with given ordered pairs.

**Greater than** ($>$)   A relation between two numbers with the greater number given first.
$$8 > 5 \qquad 9 > 1.4 \qquad \tfrac{1}{3} > \tfrac{1}{4}$$

**Greatest common factor**   The greatest number that is a factor of two or more numbers. The greatest common factor of 8 and 12 is 4.

**Grouping property**   *See* Associative property of addition and Associative property of multiplication.

**Hexagon**   A six-sided polygon.

**Improper fraction**   A fraction that names a whole number or a mixed number, such as $\frac{15}{2}$ and $\frac{2}{1}$.

**Integers**   The whole numbers and their opposites. Some integers are $^+2$, $^-2$, $^+75$, and $^-75$.

**Intersecting lines**   Two lines that meet at exactly one point.

**Isosceles triangle**   A triangle with at least two sides congruent.

**Least common multiple**   The smallest number that is a common multiple of two given numbers. The least common multiple for 6 and 8 is 24.

**Less than** (<) A relation between two numbers with the lesser number given first.

$$5 < 8 \qquad 1.4 < 9 \qquad \tfrac{1}{4} < \tfrac{1}{3}$$

**Line of symmetry** A fold line of a figure that makes the two parts of the figure match exactly.

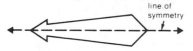

line of symmetry

**Lowest terms** A fraction is in lowest terms if 1 is the only number that will divide both the numerator and the denominator.

**Minuend** A number from which another number is subtracted. In 95 − 68 = 27, the minuend is 95.

**Mixed number** A number that has a whole number part and a fraction part, such as $3\tfrac{1}{4}$ and $6\tfrac{7}{8}$.

**Multiple** A multiple of a number is the product of that number and a whole number. Some multiples of 3 are 3, 6, and 9.

**Multiplicand** A number that is multiplied by another number.

$$\begin{array}{r} 7 \\ \times 3 \\ \hline 21 \end{array}$$ The multiplicand is 7.

**Multiplier** A number that multiplies another number.

$$\begin{array}{r} 7 \\ \times 3 \\ \hline 21 \end{array}$$ The multiplier is 3.

**Negative integer** An integer less than 0, such as ⁻1, ⁻5, ⁻7, or ⁻10.

**Number pair** *See* ordered pair.

**Number sentence** An equation or an inequality.

$$3 + 5 = 8$$
$$4 < 7$$
$$9 > 6$$

**Numerator** *See* Fraction.

**Obtuse angle** An angle that has a measure greater than 90°.

**Octagon** An eight-sided polygon.

**Odd number** A whole number that does not have 2 as a factor.

**Opposites** Two numbers whose sum is 0. ⁺5 and ⁻5 are opposites because ⁺5 + ⁻5 = 0.

**Order property** *See* Commutative property of addition and Commutative property of multiplication.

**Ordered pair** A number pair, such as (3, 5), where 3 is the first number and 5 is the second number.

**Ordinal number** A number used to tell order or position, such as *third*.

**Parallel lines** Lines in the same plane that do not meet.

**Parallelogram** A quadrilateral with opposite sides parallel.

**Pentagon** A five-sided polygon.

**Percent** (%) A word indicating "hundredths" or "out of 100." 45 percent (45%) means 0.45 or $\tfrac{45}{100}$.

**Perimeter** The distance around a polygon.

**Perpendicular lines** Two intersecting lines that form right angles.

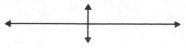

**Pi** ($\pi$) The number obtained by dividing the circumference of any circle by its diameter. A common approximation for $\pi$ is 3.14.

**Place value** In a number, the value given to the place in which a digit appears. In 683, 6 is in the hundreds place, 8 is in the tens place, and 3 is in the ones place.

**Polygon** A plane figure made up of segments.

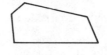

**Polyhedron** A space figure with all flat surfaces. The outline of each surface is a polygon.

**Positive integer** An integer greater than 0, such as ⁺1, ⁺2, ⁺10, or ⁺35.

**Power** $3^4$ is read "3 to the fourth power."
$$3^4 = 3 \times 3 \times 3 \times 3 = 81$$
The fourth power of 3 is 81. $4^2$ is read "4 to the second power" or "4 squared." *See* Exponent.

**Prime factor** A factor that is a prime number. The prime factors of 10 are 2 and 5.

**Prime number** A whole number, greater than 1, that has exactly two factors: itself and 1. 17 is a prime number.

**Prism** A polyhedron with two parallel faces, called *bases*, that are congruent.

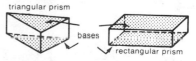

triangular prism

bases

rectangular prism

**Probability**  A number that tells how likely it is that a certain event will happen.

**Product**  The answer to a multiplication problem. In $3 \times 7 = 21$, the product is 21.

**Pyramid**  Space figures shaped like these.

triangular pyramid    rectangular pyramid

**Quadrilateral**  A four-sided polygon.

**Quotient**  The answer to a division problem. In $48 \div 6 = 8$, the quotient is 8.

**Radius**  A segment with endpoints that are the center of a circle and a point on the circle.

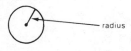

radius

**Ratio**  A pair of numbers that expresses a rate or a comparison.

**Ray**  Part of a line that has one endpoint and goes on and on in one direction.

**Reciprocals**  Two numbers whose product is 1. $\frac{3}{4}$ and $\frac{4}{3}$ are reciprocals because $\frac{3}{4} \times \frac{4}{3} = 1$.

**Rectangle**  A parallelogram with four right angles.

**Rectangular prism**  See Prism.

**Rectangular pyramid**  See Pyramid.

**Regular polygon**  A polygon with all sides congruent and all angles congruent.

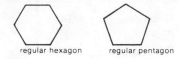

regular hexagon    regular pentagon

**Remainder**  When 20 is divided by 6, the remainder is 2.

**Right angle**  An angle that has a measure of 90°.

**Right triangle**  A triangle with one right angle.

**Rounded number**  A number expressed to the nearest 10, 100, 1000, and so on. 352 rounded to the nearest 10 is 350.

**Scale drawing**  A drawing that shows the shape of a figure but differs in size.

**Scalene triangle**  A triangle with no two sides congruent.

**Segment**  Part of a line, including the two endpoints.

**Similar figures**  Figures with the same shape but not necessarily the same size.

**Sphere**  A space figure with all of its points the same distance from a given point called the *center.*

**Square**  A rectangle with all four sides congruent.

**Standard form**  The standard form for 5 thousands 1 hundred 7 tens 6 ones is 5176.

**Subtrahend**  A number to be subtracted from another number. In $95 - 68 = 27$, the subtrahend is 68.

**Sum**  The answer to an addition problem. In $8 + 4 = 12$, the sum is 12.

**Surface area**  The sum of the areas of all the surfaces of a space figure.

**Triangle**  A three-sided polygon.

**Triangular prism**  See Prism.

**Triangular pyramid**  See Pyramid.

**Vertex**  (1)The common endpoint of two rays that form an angle. (2)The point of intersection of two sides of a polygon. (3)The point of intersection of the edges of a polyhedron.

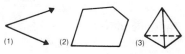

(1)    (2)    (3)

**Volume**  A number indicating the size of the inside of a space figure. The volume of this figure is 12 cubic units.

**Whole number**  One of the numbers 0, 1, 2, 3, 4, and so on.

# Index

**373**